WHAT
EVER TELLS
YOU ABOUT...

LEADING FOR
RESULTS

Best Practices from
101 Real-World Leaders

JAN AUSTIN

KAPLAN PUBLISHING

President, Kaplan Publishing: Roy Lipner
Vice President and Publisher: Maureen McMahon
Senior Acquisitions Editor: Michael Cunningham
Development Editor: Trey Thoelcke
Senior Managing Editor: Jack Kiburz
Typesetter: the dotted i
Cover Designer: Design Solutions

© 2006 by Jan Austin

Published by Kaplan Publishing,
A division of Kaplan, Inc.

Printed in the United States of America

06 07 08 10 9 8 7 6 5 4 3 2 1

Library of Congress Cataloging-in-Publication Data

Austin, Jan.
  What no one ever tells you about leading for results : best practices from 101 real-world leaders / Jan Austin.
    p. cm.
  Includes index.
  ISBN-13: 978-1-4195-8434-3
  ISBN-10: 1-4195-8434-0
  1. Leadership—United States. 2. Leadership—United States—Case studies. I. Title.
  HD57.7.A849 2006
  658.4'092—dc22

                                                        2006021100

Dedication

To my late father, Stewart Austin, the first leader I ever knew and the one who shined a light on the leader in me

FOREWORD

When Jan asked us to write this Foreword, we felt honored. We see ourselves as thinkers and futurists and thus are deeply concerned about the future. So we are happy to provide some context for this book. This is the backstory of Jan's work. This short introduction is really about why these 101 people are leaders, and why they will be the leaders of the future.

We're convinced that leaders of the future will have to have a vastly different set of competencies, attitudes, and beliefs than did the leaders of yesteryear. That's not to say that there aren't some universal qualities like vision and courage that will carry over, but that the approach and execution to leadership will be different.

What's changed? First of all, demographics, at least in the industrialized world, have changed significantly. The bulge in birth rates following World War II is slowing at the same time the demand for talent is growing. As any demographer will attest, a total fertility rate of 2.1 per thousand is needed to maintain a stable population. The United States today stands at 2.09; the EU is at 1.47, China at 1.73, and Japan at 1.40.[1] This double-edged sword means that in the future, leaders will be dealing with an ever-decreasing supply of raw talent, while at the same time those younger generations have a "whole new attitude."

The psychology of the workplace has also changed. Partly because of the demographic changes, labor (or, as we prefer to call it, talent) is clearly in a sellers' market—and thus, to mix metaphors, in the driver's seat. For example, it seems reasonable to expect a shortfall of talent in the United States alone to approach the five million mark by 2010[2] (some researchers predict an even greater shortage). Couple that with the economic shocks we have all seen with downsizing, outsourcing, pension debacles, and dying industries, and the one thing that used to bind people to organizations—loyalty—is gone. How do you lead when your follow-ers are looking out for themselves (as they've learned they must)?

Tomorrow's workforce will by motivated by growth and change rather than by security. Workers will expect their careers to be *their* re-sponsibility, not the company's; and they will want promotions based on merit, not tenure.[3] There will be fewer workers, and they will hold a sig-nificantly different set of beliefs, values, and expectations than did the baby boomers. We are going to need leaders who think and act far differ-ently than Churchill, Eisenhower, and, yes, even Jack Welch. In fact, *Fortune* magazine, that icon of the business world, recently ran an article by Betsy Morris titled "The New Rules."[4] "In with the new and out with the old." "Charisma gives way to courage." "Admire my soul, not my might." "Look out, not in." And the list goes on. The point is that what worked yesterday won't work tomorrow. So, what *is* going to work?

Our guts and our experience tell us that the most basic shift in lead-ership is going to be from left-brain to right-brain styles, values, and ways of perceiving reality. But let's get more specific. In today's lan-guage, the world is shifting from the so-called Industrial Age to what author Dan Pink has called the "Conceptual Age." In *A Whole New Mind,* Pink outlines six key competencies of the future[5]:

1. Design—the beautiful, whimsical, and emotionally engaging
2. Story—fashioning a compelling narrative
3. Symphony—the combination of disparate pieces into a new whole
4. Empathy—caring for others and understanding them
5. Play—too much sobriety can be bad for you
6. Meaning—transcendence and spiritual fulfillment

Our position is that leaders of the future will have to master these six competencies to be successful. Never fear, though, the more analytical types will still be around to make sure the numbers add up, and the engi-neers will still be with us perfecting design ideas. But the people out in front, those leading the parade, will be visionaries and storytellers. They will give meaning to the organization and its mission, and they will see that all the other parts perform in harmony. That means that they'll be motivators and orchestrators, and their role will be to forge linkages be-tween the company's mission and the individual goals and desires of "their" talent. They'll have to rally the troops à la George Patton but without the command and control authority of uniforms and the flag. The best definition of leadership we've heard is that it's "not about making people *do* what you want; it's making them *want* what you want."

But where are these new leaders going to come from? It's our contention that we are burdened today with an educational system that turns out very precise, replicable, and predictable talent that is (was) well-suited for the industrial world—but that's very ill-suited for the world of tomorrow. In short, it is rooted in medieval traditions and churns out a lot of what a dear colleague calls "material capital" designed to serve a world that no longer exists. It centers on rational intelligence about "what I think,"[6] while what we need is more social and spiritual capital—more attention to "what I feel" and "what I am." *That's* the kind of person we want to see leading the organizations of tomorrow.

The answer to the question about where those leaders will come from (and how they will learn to lead) is contained in this book. Read these 101 stories carefully; we think you will begin to see a pattern of new thinking and, more important, a new way of *being* in the world. Jan has done a wonderful job of assembling and teasing out of these leaders' stories what effective leadership is becoming—and what it must become. Her characters are not the headline grabbers of Silicon Valley, nor the cover photos from *BusinessWeek*; humility seems to be a new universal of leadership, and that's exactly the point. The rules of yore don't work today, and they certainly won't work in the future.

Charlie Grantham and Jim Ware
Executive Producers
Work Design Collaborative
www.thefutureofwork.net

Notes

1. *www.cia.gov/cia/publications/factbook/rankorder/2127rank.html*
2. *www.thefutureofwork.net/blog/archives/000202.html*
3. *www.spherion.com/corporate/aboutus/newsevents/EWFrelease.jsp*
4. Betsy Morris, "The New Rules," *Fortune* 154, no. 2, 70–87.
5. Daniel H. Pink, *A Whole New Mind* (Riverhead Books, 2005).
6. Rev. Dr. Ken Brown and Dr. Angela Merkert (*www.merkertbrown.com*).
   Also, D. Zohar and I. Marshall, *Spiritual Capital: Wealth We Can Live By* (Berrett-Koehler, 2004).

CONTENTS

Preface xiii
Acknowledgments xvi

PART 1   STANDING OUT, GETTING HEARD, AND GETTING AHEAD   1

1. "Know the organization and build relationships"   3
2. "Invest in yourself and invest in others"   4
3. "Be smart in real time"   6
4. "Plan your moves, and work your plan"   8
5. "Know yourself"   10
6. "Invest in, don't mortgage, your future"   11
7. "Get an early start to be better than best"   13
8. "Ladies, put your ideas on the table, without reservation"   15

PART 2   THE RISING STAR   19

9. "Manage the conditions that foster important psychological shifts"   21
10. "Strive to create all-star performance, not all-stars"   23
11. "Don't overrely on the assessments of others"   25
12. "Identify the broader impact you want to have"   27
13. "Constantly demonstrate self-confidence, optimism, and focus"   29
14. "Get others to see what you see without overusing authority"   31
15. "Establish a cross-functional orientation to see the whole puzzle, not just a single piece"   33

PART 3   POWERFUL DEVELOPMENTAL EXPERIENCES   35

16. "Be a credible communicator"   37

17. "Use authority to command resources, not people"   38

18. "Stand for what's right when things are unraveling around you"   40

19. "Adversity makes Teflon out of you"   42

20. "Be willing to admit what you don't know"   44

21. "Step up to courageously overcome the fear that diminishes you"   46

22. "How you manage through adversity can make or break your career"   48

23. "Transform adversity and Pay It Forward"   50

PART 4   GETTING LEADERSHIP BANDWIDTH   53

24. "Build breadth versus depth and enhance communication"   55

25. "Develop a framework that supports team versus me"   57

26. "Use the power of your personality to make people feel important"   58

27. "Seek out multiple stretch assignments to create bandwidth"   60

28. "Learn to create clarity out of complexity"   62

29. "Reinvent your brand to gain leadership bandwidth"   64

30. "Ask for assignments in areas outside of your core expertise"   66

31. "Maintain a strategic focus in everything you do"   68

PART 5   MANAGING COMPLEXITY AND 24/7 STRESS   71

32. "Get involved"   73

33. "Create scenarios and plan your actions before the day you need to execute them"   74

34. "Manage the critical few pieces of information"   76

35. "Anticipate what can go wrong and have a communications strategy"   78

36. "Managing complexity is about managing your environment"   81

37. "It's like herding cats"   83

38. "Have a simple, crisp vision that taps into people's passions"   85

39. "Don't allow 'manufactured complexity' to overwhelm your organization" 87
40. "Manage the 20 percent that drives 80 percent of the work" 89

PART 6 MANAGING UP 93

41. "Communicate, communicate, communicate" 95
42. "Understand your boss" 96
43. "Take on an advisory role" 98
44. "Be willing to seek guidance, and you'll be allowed to guide" 100
45. "Don't just know your function; know the business" 102
46. "Identify the synergies" 104
47. "Employ stakeholder analysis to effectively manage up" 106

PART 7 LESSONS LEARNED FROM BAD BOSSES 109

48. "Don't ask if you don't want to hear the message" 111
49. "The team behind you is your biggest priority" 113
50. "It's not about the results, but how you get the results" 115
51. "Don't be seduced by your power or position" 117
52. "Lead as if you have no authority" 119
53. "Practice connective leadership by getting close to people and allowing them to be their best selves" 121
54. "Don't be an energy vampire" 123

PART 8 THE PARADOX OF SUCCESS 125

55. "From me to we" 127
56. "From aggressive to persuasive" 128
57. "From tactical to strategic" 130
58. "From personal ownership to shared ownership" 132
59. "From delivering results to facilitating results" 134
60. "From local to global plans and actions" 136
61. "From self-interests to shared interests" 139

When I was presented the opportunity to author this book, I did not hesitate to offer an enthusiastic "Yes!" As an executive coach and consultant to organizational leaders, and as someone who's held a number of organizational leadership roles, I was keenly aware of the issues leaders grapple with at every level and at every age and stage of leadership. The topics in this book represent the coaching agendas of literally hundreds of leaders I've worked with over the past decade. Through first-hand experience, I also knew that much of what leaders need to know to lead effectively isn't written in management textbooks. Moreover, the personal attributes of effective leaders and many of the real-world applied skills aren't taught in leadership courses, and they aren't explicitly communicated in organizations. That's one reason so many leaders have sought executive coaching.

It's clear that the organizational landscape has irrevocably changed, and every leader must lead from a different place to deliver today's most needed results. It isn't simply a matter of being smarter and faster—that's a given. What is needed is a different kind of leader for the very different world we live and work in today. The marketplace is heated up, and global competition is creating unprecedented organizational churn—all this is against a backdrop of a fundamentally altered employment contract. Not only are jobs no longer guaranteed for the lifetimes of those who hold them, the shelf life of every job and its attendant skills is being dramatically shortened by rapid advances in technology and global competition.

Every leader's imperative today is to find ways to engage the full commitment of employees to deliver high-impact results in the midst of continuous whitewater. And that's not all. Leaders themselves must navigate steep learning curves their Industrial Era counterparts never imagined. They must hit the ground running, act decisively, and create a sense of urgency before they get run over. But the sobering reality is that the gap is widening between what leaders may have been trained to do and what they need to do to be effective in today's organization. For example, the flattening of many organizations means that the need for advanced communication and problem-solving skills are being pushed further down the organization, but the development of those skills is lagging. New leaders are finding that very few road maps are available to guide them.

No doubt, a compelling sense of urgency and decisiveness are watchwords for today's organizational landscape. The leaders who have staying power and who win the respect and full commitment of organizational members understand what they must do to lead differently while acting with urgency and decisiveness. How they think about their roles as leaders and how they lead differently is the basis of much of what you will read in this book. What they have to offer isn't simply re-packaged 1980s' management theory. Indeed, those who have created sustainable success have reinvented themselves for leadership in the 21st century workplace. They have conviction and verve, and they have a treasure trove of practical strategies born of their personal experiences to offer. They have been tested through adversity, radical and disruptive change, and, yes, even bad bosses. They have experienced serious mis-steps and setbacks, and they have had to negotiate the paradoxes of their own success. They have shared their lessons learned with the grace and humility characteristic of those who have been chastened by their experiences but who have nonetheless been grateful for having taken the ride.

The voices of leaders in this book represent a broad spectrum of leadership roles, types and sizes of organizations, and levels of leadership. There are young, up-and-coming leaders, those well on their way, and those at the twilight of their careers. There are leaders from the Fortune 500, the U.S. Government, the nonprofit sector, and even international leaders. Despite the diverse backgrounds, organizations and leadership experiences represented, what emerges is a picture of what makes a modern-day leader successful, what accelerates a fast-tracking leader's career, and what gives a leader the staying power that translates into sustainable organizational results. Delivering business results has never been tougher, but the need for leaders to lead with compassion and heart has never been more compelling. The leader who is successful today knows the business at every level, envisions and communicates success, engages commitment, and obtains results without overusing authority. The successful leader also knows how to manage peer relationships with aplomb and how to harness the intelligence of teams. And this leader possesses the know-how to artfully manage complexity rather than being affected by it and to successfully work within the system to challenge the status quo. Influence has supplanted authority as the most useful tool in the leader's arsenal.

The ability to effectively lead change may well be the single most salable capability of today's successful leader. We're not talking about incremental, internally driven change of the type that typified the Industrial Era workplace. The kind of change we're talking about is for the most part externally driven change that disrupts people and systems and that forces the reinvention of the business and its processes—repeatedly. Despite the fact that much of the change that occurs in organizations today is externally driven, those who are successful in their leadership roles see the trends that are creating change, and they steer their organizations proactively rather than reactively. To do so they must garner leadership bandwidth.

Leaders with bandwidth have a grasp on both the internal organizational environment and the external environment, and they use their knowledge to make strategically sound decisions—often without a lot of information and well ahead of the market. They know all too well that if they wait until a comfortable amount of data has been assimilated, they will have lost valuable time and a host of opportunities. But that's not all. Leaders with bandwidth understand at a fundamental level how to use themselves differently to be strategically effective. These leaders, armed with an understanding of exactly how they add value to the organization, effectively design their work to optimize their contributions and those of others.

The leaders who have shared their sage advice and practical wisdom so generously on the pages of this book are real-world leaders in real-world organizations. Interestingly, many expressed reservation about being showcased in a book on leadership. They just didn't see themselves as all that special. I came to recognize that their humility is, in fact, one of the attributes of leadership most worthy of celebrating. We only need to look as far as the recent spate of corporate scandals and associated meltdowns in executive integrity to appreciate what a leader's humility can bring to the table. But there is something even more compelling to consider, and that is that leadership is not a role or a position. Leaders are nominated. There is no leadership without followership. The personal attributes of a leader that inspire and engage followership will in all likelihood be ultimately recognized as more instrumental to an organization's success than any formula for casting organizational strategy or waging a competitive marketing campaign. The leaders represented here make a solid case for melding business acumen with compassion and heart. Armed with courage and conviction and a passion to succeed, they are redefining organizational leadership excellence.

Acknowledgments

I am deeply grateful to the 101 leaders who made this book possible. Some of them are my clients, each a servant leader in his or her own right. Some of them are the gifts of my esteemed colleagues, and they are truly models of leadership excellence. To my colleagues who knew just who I needed to talk with to make this book come together, I offer my heartfelt thanks. I am especially grateful to my husband, Dan, who not only coordinated 101 interviews, but is my biggest fan and constant supporter in all I do.

PART 1

STANDING OUT, GETTING HEARD, AND GETTING AHEAD
SECRETS OF FAST-TRACKING SUPERSTARS

■ ■ ■

You've watched them with a measure of envy and awe—those fast-trackers who seem to climb the career ladder at a faster-than-life pace with effort and ease. How do they do it? What makes them standouts so early in their careers? And just how do they define success? You'll be inspired and more than a bit surprised as you read the stories of the fast-trackers on the following pages. What these individuals have learned about creating success on their own terms offers a road map for those with ambition and attitude whose aim is to stand out, get heard, and get ahead.

Putting a career on a leadership fast track requires nothing less than an entirely new scorecard for success. The conventional wisdom that informed career progression in an earlier era has been eroded by a highly competitive global business landscape. What's more, standing out against a noisy background requires novel means of communicating with your audience, driving the highly visible results that matter most to that audience. It doesn't just happen by showing up, and it isn't a matter of luck.

Fast-trackers understand what few others do: getting ahead in today's marketplace is not about keeping one's head down and working harder than one's peers. They understand that simply working harder is often a prescription for a parked career. Fast-trackers know there is no single formula for being a standout success. Multiple strategies succeed but not all succeed for everyone. More than anything else, having a clearly identified plan that is executed with nimbleness and confidence registers with fast-trackers as a central organizing principle. They also understand that while solid business acumen is a requisite for success, key personal attributes score the most wins along the way.

Ana fervently believes that being a fast-tracker doesn't just happen; it takes an active, thoughtful approach. You're not going to fast-track in a company that's static, for example. You must be able to move within the company or at least be able to take on specific projects with which you can develop yourself and your career. According to Ana, the aspiring fast-tracker must evaluate these factors up front. You can't simply assume that people above you are going to see you doing a good job and move you up. That's a passive approach. "Instead," Ana says, "you have to look for the opportunities to get you where you want to be." In fact, every move you make should be based on an outcome that you've envisioned. Ana relates that she pursued every one of her jobs except one based on her assessment of what skills she needed to develop to prepare for the next level. She advises, "Look at what sells and what will make you attractive, and aim to get that for yourself."

Being a fast-tracker is not without risk, and you can't afford to ever get too comfortable. Ana observes that you can't settle or compromise, and that you've got to stand up for what you believe in. "Look for the most critical things that need to be fixed, and then *be willing to put yourself at risk* to make the difference that matters." When it comes to executing ideas, Ana maintains that it's important to realize that you may know a lot, but you don't know it all. You simply can't afford to control everything, and you need the help of others to be successful. So while being a fast-tracker is a full-risk proposition, it's a showstopper if you don't intelligently engage the support of others.

2. "INVEST IN YOURSELF AND INVEST IN OTHERS"

■ ■ ■

Pedro Garcia is senior consultant for Drake Beam Morin's Florida district. Since joining the firm six years ago, he's held three different positions. In his work with DBM, a global human capital management services firm, Pedro works with clients throughout Florida and other southeastern states. Not only is he a model for what it takes to be a fast-tracking success, his work involves supporting executives in making successful career transitions.

Pedro suggests that some very specific personal attributes, when present, contribute to an individual's ability to stand out, be heard, and get ahead:

- *A palpable, contagious drive and a passion for the business and its mission.* Those who succeed make the success of the business a priority; it isn't just their own success that's important to them.
- *A high degree of personal humility.* Fast-trackers are achievers and doers, but they also recognize the value that others bring to the table.
- *Respect for others.* They show respect by being good listeners, integrating the ideas of others with their own, and engendering a high level of mutual positive regard that transcends professional boundaries.
- *Hard-working.* They believe "We're in this together," and they are willing to get their hands dirty. It's a continuum, not a hierarchy.
- *Accessible.* They're willing to be helpful to others. "This isn't a solo flight." Pedro stresses that the successful trackers bring others along with them on their way up.
- *Committed.* Fast-trackers are committed to their work, to the organization, and to others' success.

Pedro suggests that while these personal qualities are important, they are by themselves insufficient. They must be integrated with specific strategies that are executed on multiple levels. He says you need to establish personal goals for your career direction and the skills you will need to move up. He adds that you also need professional goals for getting involved in initiatives, partnering up and down the organization, and doing what contributes to your broad visibility, especially with organizational decision makers. This involves taking an active, proactive approach to your career. He stresses the importance of taking your career by the reins and not simply sitting back and hoping others will notice your work and your contributions.

He maintains that *knowledge is critical* because it gives you credibility and authority. But it's not just technical knowledge that's important, but a broader base. Knowledge areas that Pedro views as important to the aspiring fast-tracker include organizational management, leading people, communication style, and industry trends. The fast-trackers he's known get involved in professional associations or industry trade groups, read professional publications, and network with colleagues— routinely. "The bottom line," he says, "is you have to be willing to invest in yourself. It's an investment that will return itself in the form of opportunity." Pedro relates that he's seen many people who've been burned out in their jobs or suffered the disappointment of seeing their careers stall. He believes that they've really sabotaged their own success by not investing in themselves and by not honoring healthy boundaries between their personal lives and work. Pedro says, "Fast-trackers are self-responsible. They take care of themselves."

Finally, Pedro observes that fast-tracking is about *creating success on your own terms,* and not trying to conform to standards of success established by others. "It's your career, and you need to establish what success looks like for you. And at the end of the day, it's about arriving, not about having arrived. It's a process of continual growth and renewal."

3. "BE SMART IN REAL TIME"

■ ■ ■

Karen Heitzman believes that networks may well be the most critical success factor for an aspiring fast-tracker. Heitzman is vice president of human resources at Pearl Meyer & Partners, an executive compensation consulting firm. She's also held senior-level roles at Drake Beam Morin and Quality Metrics.

For Karen, *networks* have been invaluable to her fast-tracking success. She says, "I've been referred in to every one of my best career opportunities." She meets monthly with a group of professional women for dinner. She says, "It's informal and fun. We're not there to talk business, but it's amazing how many business leads come your way when you're not trying to force anything to happen." For Karen, it's critical to look for ways to give to your network, for when you give generously to your network, you can take from time to time.

Karen recommends *joining professional associations* to expand your networks and build your visibility. With association membership, you have instant access to thousands of contacts who have information, advice, and resources to offer. "You don't have to know everything about everything when you have a network. Moreover, it's not always what you know but who you know who does know. Your success doesn't depend so much on how much expertise you have but how expert you are at accessing information when you need it."

Karen fervently believes that *fast-trackers are fast learners.* "Be willing to accept challenging assignments, even if you don't have everything it takes to deliver at the outset," she advises. Adopt a "can do" attitude and be willing to accept some personal risk. She says, "Gulp and then *get busy learning what you need to know in real time."* She adds that with technology at your fingertips, information on an almost limitless number of subjects is instantly available. "Fast-trackers aren't experts," she observes, "but they are courageous at stepping up and stepping out."

Networks are important, and being a fast, resourceful learner is important, but there's more. Karen says, "When I've been my most successful, I've created a powerful intention and then focused my attention and actions in the desired direction. You've simply got to get out of your own way." Karen says she's seen people sabotage themselves with self-defeating thinking and behavior. "These things are killers," she says. "You can't act courageously on what you don't believe in, and when you fail to act, you reinforce the self-defeating thinking."

For aspiring fast-trackers, Karen endorses *reading across a broad range of topics to be able to integrate and customize.* She believes you're better on your feet—smart in real time—when you know how to be resourceful, how to integrate, and how to customize a broad range of knowledge to your current challenges. You effectively expand your personal bandwidth when you do this.

Karen warns that fast-trackers need to *guard against the tendency to become smug with their success.* She says, "Never think that you've arrived and that you don't need others. On the other hand, you must be confident in who *you* are. Don't suffer over unfair criticism that undermines your core confidence."

Finally, Karen suggests that the fast-tracking career path doesn't have to be a clearly laid out linear path. You *don't have to move in a lockstep fashion* in a company. Instead, she suggests it's better to embrace the possibilities in multiple spheres. So what if your path looks more like a checkerboard than a ladder? Fast-trackers are grounded, and they create success with their personal signature on it.

4. "PLAN YOUR MOVES, AND WORK YOUR PLAN"

■ ■ ■

Named one of Calgary's Top 40 under 40 in 2004, **Drew Railton,** at 31, is vice president and general manager of business development at Toombs KWA, an outplacement and career management firm located in Vancouver, British Columbia.

Drew seems mature beyond his years, but this is no accident. He got an early start. He worked full-time while attending college in Calgary, after which he joined TELUS, one of Canada's largest telecommunications companies. While working at TELUS, he sought out a mentor who helped him connect with community organizations. Before long, he joined the board of a community theater. The theater was financially troubled and in desperate need of volunteer help. "Doing community volunteer work put me on the map," Drew says, "and I gained experience in areas that I wouldn't have had exposure to otherwise. Moreover, when you're young, you can make a lot of mistakes because others will chalk it up to inexperience and naïveté. You can tackle a steep learning curve, and when you fall off, forgiveness comes easily." Drew cautions against shying away from opportunity simply because you're young or you lack certain experiences. "Many community organizations are desperate for help, and your contributions don't go unnoticed or unappreciated."

While community involvement has been an important accelerator in Drew's career, he offers the following tips and strategies for successful fast-tracking:

■ *Diversify your networks.* Doing so will expose you to different people and different opportunities. Don't get pigeon-holed in a job or in a specialty area that could limit your future moves.

- *Tackle the opportunities that will stretch you and develop you as a leader.* If the stretch is big enough, you won't be ready, but you can't get ready where you are. You have to dive in and learn on the go.
- *Don't just talk about what you do.* Instead, talk about the impact you want to have or the impact your efforts have already had. Focus on accomplishments, not activities.
- *Invest in your personal development.* Don't be too proud to ask for help. Seek out outstanding individuals who can mentor you.
- *Have a plan.* Without goals, you have very little chance of moving on and moving up. Identify what progression of roles will best position you, but be realistic. "You're not going to go from being the head of human resources to being CEO of a company—you've got to broaden your experience."
- *Be flexible.* Be willing to move laterally and maybe even take a step back to get the right mix of skills and experience.
- *Be persistent.* Build the plan and work the plan. Drew takes the prize for persistence. He took part in 253 informational interviews before landing the consulting role he wanted. Drew fervently believes that few people are willing to put in that kind of sweat equity, so when you do, you distinguish yourself.

Drew maintains that it's just as important for aspiring fast-trackers to know what *not* to do as it is to know what to do. For starters, *don't work yourself to death.* It's easy to get sucked into the trap of working 12- to 14-hour days. "You think that by making a yeoman's effort, you'll get ahead, but that thinking couldn't be more misguided. You'll be in the background while others are running in circles around you."

Drew also fervently believes that *you should never show disrespect,* no matter how disappointed you might be about someone or something. "You never know who the person you're talking to knows and how your remarks could come back to bite you."

Finally, aspiring fast-trackers should *never refuse to help others.* You can almost always be of some help, even if it's just providing information or a lead. He believes that when you help others, your generosity always comes back in the form of a gift down the road.

5.   "KNOW YOURSELF"

■ ■ ■

The world of nonprofit organizations provides fertile ground for as-piring fast-trackers. **Mario Siciliano** is, at age 40, president and CEO of Volunteer Calgary. Part of a network of volunteer centers across Canada, the organization serves as a clearinghouse for volunteerism, connecting individuals to volunteer opportunities. The organization also conducts social marketing campaigns to promote the value of volunteerism and provides social policy advocacy.

Mario got an early start in his leadership career. He was the night maintenance cleaner at a McDonald's restaurant when, at age 19, he found himself leading a staff of 100 and holding multimillion dollar financial responsibility for the global fast-food giant. Mario says he worked with McDonald's for about four years before making the decision to move into the nonprofit arena. He took a management job in a nonprofit orga-nization and became CEO six months later. Mario has since held a vari-ety of regional nonprofit leadership roles, including serving on the boards of local, regional, and international charities.

He says he's very grateful for his early experience and his rapid ad-vancement in the for-profit sector. "I've been allowed to operate contin-uously in a learning zone—doing things I'd not done before—just enough but not too much stretch." Mario believes it was synergistic. "I brought my aspiration and my yearning to learn, and there were oppor-tunities to match." In his view, when individuals don't take advantage of opportunities to learn, it's typically because of diminished confidence or other personal factors such as tentativeness. So his first success tip for aspiring fast-trackers is to *stay in a learning zone.*

His second tip is to *access mentoring by colleagues.* Mario observes that there's a world of knowledge beyond what any one of us can know. The flow of information is overwhelming, making it hard to incorporate anything new. What he's learned is that working with people who can share their practical "live on the floor" insights on leadership can help you cut to the chase and get what you need in real time.

Mario, who earned a master's degree in workplace learning, believes that understanding the way adults learn has helped him to understand himself—to be more conscious of himself and his impact on others. For example, he says he learned how autocratic he was in his thinking. "Understanding myself helped me to make giant steps forward as a person, and in so doing, I saw more opportunities I could take advantage of. When you understand yourself, you can see a bigger future."

Mario also believes that it's important to develop *awareness and skill in working with difficult people.* Knowing yourself first and others second, with sensitivity to individual differences and others' personal context, can increase your chances of successfully navigating through difficult interactions. "You have to take people out of the boxes you've placed them in as well as the box of judgment you've put yourself in." He's found that doing this has had a tremendous impact on his success.

According to Mario, *fast-trackers should volunteer their time in leadership roles in the community.* These roles can be powerful because you're given more room to grow and develop, well beyond what you might experience in your regular job. In fact, you might acquire responsibility in a volunteer role that you might not even qualify for with a full-time job. You build valuable experience, exposure, and networks through volunteering for community leadership roles. He adds, "There's a limit to what you can learn in one organization. By volunteering, you're able to work for several organizations at the same time, thus increasing the scope of your learning. It's leverage, too, because you can get a lot of learning through several part-time commitments."

6. "INVEST IN, DON'T MORTGAGE, YOUR FUTURE"

■ ■ ■

At 29, **Russ Benes** is chemical manufacturing area production manager at Abbott Laboratories in North Chicago. This is his fourth leadership role since joining the company at age 22. Russ was initially hired into a technical-support engineering role to provide support to shop-floor operators. He recognized right away the importance of forging strong peer relationships and learning to use skills of positive influence.

"I wanted to be the guy they called when there was a problem." He explains that while he was using his engineering skills, he also established credibility with the shop-floor people by being attentive to details when completing reports and by being easy to work with.

In Russ's estimation, the people who advance their careers are those who, in addition to knowing the science, know the business. "Those who just sit back and do what's required in the job description don't get ahead." Russ says that in addition to being curious and asking questions about the business, he learned a great deal by pursuing challenging stretch assignments, which kept him on his toes and stretched him in new directions. He adds, "I couldn't justify being in my job if I were the kind of person who threw in the towel at the outset. You can't run just because the assignment is demanding or is difficult to get a grasp on." Not only that, but taking on a challenging assignment gives you visibility inside and outside your organization. You get to interact with people from other disciplines, and you broaden your perspectives—and your networks.

Russ suggests that you can often find ways to create stretch within your current job. "Don't think that you always need to ask for permission to add value in your job. If you feel strongly about a gap in the business, be willing to take the initiative. Put together a program or develop a methodology to improve a process." The upshot is that if you are creating value, it would be the rare boss who would slap your wrists for that. In a similar vein, Russ notes that if you want to get ahead, it's your responsibility to manage your career. People are busy, and getting face time with a boss to do career planning can be difficult. You need to ask the questions and present your goals for career development. *Identify the opportunities you see and ask for the assignments.*

Russ believes that his career has benefited from his willingness to learn from his boss, coworkers, and direct reports. He's proud that the relationship he has with his current boss is terrific. He adds, "I know that part of my job is to provide updates, but I'm always looking for his perspectives to broaden my own." Use the relationship with your boss to support your learning, but don't confuse getting input to expand your perspectives with asking for guidance and direction. Use the relationship with your boss to expand *your* decision-making and problem-solving skills. Russ is equally enthusiastic about learning from peers and direct reports. He believes that when you entertain perspectives from those who are in different roles, you get a new lens with which to view the landscape.

Another aspect of Russ's fast-tracking success has been his *willingness to seek out mentors and coaches* to support his development. He insists that by working with mentors, you can accrue benefits in a host of subject matter areas. Relationships can be formal or informal, but find people who are willing to connect with you. Russ has taken full advantage of his company's sponsorship of coaching, training, and continuing education. In addition to attending numerous professional conferences, he has worked with an executive coach, and he's pursuing his MBA. Russ says each of these opportunities has helped him to develop additional expertise, hone best practices, and apply new concepts and principles in his day-to-day work. "It's critical that you stay on top of your game if you want to advance your career. And, by the way, this means *being willing to invest in your development outside of work.*" He insists that you can't be stingy in applying your personal resources. He sums it up by saying, "Invest in, don't mortgage your future."

7. "GET AN EARLY START TO BE BETTER THAN BEST"

■ ■ ■

As a college freshman majoring in human resources management, **Sherry Cassano** was already charged up about her career. While attending classes full-time, she enrolled in INROADS, a program that helps minorities get a head start and a competitive advantage in their careers. Throughout her four years of college, Sherry participated in INROADS seminars and mentoring sessions on topics ranging from financial planning to corporate savvy, managing up, image enhancement, and interviewing skills. She also did summer internships with INROADS corporate sponsors. Her first placement was with Clairol, where she was able to jump directly into human resources work. "As a sophomore in college, I was doing recruitment. I got a lot of experience early on that gave me an edge over my peers." At the end of four years, Sherry had job offers from Clairol's parent company Bristol-Myers, but she decided to take a recruitment job with a consulting firm. She then joined People's Bank in 2001 as a recruiting specialist by tapping into the INROADS network of corporate sponsors. Sherry saw recruitment as a good way to get into a company, but she had a much bigger game plan.

Sherry explains that because her recruitment specialist role was in a regional office of the bank, she became "the face of HR" there. She was approached on a broad range of HR issues by people in the regional office. After conferring with colleagues in the bank's corporate offices, she responded to the issues. In this way, she began to develop human resources acumen, and she won the confidence of coworkers in the regional office. The following year she was offered the opportunity to move into corporate headquarters where she actually got to manage the INROADS program for the bank. Her role gave her direct visibility with the bank's senior managers. Her next role as an organizational effectiveness manager reporting to the senior executive officer for one of the bank's lines of business was a natural move, given the visibility she'd attained.

Sherry says that you can also *influence your boss to give you the type of work you want.* As a young recruiter at People's Bank, she told her manager that she wanted to get involved in the Equal Employment Opportunity reporting for the bank. She relates, "It was a natural extension of the INROADS program management work I was doing, and I got some very valuable and highly specialized experience in the process." She adds that you can *leverage your assignments to gain exposure.* She used the EEO reporting assignment as an opportunity to identify trends in hiring by the bank and to flag retention issues that she then presented to the bank's senior management.

In Sherry's view, aspiring fast-trackers must *be deliberate and armed with a plan from the outset.* She says you have to *set your own goals* for your professional development for you can never defer that process to others. Moreover, she insists that you can't get too comfortable. You have to *expand your learning curve as you reach mastery,* before there is any chance that you'll get stagnant. In addition to having and working a plan, it's critical to do an excellent job. She says, "Don't just do a good job; be the best by learning the business and mastering your craft." For Sherry, this meant taking industrial and labor relations courses at Cornell University to hone her HR acumen. Not only that, she enrolled in a master's degree program in organizational development. The payoff for Sherry was that she developed a deep and broad understanding of the business environment that enabled her to speak intelligently on a variety of issues. In the process she enhanced the quality of her contributions to the business, and she built credibility.

Then one day Pfizer called.

Sherry knew that she needed global business experience if she wanted to get serious career traction. And Pfizer, with more than 144,000 employees worldwide, represented a golden opportunity. Nevertheless, with typical planning precision, Sherry looked at the pros and cons of shifting out of a job she loved into working for one of the world's biggest brand-name companies. She asked herself the same tough question that she's asked herself at every previous career intersection: "What does the opportunity offer that I've not already done?" Pfizer won out, and at age 27, Sherry Cassano is HR manager for Pfizer Global Research and Development.

8.   "LADIES, PUT YOUR IDEAS ON THE TABLE, WITHOUT RESERVATION"

■ ■ ■

Carolyn Donaldson has spent 30 years in human resources in the pharmaceutical and medical-device industries. She is currently the vice president of human resources for Noven Pharmaceuticals, Inc. She has taken a particular interest in fostering women fast-trackers during her time at Noven, for bioscience has largely been a male-dominated industry in which women are just now making serious progress.

What Carolyn has observed about the behavior that makes or breaks an aspiring woman fast-tracker's career is instructive. She notes that women have been socialized to be more passive than their male counterparts. "They wait for others to push them along, while males are more likely to recognize where they want to be." Women are also more likely to ask questions, while their male counterparts put solutions on the table. They use more tentative language, take fewer risks, and have an annoying tendency to defer power and credit to others. Carolyn notes, "You don't see males letting others take credit for their ideas, but you sure see females doing it."

Carolyn has identified the behavior that accelerates careers for women in her company:

Have a plan. Know what you want and need, and plan for how you're going to get there. Then exercise the courage to make the plan actionable. Carolyn cautions, "Don't fold just because the plan doesn't sell initially. Use the experience as a basis to reassess your personal strengths and liabilities and reset the plan with more realistic alternatives." In Carolyn's experience, the best plans come from a deep self-knowledge. "It's about calibrating your internal compass as opposed to adhering to external expectations, and having a realistic plan for creating success on your own terms." For Carolyn, this means doing the soul-searching to identify personal drivers that fuel one's passion for work.

Put your ideas on the table, without reservation. Do your homework to ensure that your ideas are substantiated, then put them out there unabashedly and confidently. Carolyn maintains that this point can't be overemphasized. "Women have got to stop asking so many questions and apologizing for having a point of view. Questions and apologies only make people wonder about your capability—and your confidence." You've got to demonstrate the kind of professional respect that all your colleagues deserve, so listen to make sure you fully understand what others are saying, and then make your points powerfully. Carolyn notes that when women do this, the differences between genders disappear. "Don't give away the opportunity to demonstrate value." You also have to be willing to act without asking for permission. Power players take charge; they take initiative. They don't apologize or ask for permission to make a contribution.

Establish and maintain strong networks. Networking is not about socializing but about selectively approaching the audiences that can impact your career. Carolyn maintains that a lot of impact can be seen in internal networks as well as in affiliation with professional associations. "Women naturally shy away from networks. It goes back to the way they are socialized to be gracious—waiting to be noticed and invited," she notes. Carolyn maintains that fast-trackers are good resources for others in their networks. They are known for the ways they can be help-ful to others for they are able to effectively balance their self-interests with supporting the interests of others.

Be resourceful. Know enough to be able to access the information you need to support your success. Carolyn warns that not being resourceful is a ticket for derailment. Successful fast-trackers are smart enough to compellingly communicate what they know and then gather the addi-tional information they need. They're quick turnarounds, and they never look like they're not on top of things. They work the system to maximize their contributions. She quips, "You never wonder why a fast-tracker is at the table."

PART 2

THE RISING STAR
WHAT SUCCEEDS AND WHAT DERAILS
THE INDIVIDUAL CONTRIBUTOR
IN A NEW LEADERSHIP ROLE

■ ■ ■

Assuming a new leadership role is, in many respects, a right of passage that is not particularly well annotated in management literature. In fact, many individual contributors new to leadership roles discover to their dismay that what served their success as individual contributors can fail them miserably as rookie leaders. Nailing down the attitudes and behavior that will sustain success in leadership roles can be a humbling and confidence-shattering experience for those who are left unguided on the playing field. No one wants to see a new leader fail; in most cases, failure occurs because important success strategies for the new leader have not been made explicit. Much is left to chance occurrence, resulting in unsettling aftershocks when mistakes are made or people are inadvertently mismanaged.

The rising stars as well as the advisors to rising stars who appear on the following pages offer a prescription for success in what has by all accounts become a fast lane. New leaders today must hit the ground running. The learning curve is steep, less margin for error exists than ever before, and leaders must engage the full commitment of their employees as a first order of business. Missteps occur when new leaders overplay the hand that made them successful as individual contributors or when they misguidedly overuse authority. The new leader must shed the attitudes and behavior of an employee to make the full shift into the role of leader. Much of what needs to shift is psychological and emotional. What was rewarding as an individual contributor must be supplanted with a new picture of success that conveys distinctly different rewards.

There is wisdom here for the aspiring leader, for the individual in a new leadership role, and for those who advise and guide new leaders.

9. "MANAGE THE CONDITIONS THAT FOSTER IMPORTANT PSYCHOLOGICAL SHIFTS"

■ ■ ■

In her role as vice president of learning and development, **Barbara Healy** manages the corporate university, talent management, succession planning, and executive coaching for People's Bank, a northeastern U.S. banking chain. In her view, organizational leaders in general fail to understand the requisite psychological and behavioral shifts for people moving from individual contributor to leadership roles. She notes that because it's quite common to reward great individual contributions with promotions to leadership roles, many managers who are technical or professional experts don't know how to delegate, how to develop and coach others, or how to create contribution through others. Barbara points to research by ClientSkills® that suggests that 70 percent of new and incumbent managers never fully make the transition into manager role behavior and therefore don't contribute to their organizations the way they should. The biggest consequence to the organization when rising stars are not able to transition fully into the role of leader is an inability to leverage the distributed intelligence of a team. She points to the requisite shifts that an individual contributor new to a leadership role needs to make to be successful:

A shift in behavior and values. Fundamentally, this is the shift from "me focus" to contribution through others, and it can be vexing for those whose identities have been cultivated based on their subject-matter expertise. After all, these experts have been valued and rewarded for what they know, not for the knowledge they can harness from others. And the promotion itself is often a signal that the individual's expertise is his or her most important asset. Moreover, because the value of the person lies with his or her personal expertise, the tendency is to continue to rely on this expertise as a success formula despite a positional change.

A shift from tactical to strategic. The rising star needs to garner a broader perspective on the work in his or her area of management responsibility, particularly how it integrates across other areas in the organization. He or she also needs to be able to articulate and clarify direction for others and help them understand how they can make a difference. In an entry-level leadership role, the strategic shift that's needed isn't so much about organizational strategy as it is about understanding more of the organization than just one's own area and how the work that gets done adds impact.

A shift from managing one's self to managing the flow. With this shift, the new leader understands how to manage the work of one's team—to organize the work and coordinate through making assignments. The leader also understands the need and has the skills to represent the work of the team to the broader organization.

A shift from possessive to open communication. If a new leader still thinks that he or she is a specialist and has all the answers, he or she may be unwilling to share information—to communicate what he or she knows. In Barbara's experience, experts tend to be possessive of their information. It's their identity and their badge of honor, but they can't succeed in leadership roles unless they shift the way they communicate.

A shift from personal knowledge to networked knowledge. Successful new leaders understand the importance of acquiring information and resources that can be passed on to their teams for them to do their work. The emphasis is on acquiring information that can be useful to others rather than to just the leader.

A shift from emphasizing self-development to developing others. Because many new leaders don't understand that developing others is a part of their job, much less how to go about it, they may overrely on their own expertise to direct the actions of others. Or they may send people to corporate-sponsored training programs to handle this development. The new leader needs to partner with employees to create individual development plans. These plans can include attendance in corporate-sponsored training, but they build on it by identifying strategies for integrating and applying such learning in the work area. They also create opportunities for the new leader to give feedback and identify further opportunities for stretch development.

A shift from reacting to change to leading change. The very nature of change has changed, and new leaders must be able to deal with radical, disruptive, continuous, externally driven change. Not only do they need to learn to be personally resilient, they also must be able to help others manage their way through change. Barbara observes that yesterday, a leader could see the end state with change. The change process had an observable beginning, middle, and end. Today, the end state is always emerging, and leaders must be able to help people live with the ambiguity. They must also be able to anticipate change and lead others into it.

10. "STRIVE TO CREATE ALL-STAR PERFORMANCE, NOT ALL-STARS"

■ ■ ■

With more than 30 years of experience working as a human resources professional, **Bob Joy** has had a lot of opportunity to foster rising stars. His most recent role, senior vice president of human resources at the Colgate-Palmolive Company, is a position he held for 11 of the 20 years he was with the company. But Bob believes that because he got his start in the world of business working as a store manager at a Krystal restaurant, he's been able to observe the challenges confronting rising stars from both sides of the fence. That experience, he says, is what helped him identify and translate success strategies in very practical terms.

The first thing Bob says he's always told a new leader is, "Everything that's worked for you up to now has the potential to work against you as of now." He says this because, in his experience, individual contributors tend to believe that they control their own destinies. They think that all you have to do is work hard and you'll outperform everybody else. The trouble with this thinking is that as a leader, the focus is no longer on you and how you personally perform. *It's about how well you can lead a team.* Bob offers some sage advice for new leaders in this regard:

You have to focus the group. People will not naturally follow you simply because you've been promoted to the role of leader. You have to align in the right direction on the right things. Get them excited and in action around a vision that you clearly communicate and that creates exciting work with plenty of the right kind of challenge.

You have to earn the trust of others. Just as people will not naturally follow you, they will not naturally trust you. People will question your honesty and your dependability. If you are straightforward in your communications, set clear expectations, and deliver on your promises, you have a good shot at garnering the trust and respect of those you lead.

Deliver effective feedback that develops people. In Bob's opinion, everybody's great at giving good news, but many new leaders don't know how to deliver the less-than-positive news. The skills of delivering feedback take some honing, but what's most important is to deliver the message in a clear, concise way that creates awareness but protects the dignity of others.

Embrace no-nonsense accountability. For Bob Joy, the formula for no-nonsense accountability is simple. When things go well, the team gets the credit. When things go badly, the leader assumes responsibility without being defensive or attributing outcomes to others or to circumstances. The leader doesn't try to dodge the bullet. In Bob's experience, a leader's courage in this regard will be rewarded a hundred times over.

Don't try to clone yourself. Instead, focus on balancing the skills of your team, being sure to complement your skills as the leader. To do this effectively, you must take the time to understand your strengths as well as your liabilities and surround yourself with people whose strengths balance your liabilities. Then be sure to support those people to play fully to their strengths. A pet peeve of Bob's is the all-too-often tendency of leaders to focus on improving people's liabilities instead of helping them manage the liabilities while playing to their strengths. As he puts it, "There is all-star performance, not all-stars." Individual liabilities can essentially be rendered irrelevant when they are balanced by the strengths of others on a team.

Continuously talk about and prepare your team for change. It's no secret that you're going to be faced with rapid change, and your people need to become adaptable and flexible. Bob suggests that answering two fundamental questions can supply much of the support people need to deal with change: "Why is the change necessary? How does the change affect me?" The leader must be able to define what is changing, even if the change isn't yet real. The ability to anticipate change is developed by identifying trends and anticipating how they will likely impact the team. Then defining roles in light of the anticipated change gives people what they need to make change personally actionable.

11. "DON'T OVERRELY ON THE ASSESSMENTS OF OTHERS"

■ ■ ■

Bill Brenner got the shock of his life with his first leadership role. He observes, "Even though I had a college degree in business, I realized in a hurry that I had an awful lot to learn about being a leader." Today, Bill is the director of finance and administration for the American Red Cross's National Testing Laboratory in Charlotte, North Carolina. He got his leadership start, though, as the housekeeping manager for a private high school and later a nursing home.

While his college education prepared him with the basics for running a business, it didn't prepare him at all for the daunting task of managing people. "The book learning was all about the principles of business and finance, but little else." He says he just had to throw himself into the fire and hope he didn't burn up. He did it because he was determined to be successful. He readily admits that he made plenty of mistakes early on. "I was overly directive with people. I was rough, and I overused my power as a supervisor. I learned the hard way that you can't make people do stuff,

and you can't overreact when people screw up. I had to learn to understand people, and I had to learn that respect breeds respect."

Bill also discovered the pitfalls of overrelying on the assessments of
others. He allowed others' assessments of the people who reported to
him to color his perceptions of them and how he treated them. "I just
didn't have the confidence in my own assessments. I let politics shape
my attitudes and my behavior more than I should have. I was unable to
look at a person or a situation with my own eyes out of fear that I would
fall out of favor with my bosses." Bill says that he's always respected
his bosses, but that early on he didn't fully appreciate the importance of
knowing how to handle himself with his bosses. "I didn't manage up
when I should have, and I erred in always deferring to my bosses' opinions." Bill is keenly aware these days of how much his deferring to the
assessments of others limited him. Now his own integrity requires him
to make his own assessments and develop his own conclusions.

Bill also didn't understand the importance of building relationships
across the organization and being able to influence and be influenced
through those relationships. "I was a loner early on, and I had tunnel vision as a result. I just didn't see how important others were to my success." Today Bill has a much better definition of who his customers are,
and he realizes that success is about more than simply delivering on individual objectives. "I have to have a broader perspective and be willing
to engage with others and integrate their needs and standards. It's not
just about me anymore."

Bill observes that he learned more when he became a manager with
other supervisors reporting in to him. He had to learn patience. "When
you're a direct supervisor, you're in the weeds; but as a manager, you've
got to entrust the responsibility to others. You've got to have patience
when they don't work in the same way you do and when they make mistakes. It's a long-term investment you're making."

Bill maintains that he's a work-in-progress as a leader, but today, he
has much more patience and understanding than when he was a new kid
on the block. He says he has huge respect for what new leaders go
through, and he endeavors to use the wisdom he's gleaned to support them
through the rough spots.

12. "IDENTIFY THE BROADER IMPACT YOU WANT TO HAVE"

■ ■ ■

As the superintendent of one of Maine's school districts and a part-time adjunct faculty member in a graduate program for school administrators, **Mike Cormier** has had plenty of opportunity to observe rising stars and to support their success in new leadership roles. Mike observes that assuming a leadership role for the first time requires an individual to embrace the opportunity to have broader impact on the organization and its stakeholders, and then to embrace the responsibility that goes with it. He maintains that as a leader you don't turn it off. You can take breaks and distance yourself when necessary, but leadership is a commitment that's full-time plus. Mike has identified some additional rules of the road for the new leader:

Reframe former peer relationships. People who were your friends now are your employees. What's most important is the need for the new leader to confront issues of personal insecurity. When he was a new leader, Mike was afraid that his former peers were going to abuse the new relationship because they'd been personal friends. So he pulled back to create distance, and that's something he later regretted having done.

Ask for help and guidance from a mentor. It can be helpful to confide in someone about feelings of insecurity or ask for advice on a challenging issue. Mike admits that as a new leader he wasn't very good at doing this, thinking that if he asked for help, he'd be viewed as a failure. He thought that if he made a mistake, it would be even worse. Today, he says that admitting a mistake is about an action, not the person. And while it's important to own mistakes, you can't overidentify with them. The latter, he thinks, is a prescription for loss of sleep.

Tell the truth, regardless. In Mike's view, telling the truth is more important by far than posturing, profiling, or becoming defensive. You'll be remembered for how much integrity you have in this regard.

Mike Cormier also has some insights about what he believes can derail a new leader. *Overusing power* is one way that he's often seen new leaders derail. *Rushing to judgment* because of not being well informed is another derailing factor, as is *failing to include others.* In Mike's view, the notion that "I'm the boss" is a myth when it comes to gaining the cooperation of others. A leader must not overuse authority and must foster the willingness in others to follow by engendering trust. Rushing to judgment may be a tendency of those who overuse power as well. Taking a more deliberate, inclusive approach by gathering all the salient information can lead to better conclusions without creating resentment in the process.

Another way that Mike has seen new leaders derail is by *not dealing directly with issues when the issues are still small and manageable.* The new leader may be reluctant to tackle a tough challenge or lack confidence in bringing the issues to the table. Whatever the reason for holding back, the new leader should not allow things to get to the stage of a crisis before dealing with them. By dealing with issues when they are small, the new leader saves valuable time and resources and creates goodwill in the process.

Two additional areas that Mike identifies as potentially problematic for new leaders are *failing to be clear about expectations* and *failing to delegate properly.* A leader has to be crystal clear about what kind of input is needed from others. When a new leader isn't comfortable communicating, the result can be angry reactions and people not feeling heard. When a new leader isn't delegating appropriately, often he or she has a heightened sensitivity to getting everything right and a need to personally control the work. Mike advises that new leaders must sift through the issues and be willing to let go of things. You can stay involved and manage accountabilities, but you don't have to control every action. This is an important distinction that every new leader has to learn.

13. "CONSTANTLY DEMONSTRATE SELF-CONFIDENCE, OPTIMISM, AND FOCUS"

■ ■ ■

As senior vice president of Chase Home Finance and a 30-year banking industry veteran, **Maureen Erwin** has fostered a lot of rising stars. She offers her perspective on what can derail new leaders, including some key gender distinctions derived from her firsthand experience:

Failing to make the full transition from peer to leader. This can be especially tough for the rookie leader who must renegotiate roles with former peers. The new leader must put some distance in those relationships, but not become aloof or out of touch. When the appropriate distance isn't there, the individual fails to establish himself or herself as a leader and essentially remains one of the pack. This can blind the individual to the different expectations for his or her leadership role performance, and it can also blind the leader to the expectations direct reports have for those who lead them. It takes a measure of self-confidence for the new leader to make this shift—to be able to see himself or herself as a leader who creates value for the organization through relationships with others.

Not being decisive or being overly decisive. While consensus building may be a preferred strategy when functioning as a team member, overusing it in a new leadership role is derailing. On the other end of the spectrum, a new leader who charges ahead without ever considering the input of others will likely get pegged as arrogant. Maureen says, "It's a balancing act that every new leader has to learn to be effective."

Lack of awareness of political undercurrents. The rising star may not pick up on the dynamics of a situation and, thus, may jump in too quickly without first allowing others to "tee up" and then observing how things play out. The result can be premature input that is not well thought out or that fails to integrate the viewpoints of others. Moreover, the young leader may not read subtle social cues because of extreme self-consciousness or trying to make a good impression. Political savvy can be developed through mentoring as well as by observing process and timing.

Failing to get connected. It's easy for a rookie leader to remain isolated in his or her role, preoccupied and sidelined with what can be a daunting amount of new things to learn. Moreover, having become overly comfortable relating to a small group of peers, the rookie may not see the need for broader organizational networks. Maureen maintains that such networks are not only important to career advancement, but they also make all the difference in a leader's having access to important information to do the job and to represent the organization well. In her experience, women tend to be slower getting on the network bandwagon than their male counterparts because they are socialized to wait for the invitation. Because women are less likely to be tapped on the shoulder and invited than men, they must take the initiative.

Not managing the new leader's performance and that of the team. Maureen cautions that this is not simply about being able to accomplish tasks and hold others to task. It's much bigger than that; so big, in fact, that many young leaders don't get it. What young leaders often don't see and connect to their day-to-day work are things such as profit and loss, strategic goals, and the company's reputation. It's like they have tunnel vision. They must make the connection that profit and loss is the underlying driver for everyday activities, and when they can do that, they can more effectively manage high or low performance levels beneath them.

Failing to clearly communicate success in a succinct way. Think of this as personal brand management or, as Maureen puts it, "the elevator ride speech." She's observed many a rising star blow the opportunity to make a positive impression on a senior executive on the ride up the elevator. The executive asks, "How are things going?" The young leader responds, "Very well, sir." Maureen maintains that the young leader must relate what the team is doing that is strategically aligned and that speaks to results. It's about having self-confidence, optimism about the future of success, and a focus on what's strategically important. She adds, "Senior-level executives want to know that junior leaders are thinking like they're thinking—that strategic goals are being internalized and communicated."

Lack of attention to self-development. In Maureen's view, if you think you're finished with learning, you're finished with your career. Yet, she's seen junior leaders step back from the imperative to constantly improve their knowledge and skills. Improvement opportunities come in many packages, including taking courses, doing stretch assignments, and getting involved in leadership roles in the community.

Absence of discipline in work and personal life. Maureen says, "It's all conveyed. A lack of discipline shows up as a lack of presence or stress-induced reactivity. When you're not in control of yourself, it erodes your credibility, and it erodes others' confidence in you."

14. "GET OTHERS TO SEE WHAT YOU SEE WITHOUT OVERUSING AUTHORITY"

■ ■ ■

John Lee is a career health and human services executive. As president of Coordinated Care Services, Inc., a Rochester, New York nonprofit, he leads state- and county-funded initiatives to bring innovative solutions to mental health, substance abuse, and social service problems. CCSI's reach is statewide, with programs impacting 50 percent of the counties in New York State. John says, "We help government do the job better." John feels privileged to have fostered many rising stars in the health and human services arena during his more than 20 years in the field, and he knows firsthand what succeeds and what derails the junior-level leader.

In John's view, many young leaders don't have a good understanding of the power that comes with leadership, and how that power must be used to be effective. He distinguishes between what he calls reverence power and authoritative power. He suggests that young leaders need to learn how to use reverence power to inspire others—to get them to see a vision and commit to it. "Especially when a leader is working with a team, it's important to get the team members to see what the leader sees without overusing authority. The best way to do this is to engage the team and demonstrate respect for team members' opinions."

Young leaders also need to understand how to delegate effectively. In John's experience, rookie leaders tend to oversupervise their direct reports and thus oppose agreeing on plans of action and enabling individuals to move forward confidently and independently. He believes this tendency is rooted in the fear that others will make mistakes that will reflect badly on the leader, who feels overresponsible. He believes that a young leader is well served by reassurances that mistakes are expected, and that learning is the desired outcome when they occur.

Possessing the right level of self-confidence is important for a young leader. Self-confidence can be generated by building on prior successes, as well as committing to stretch goals and succeeding. But an overly confident attitude can be a derailing factor, resulting in a young leader's being less receptive to feedback or being viewed as arrogant by others. John believes that the rookie needs to have a "realistic view of his or her capabilities coupled with an optimistic outlook."

How an individual approaches the broader scope of responsibility that comes with a leadership role is another important consideration. John expects his rising stars to be prepared for meetings and be prepared to follow up. He also expects them to be able to hold conversations at strategic versus operating practice levels. The leader must be thinking continuously about how his or her own work relates to the work of others and to the overall success of the organization.

John has observed that some young leaders are reluctant to ask for feedback, and when they do receive it, they may not be receptive. This may stem from either overconfidence or a fear of failure. He believes that incorporating regular "off-cycle" feedback—that is, feedback that occurs outside of formal feedback processes such as performance reviews—can create a context for developmental feedback that people are likely to be more receptive to. Feedback, then, is an ongoing process embedded in the organizational culture rather than an event. John places a high value on using behavioral and communication-style assessments and tools to help the rising stars in his organization develop situational awareness—the ability to read people and situations and adapt to manage them effectively. It's a framework that enables people to obtain feedback by discerning the cues in their environments.

Finally, a rookie leader needs to learn to manage what John calls "decision rights." It's about determining who owns a decision—the leader or the entire team. If it's the leader, then the leader must be clear about what kind of input is wanted from team members. If the entire team owns a decision, then the leader must create shared ownership by clearly communicating the decision parameters and how far a team can go. This can get tricky if the young leader is working to develop more self-confidence or is learning to let go of control, but it's an important developmental milestone to be able to effectively lead others.

15. "ESTABLISH A CROSS-FUNCTIONAL ORIENTATION TO SEE THE WHOLE PUZZLE, NOT JUST A SINGLE PIECE"

■ ■ ■

Bill Edwards is a rising star at Xerox. His current role of project manager with the Production Systems Group at the company's Rochester, New York, site is his second leadership role since joining the company 16 years ago. As an up-and-coming leader, Bill, who is trained as an engineer, relates that the first thing he had to determine was what success meant. As an individual contributor, he was defined by what he accomplished under his own steam. As a leader, he realized that success is about knowing where you and your team are going in the big scheme of things. Bill observes that as a new leader, he also had to understand what was being asked of him by his management because he not only had to communicate the actions needed but also the overall direction. He says it was necessary for him to make a shift out of thinking about activities to thinking about the whole system. To become more effective in systems thinking, he learned that he needed to ask more questions—to be able to see the entire puzzle, not just a single piece. For him this translated into establishing more of a cross-functional orientation.

As a young leader he learned that *how* you go about getting results really matters. "It's important to realize that treating people fairly doesn't mean treating everyone the same. You have to respond to differences in style, motivation, and skill levels." Bill is quick to add that he used to worry a lot about what people were feeling, but he learned that he couldn't abdicate his responsibility when decisive action was called for. In a similar vein, Bill says he learned that while it's important for a leader to anticipate and expect employee engagement, the leader must be prepared to enforce performance expectations. He admits that he still struggles with managing unproductive employee conflict. "As a younger leader, I shied away from dealing with it altogether, and even now, I struggle with knowing how quickly I should move in to enforce expectations when employees are performing but are creating conflict. I've learned that it's important to have a well-thought-out approach ahead of time."

Bill observes that dealing with employee behavior and the related human resources issues represented his single biggest challenge as a new leader. "You want things to go well; after all, it's a reflection on you if they don't. As a leader, you're measured on the results of the team, but you can't take on the work of the team if it's not being done. I learned that I had to have the tough conversations and then take a step back to not take on too much responsibility for other people's reactions." Bill acknowledges that as a young leader he was fearful of the human resources people. "I didn't understand their role, and I worried that I would be viewed negatively if I sought help or revealed my vulnerabilities. I was also worried at times that HR might overreact if I brought an issue forward." Bill says that now his relationship with HR is more relaxed and he now views his HR colleagues as partners.

When asked what he considers the single most important piece of advice he could offer other up-and-coming leaders, Bill says that every leader has three primary stakeholder groups: his or her manager, peers, and employees. "All three groups are pulling on you, sometimes in different directions. As a leader, you have to find the right balance in managing the expectations of all three without compromising any one of them." A young leader might tend to overemphasize the needs of his or her manager and thus be overly directive to the exclusion of building employee teamwork. Alternately, a young leader might overemphasize team consensus to the exclusion of decisive leadership. Striking the right balance comes with time, experience, and plenty of mistakes. Bill adds that effective leaders use their authority wisely. A leader must understand and manage decision rights effectively to gain the respect of team members. "Be clear about what input is wanted and when it is wanted."

PART 3

POWERFUL DEVELOPMENTAL EXPERIENCES
LESSONS FROM STRETCH ASSIGNMENTS AND ON-THE-JOB ADVERSITY

■ ■ ■

Experience *is* a great teacher. Leaders at all levels benefit from stretch assignments designed to deepen and broaden their experience and sharpen their skills. Moreover, stretch assignments, by shifting the landscape of players and perspectives, introduce new frameworks for solving vexing business challenges and making good decisions. The best stretch assignments align a leader's personal strengths and aspirations with organizational strategy. They are often special project roles that are both high stakes and high visibility. Thoughtfully executed, they can rapidly develop a career.

Not all developmental experiences are anticipated or planned, however. Nor are they always welcome. Some experiences come in the form of on-the-job adversity, representing the kind of challenge that no leader actively seeks, and many outright reject. It's typically in retrospect that such experiences get the recognition they deserve. When they are fully integrated by the leader, new insights and fresh perspectives almost invariably follow.

The leaders on the following pages have shared the richness of the experiences that have developed them, whether they sought out those experiences or they found themselves immersed in them. What they discovered about themselves sometimes surprised but always gratified them. Often humbled by the gut-wrenching ambiguity they faced during times of adversity, they developed resiliency to face even tougher challenges down the road. And enlarged by their experiences, they made themselves more salable as organizational leaders.

16.   "BE A CREDIBLE COMMUNICATOR"

■ ■ ■

LoJack is a household word, thanks to people like **Sarah Montague**. The company, which manufactures radio frequency–controlled location devices for cars, motorcycles, and commercial applications, has an overall "aided and unaided" brand recognition of 98 percent. This is comparable to the brand recognition enjoyed by Coca-Cola. That's brand recognition. Sarah is the director of advertising and marketing communications for the LoJack brand.

She describes her most powerful developmental experience as that of presenting to the LoJack board of directors for the first time. According to Sarah, it's one thing to present to your team or to your boss, but it's quite another to present to the company's board. Her stretch assignment to develop and present the LoJack brand advertising plan to the board was both energizing and inspiring. "I am really passionate about this, and it felt wonderful to have the opportunity to bring my ideas to life with the board."

Sarah relates that she felt more than a little nervous about presenting to such an auspicious group, and she realized that her biggest stretch was in learning how to manage herself. She believes that her tips for talking in the boardroom or to any powerfully influential audience will lead to a polished, poised presentation.

"The first thing you have to do is learn to *use your nervousness to energize and empower yourself.* You are, after all, an expert in your area, and that's why others want to hear from you." Sarah is on the mark here. Professional speakers who have mastered podium panic know that when you focus on the ideas you want to share with your audience, rather than on how others might be judging you, nervousness can seamlessly shift into excitement. And that excitement, when telegraphed across the room, can be absolutely captivating.

The second thing Sarah says she learned is that you must *engage the conversation.* "When you can engage the conversation, you have a certain amount of poise that isn't possible when you are merely making a presentation. Moreover, if you are naturally curious, you can communicate that and create a 'meeting of the minds.' When you are at ease with yourself in this way, you get into a state of flow, and your natural strengths come to the surface."

Sarah quickly adds that the third thing she learned is that there is no substitute for mastery of your subject matter. But that's not all. Expertise is by itself insufficient, and that's where so many people miss the boat in their communication. You have to have a *well-honed point of view*. This is what brings your experience and expertise to life in the real world of tackling challenges and creating opportunities that add value.

Finally, Sarah offers that she's learned that there is great power and strength in knowing what you know and what you don't know. It's easy to get lulled into thinking that you're an expert whose opinions are respected, but just when you settle into a comfort zone with that, something will invariably trip you up. The secret to success, she says, is being willing to admit what you don't know while being resourceful about closing your gaps. "People respect a person more who's honest and resourceful."

17. "USE AUTHORITY TO COMMAND RESOURCES, NOT PEOPLE"

■ ■ ■

Jaime Figueroa has worked for the U.S. Government for more than 20 years, including 7 years with the Department of Defense and more than 13 years with the Federal Aviation Administration. In his role as program manager of surface technologies, Jaime oversees research and development of technology improvements to airport runway lighting and signaling systems. The goal is to prevent runway incursions and make flying into and out of airports safe.

Jaime relates that over the years he's had a number of opportunities to take on stretch assignments in the form of special projects with, as he puts it, "high visibility and little margin for error." In the process, he's learned a lot about how to manage his way through both technical and interpersonal challenges.

"The first thing you have to do with any stretch assignment is get a thorough understanding of the scope and complexity of the assignment *before* you accept responsibility for it. This includes clarifying criteria for success, time frames for deliverables, and the resources that will be available to support successful execution. Moreover, you need to determine if you have the requisite skills and functional expertise necessary for the assignment." In other words, don't sign up to build a rocket if you are a bridge builder.

Jaime relates that it's easy to make the mistake of overrelying on other people's assessments of things such as project complexity, skill requirements, and resources. He insists that you must make your own assessment, with a special emphasis on the availability of resources to support execution. An inaccurate estimate of resources can result in delayed execution and a failure to deliver expected outcomes in a timely fashion. As he puts it, "When you are already chest-deep in a stretch assignment with a short-term turnaround and little margin for error, you don't have time to engage in discovery, and you have little leverage to renegotiate the parameters of your assignment. It's 'after the fact.'"

In the high-tech world of aviation, projects routinely require the support of a number of technical experts. Jaime observes that this can be a treacherous slope because you never want to have to rely 100 percent on the technical expertise of others. "You have to personally bring sufficient technical expertise to the table to be able to judge quality and to know when something is 'good enough.' Especially when you are spending taxpayer dollars, you want to deliver but not 'overdeliver'; it's a 'best-value proposition.'"

Jaime offers some specific advice on the use of authority. "While authority is important, and it has its place in any organization, you cannot overuse it to get things done. *Leaders should use authority for commanding resources, but resist the tendency to use it to garner people's cooperation.*" For that, he says, you must invest in creating a *shared vision of success and operational alignment.*

Finally, Jaime suggests that it's important to *fully understand the organizational politics surrounding an assignment.* If the project represents a fundamental and disruptive change in the organizational culture, odds are challenges may occur when creating operational alignment around integrating and implementing the change. Special attention will need to be given to "selling" the ideas up, down, and across the organization, and the pace of implementation may need to be adjusted to maximize acceptance and buy-in.

18. "STAND FOR WHAT'S RIGHT WHEN THINGS ARE UNRAVELING AROUND YOU"

■ ■ ■

Rachel Moore is vice president of human resources at Enerflex Systems, a Calgary-based manufacturer of heavy equipment for gasoline processing. She laughs as she shares that there are hardly any women in the industry she works in these days. But her story of on-the-job adversity goes back to 2001 when she was at Selectron, a high-tech manufacturer of switching systems and other components of mobile phone systems.

"Two years into my job at Selectron and having just returned from maternity leave, I was told that my boss was going on an extended leave and that three factories, representing our entire Calgary operation, were going to be closed. The closing of those three factories would cost 550 people their jobs. I was asked to take the lead, despite the fact that I was a mere 30 years old and was not the most senior person. I had no experience with the human resources side of decommissioning factories."

Rachel explains that people were told of their termination dates, but they were also asked to participate in decommissioning their areas and training their Malaysian counterparts to do their jobs. "We had multiple members of the same families employed at the factories who were being confronted individually and collectively with the loss of their jobs. We had people with salaries of $100,000 facing the prospects of earning $8 per hour. It was painful beyond words. As if all this weren't enough, I knew that my job was to end as well."

But the reality remained—there was a job to do. Rachel says that she had to figure out how to manage a lot of complex things simultaneously, including the regular and ongoing job demands, organizational communications regarding the change, legal issues, continual emotional upheaval, and some thorny American parent company issues regarding the Canadian context. "We were a Canadian company with deeply engrained cultural values. The parent company's plan was to give everyone the same severance package of 12 weeks of pay. But we had employees who had given us nearly 20 years of service, representing their entire working lives, as well as those with very short tenure. We were not about to be treated like the 51st state; we needed to have our cultural values honored."

Rachel feels that her experience of on-the-job adversity was a great teacher, and she offers some rules of the road for fellow travelers:

- *Acknowledge that adversity is happening to you, too.* Rachel insists that it's just not true that you can't show emotion as a leader. Acknowledging what's going on for you can help you connect with others who are in pain. Moreover, you can use your empathy to help them to move beyond the emotions that may be overwhelming them. It's important to move beyond your own emotions in order to do the job, however. Rachel believes it's about being mature enough to manage yourself despite painful emotions.
- *Continue to celebrate.* "As people were leaving, we had graduation ceremonies. We strived to find ways to make it worthwhile for people to still show up. We had staged reductions in staffing, so it was important to provide closure as well as to maintain an esprit de corps for those who still remained."
- *Stay positive.* Rachel believes that this is a powerful differentiator with leaders. She observed that when leaders were able to move beyond their emotions and look for the positives about people and the future, their employees rallied and managed their circumstances well. When leaders weren't able to do that, things didn't go well and there was a lot of mopping up to do.
- *Establish a legacy.* Rachel exclaims, "I was astounded by the personal character I saw emerge in others in a time of adversity. Their generosity and sense of community persisted, despite their losses." She believes that a leader's job is to call forth the best in others. "When we saw bad behavior, we said, 'We're better than this. This is not who we are.' And you know what? People agreed." Rachel believes that people will rise or fall to a leader's expectations of them. "We asked them what they wanted our reputation as a company to be, and they responded by continuing their charitable giving to the community until the very end."

■ *Preserve people's dignity.* Rachel believes that it is possible to maintain standards of respectfulness and fair treatment despite adversity. "You may not be able to control the what, but you can control the how." For example, terminated employees weren't escorted out by security or denied access to their computers. Their dignity was honored throughout the process.

19. "ADVERSITY MAKES TEFLON OUT OF YOU"

■ ■ ■

When **Matt Stasior** was asked to take on the job of vice president and general manager of the Las Vegas division of Nationwide Lending, he didn't hesitate. He thought he would be taking over a business unit that needed a boost to get its profits back on track. After all, he'd been one of the early Microsoft millionaires with four business start-ups to his credit. What he found out, however, was that the Las Vegas division needed a lot more than a boost. As he puts it, "I realized pretty quickly that we needed to be in a start-up mode. Things were in decay."

Matt faced a number of unanticipated and highly unwelcome problems when he arrived on the scene. He discovered that no one had been managing the business for some time. Because the managers were frustrated by what they viewed as unfair management compensation, they had been focusing on sales to scale up their earnings. Matt also discovered customer-service problems, a facility badly in need of repair, and a business model that didn't support profitability. As if that weren't enough, he learned that a full-time salaried employee was attempting to set up a competing firm and an employee he had had to terminate threatened his life. It's no understatement when Matt says that the situation required a degree of "overmanaging" at the outset.

One of his biggest personal challenges, Matt says, was coming into a new organizational division without any of his own lieutenants. Then there was the loss of two key mortgage-banking staff and others in the aftermath of three successive increases in fees that impacted staff commission earnings. "The fee increases were necessary to restore the division to a profitable status, but there were personal sacrifices that went with them." Still another challenge Matt faced was a dearth of job candidates who brought mortgage-banking acumen. "We were attracting people with great sales skills but no business acumen, and that was a big problem."

Matt says unhesitatingly that his religious faith gave him the strength to persevere in the face of the daunting challenges he faced. Nationwide Lending is a privately owned faith-based organization, so bringing faith explicitly and openly into a leadership role is consistent with the organization's culture.

Matt also looked to the company's CEO as a colleague and trusted advisor in the process. "We had open and honest communication from the start, and we engaged in an active partnership in which he was integrally involved with the issues." Matt relates that he worked hard to stay aligned with the CEO, adding that it was a kind of cover for him given his newness in the division. "He provided very visible corporate leadership to our business unit, and he helped me resolve conflicts with some long-standing employees. He had the respect of people, and he had a credibility that I didn't initially have." Matt states that even so, he communicated frequently with employees about what was happening and why changes were being made. "Everyone understood even if they didn't agree."

Matt's next intervention was to rebuild the senior management team from the ground up. He had some great producers who were creating strife in the organization, and their toxic impact could not be tolerated if things were to improve. He kept them on until new hires were up to speed, and then he let them go. He also groomed some existing managers to take on additional responsibility. He explains that as part of creating a new foundation for the management team he'd put in place, he brought prayer into the team meetings. "While it may seem odd to do that in a business setting, I can say unequivocally that it made a difference in our organization. It strengthened the team's bonds and connected us to a higher purpose."

Matt then refurbished the physical environment with new paint, carpets, a multimedia-enhanced conference room, and, of course, a new sign in front of the building. The changes, he says, were uplifting and energizing, and fostered a renewed spirit in the workplace.

How did his experience of on-the-job adversity develop Matt as a person and a leader? He says, "It made me tougher—like Teflon. I learned

to let more stuff just roll off of me. Now I don't take things as personally. I look at the full context of a problem and try to understand it. I'm
more accepting of others and their very real frustrations."

20. "BE WILLING TO ADMIT WHAT YOU DON'T KNOW"

■ ■ ■

When **Terry Maxwell** was regional vice president of Cracker Barrel's
restaurant operations, he never thought about leading the retail side, that
is, until the day he was asked to do so by his senior management. Terry
is now the senior vice president of retail operations for the entire Cracker
Barrel chain of country stores. His move into the retail side of the business represented a powerful developmental experience. About the move
he says, "You think you know a business when you're looking on from
the periphery, but it's much different once you're up close and personal
with it." But he soon learned that the retail side of the business is much
different, and the skills he had garnered on the restaurant side needed
some retooling.

Terry says he was initially challenged by the need to assess talent,
build credibility, and shore up his knowledge of what for him was a new
part of the business. On the subject of talent, he learned that while certain attributes such as customer friendliness are "must-have" attributes
on both sides of the house, certain differences exist. He learned that the
retail side is very product- versus service-oriented, and that the product
line is shifting constantly. Success on the retail side requires positive energy, a proven retail track record, and organizational skills. So he needed
to rethink his assumptions about the talent requirements within the retail
operations.

Perhaps more important, he needed to build credibility with retail
employees. "I had to stop jumping to conclusions and overrelying on
my restaurant experience and learn to work more collaboratively with
the retail folks to move that business forward. When you don't know a
side of the business, you've got to be willing to be more deliberative,

ask more questions, and be willing to learn from others." Terry agrees that these are things every leader should do, but a developmental experience such as the one he had really levels the playing field and forces certain behavior. The bottom-line learning for Terry is that as a leader you cannot overrely on past experience and think that you know what you're doing in a new environment.

Terry is glad that he took on a stretch assignment, and he thinks other up-and-coming leaders should seriously consider doing the same. He believes that taking on a developmental experience of this type actually made him more promotable in his company because the experience broadened his perspective and made him more knowledgeable about the business as a whole. What advice does he have for other up-and-coming leaders?

- *Be willing to take some chances.* Get out of your comfort zone, even if the stretch assignment looks like a lateral move. You will increase your value to your company by understanding a broader scope of the business. You won't step into it knowing everything, and you'll be taking some risk. But if you stay put in a narrow area, you might be comfortable, but you'll be less and less valuable to the company over time. So what seems safer may, in fact, be riskier in the long run.
- *Understand the impact of your role.* It's not about you; it's about what you can do to help others perform better. With every increase in responsibility comes more responsibility to help others succeed.
- *Maintain a level head.* Terry says it well when he observes, "You're never quite as good as or as bad as people say you are." So maintain an even temperament or, as he puts it, "Focus on your 'true north.'" Doing so will enable you to make better decisions despite internal pressures. He adds, "Don't overvalue or undervalue yourself, and don't allow the ebb and flow of business cycles to control your mood."

Terry sums it up by saying that powerful developmental experiences in the form of stretch assignments can be humbling, but when you expose yourself to situations in which you are not an expert, you can use your humility to help other people grow. "After all," Terry says, "everyone else knows you don't know everything. The question is, are you willing to admit it?"

21. "STEP UP TO COURAGEOUSLY OVERCOME THE FEAR THAT DIMINISHES YOU"

■ ■ ■

Janey Gregory is a principal at MulvannyG2 Architecture, a Seattle-based architectural design firm. She's also the design group leader for the Costco account, which has 150 employees assigned to it. Janey has been an architect since 1986, but only recently has she been a fearless podium speaker. Her story is one of courage and fierce resolve in tackling an area of personal development that many people fear more than death.

Janey describes herself as having been painfully shy and reserved growing up. She says, "I was highly creative, and I was articulate, but I avoided situations where speaking was required. In fact, I don't think I would have gone to architectural school if I'd known that I'd have to make presentations in front of groups." She relates the excruciatingly painful story of the first time she was required to make a presentation in architectural studio. "I'd spent weeks preparing my presentation. I was overprepared. But when I stepped up to the podium, I had a panic attack. I froze, everything went black, and I just stood there, unable to utter a word. Finally, still speechless and thoroughly humiliated, I just walked away from the podium and sat down." The second time she had to present in architectural studio was better—barely. Janey says she read her entire presentation without ever looking up at her audience. At least she got through it without blacking out. "I knew I had a problem," she says, "and I really wanted to get over it, because by this time, I realized that speaking was going to be important to my future success."

Janey says that reading poetry out loud enabled her to get outside of herself by actually hearing herself talk, and, as a result, feel less anxious. "In order to read poetry, you have to be able to connect emotionally with the poet, and when you do this you move beyond your self-consciousness." She also took a Dale Carnegie public-speaking course, adding that to her utter surprise, she won numerous awards for her speaking during the course. Janey explains that she was able to get through the speaking exercises by intensely focusing. It also helped that the facilitators and participants were hugely supportive. "Still," she says, "I wasn't comfortable, and speaking was not something I would volunteer to do."

As she moved into her early professional architectural roles, Janey managed her way through client presentations by overpreparing and excessive rehearsing. While she got better at delivering presentations, she still was not able to move past the fear and dread that came with each one. "I was afraid that people would laugh at me or that I'd forget what I was going to say and look foolish." She says that while she's always had an incredible drive to succeed, she believed for a very long time that the only people anybody wanted to listen to were the gregarious types. Clearly, it was Janey's fear of public humiliation that kept her in a painfully self-conscious and diminished place. But that's not all. Because architecture is still very much a male-dominated profession, Janey didn't initially find it an easy place for a woman to be successful.

Janey had been with her current firm for a while when she learned that the firm was going to sponsor a seminar series called Women in Leadership. "Because my firm was a sponsor, the seminar organizers wanted a woman from my firm to participate on a panel. And wouldn't you know, I was the only senior female designer in my 350-member firm! I was scared out of my mind, but I agreed to be on the panel on the condition that my management provide me with help in overcoming my speaking anxiety. They readily agreed, so I went to several sessions with a hypnotist. I chose a hypnotist because I felt that my brain needed some rewiring, and I thought that a hypnotist was the best-qualified professional to help me. The sessions were terrific, and not at all like the perceptions that many people have of hypnosis. I came away with three tapes, which I listened to every single day. I listened to them in my car and at home—as often as I could. I also practiced with my son's karaoke equipment to get used to working with a handheld microphone."

So how did Janey's panel debut go? She exclaims, "The day of the panel came, and there was an incredible turnout. I did a brilliant job, with no notes whatsoever. It was completely from the heart. I was totally at ease, without fear or self-consciousness, and I delivered."

Initially a bit stunned but enormously delighted with her newfound success, Janey says you can't shut her up now. She literally beams as she shares that she met the biggest fear in her life head on, and nothing, absolutely nothing, frightens her now. She adds, "My breakthrough was getting over the fear that when I opened my mouth, what I had to say wouldn't interest anyone else. I realized that what I have to say really does matter to other people. Now that I absolutely know that deep down, I speak all the time."

22. "HOW YOU MANAGE THROUGH ADVERSITY CAN MAKE OR BREAK YOUR CAREER"

■ ■ ■

Don Bornhorst has experienced the perfect storm firsthand. It's not that he was asking for a challenge of that magnitude, but it showed up in the most unwelcome way on December 22, 1994, a day that he says he'll remember in vivid detail for the rest of his life. Don is senior vice president of finance and CFO for Comair, the Cincinnati-based discount air carrier now owned by Delta Air Lines.

Don describes the wintry mix that pelted Cincinnati in the height of Christmas travel in 1994. "We knew there was a storm headed towards Cincinnati from the Midwest, but we thought we had everything under control. What we didn't anticipate was the three inches of ice that fell during what we call a 'push,' when a lot of airplanes are scheduled to leave the airport at around the same time. We had de-icing equipment on hand, but we were totally unprepared for the magnitude of the problem we were facing. We deployed our de-icing equipment, but found to our utter dismay that the 30 to 40 gallons of deicing chemicals we typically use didn't begin to budge the ice. After more than 1,700 gallons were applied to one aircraft, it still couldn't be operated. To make matters worse, because the roads leading in to and out of the airport were all covered with three inches of ice, there was no way we could bring more de-icing chemicals to the numerous aircraft that were parked at the gates. There was also no way that the more than 1,000 passengers who were stranded in the airport could be transported to area hotels. Any thought of a quick thaw was eliminated when record-breaking cold temperatures pushed in right behind the ice storm."

You think it can't get any worse than that, but it does. Don describes the chaos that ensued when the computer-based crew-scheduling system experienced a catastrophic failure: "We couldn't dispatch any crew members to airplanes, so on December 24th we were forced to shut down the entire airline until we could recover our computer system. That didn't happen until the 26th, when the ice melted, and the airline was able to resume normal operation." But that's not all. Don explains, "Of the 12 members on the airline's senior leadership team, only three, including me, were working through the storm. The other team members, who were on vacation during the storm, didn't call in or come in to help with the crisis. I personally went 72 hours without a shower or any appreciable sleep, and it wasn't any better for the skeleton staff who hung in with me. Amidst all the pressure that people were under, the perfect storm turned into a national media story. In my unkempt and overtired condition, I became the spokesperson for the airline."

Don asserts that the most important lesson he learned is that how a leader responds to and manages through adversity can make or break a career. He doesn't think it's any coincidence that the same 3 executive team members who stepped up during the ice storm in 1994 were the only ones of the original 12 who were retained when Delta took over Comair in 2000. In fact, Don believes that adversity is not only a great teacher but also a great sorter of leaders. He says, "The real test of a leader isn't in the day-to-day but in the organization's most vulnerable moment."

Secondly, he's now keenly aware that in a crisis, leadership has to be paced, and it has to be flexible. You can't have everyone be "on"—sleep-deprived and on edge all at the same time. The result is that everyone fades at the same time. Moreover, some people are quite decisive and able to maneuver under pressure, while others need to take on more of a support role. Don says he observed that individuals who were less successful in managing through the storm were not flexible in their approaches to problems when situational leadership was required. "We didn't have the luxury of collaborative decision making. People needed to individually step up, assume a certain amount of risk, and act decisively in the absence of a lot of data."

Don maintains that another important lesson he gleaned is the importance of communication and visible leadership in a time of crisis. People need information to cope with their circumstances. He explains that during the crisis he went down to the ramps where employees were trying to de-ice to observe the scene from their point of view. He also talked with those on the front line who were dealing with passengers and those behind the scenes who were struggling with the mounds of baggage and caged animals. And he talked with parents whose unescorted minor children were stranded in the airport. He says, "There are multiple points of impact in a system in crisis, and a leader has to see and touch all of these." Don's motto for times such as these is "Serve, lead, and succeed."

23. "TRANSFORM ADVERSITY AND PAY IT FORWARD"

■ ■ ■

Kevin Tuerff is president and principal of Enviromedia, Inc., an Austin, Texas, advertising and public relations agency. Established in 1997, the firm is solely dedicated to improving public health and the environment and won't take business from companies that its leaders deem to be socially irresponsible. His story is about the courage required to manage through adversity and the redemptive power of servant leadership.

Kevin explains that he's always been cautious about hiring and staffing, endeavoring to create an environment that supports employee commitment and retention. A set of unfortunate circumstances conspired to thwart that noble intention, however. "We had been informed that we were to be awarded a multimillion-dollar contract by the state to develop a series of public service ads. Then, abruptly, the contract was canceled. We learned that this was a result of political pressure by a competing firm. We were devastated when we realized that we had to let several of our employees go as a result of the loss of the contract. One of the employees selected for layoff was a fairly new employee who, just a few months into his employment, had been missing a lot of work. He was already at risk of being terminated, so when we had to make the tough call about who to let go, he was among those selected. Then, two days after the young man's layoff, I learned that he had committed suicide. It was shocking news, and everyone felt terrible, perhaps no one more than me, given that he'd been my direct report.

"I knew we needed the assistance of outside professional support, so I called the executive coach who'd been working with our firm. She also happens to be a psychologist experienced in working with critical incidents such as the one that had occurred in my organization. She came in right away and met with the staff as a group and then with anyone who wanted to have private time with her. There were a lot of feelings of guilt. People were worried that the young man may have felt mistreated by others in the organization. For me, the toughest part was realizing that the decisions you make as a leader can have tragic implications for people. Moreover, you don't have any control over how people will react in the face of bad news."

Kevin relates that he was keenly aware that he needed to provide leadership in the aftermath of the tragedy that would enable people to manage through it and then find a way to acknowledge it as a part of the organization's history. His experience with the 9/11 terrorist attacks on the World Trade Centers provided inspiration. He shares that he was on a plane headed for Texas from Paris when the attacks occurred, and his plane was diverted to Newfoundland for three days. During that time, he says, he experienced incredible generosity from his Canadian hosts. "They brought us food and blankets and pillows, and they drove us to the store to buy clothes, since we had no access to our luggage."

Kevin says that as a result of his experience in the immediate aftermath of the 9/11 attacks, his firm does a Pay It Forward project each year in September, based on the principles in the movie of the same name. The employees are split into teams of two, and each team is given cash to spend on individuals in the community. He adds, "The young man we'd laid off had been an enthusiastic participant in the Pay It Forward project, so the year after his suicide, we dedicated the project to his memory. The employees used the money to buy school supplies and Christmas gifts for kids in a group home who were recovering from substance abuse." Kevin believes that by turning the adversity his organization had experienced into something powerfully and positively directed was healing for the entire organization.

How has adversity made Kevin a stronger leader? He says that he's no longer afraid of adversity. It's stressful, to be sure, but he knows now that he can manage through it, and that he can separate the painful emotions from the reality of what needs to be done. He found that he could be resourceful and that he could use that resourcefulness to create positive impact. He's clear that it's not about being heartless, but about being able to manage the disruptive emotions so that they don't overwhelm his ability to act decisively.

PART 4

GETTING LEADERSHIP BANDWIDTH
WHAT IT REALLY TAKES TO SUCCEED AS A LEADER WITH BROADER ORGANIZATIONAL LEADERSHIP RESPONSIBILITY

■ ■ ■

Garnering organizational leadership bandwidth takes discipline and tenacity. And it takes vision. Leadership bandwidth is, quite simply, the capacity to assume a broader scope of responsibility and lead effectively at progressively higher levels of the organization. Those who successfully acquire the necessary bandwidth to shoulder broader organizational roles are emotionally mature, and they are tireless in their pursuit of the right stuff for managing themselves and the multiple competing priorities they confront every day. They are willing to reinvent themselves at each new level of contribution, shedding what no longer serves them and cultivating important new skills, behavior, and relationships.

Leaders seeking to garner leadership bandwidth often discover that the path is replete with paradox and contradictions. For example, developing the capacity of a team may mean that a leader needs to invest in the development of individual team members. Moreover, while leaders with bandwidth have considerable authority, they understand that they can easily overplay that hand, and that they must develop the capacity to influence without overusing the authority of their positions. It's the power of personality over positional authority. And there's more. They understand that acquiring bandwidth can be and often is about developing skills outside of one's core expertise. In fact, clinging too closely to a specialty can be an impediment to creating leadership bandwidth.

Perhaps most important, leaders with bandwidth have the capacity to step up courageously and act decisively in the absence of a comfortable amount of data to support decision making. This is about accepting risk and using the skills of synthesis to filter out the critical pieces of information that will lead to decisions that are ahead of the market. These leaders are nimble at creating clarity out of complexity.

24.

"BUILD BREADTH VERSUS DEPTH AND ENHANCE COMMUNICATION"

■　■　■

When I first met **Fred Muhleman** in 1999 during an extended consulting assignment at the Eastman Kodak Company in Rochester, New York, he was already building extensive leadership bandwidth. While he was trained as an engineer and recognized for his solid contributions in that arena, it was clear that his interests lay more in the business. He soon moved up to a highly visible role as director of worldwide manufacturing for single-use cameras, and later he moved on to the role of CEO of Cross Bros. Company, a manufacturer of power transmission equipment and integrated conveyor systems.

Fred has been very strategic about building leadership bandwidth. He relates that two things are critical to success in this arena:

■ Taking on broad assignments versus building depth in a specialty
■ Taking on tough assignments that stretch you in many directions

The benefits of taking on stretch assignments can be measured in attracting more of the right kind of opportunities and in upward mobility. And, he says, "Taking on a number of assignments with some of the best people as collaborators really broadened my perspective."

Fred's assessment is that *the higher you go in an organization, the more your being a specialist is a detriment.* "And what's more," he says, "you must be willing to make the leap, *get out of your comfort zone, and take some risks.*" He observes that many people fail to stretch beyond their comfort zones out of fear of failure. He's quick to point out that while many stretch assignments do carry risk (that's what makes them a stretch after all), it is possible to calculate the risk ahead of time and manage it in real time. He advises, "You don't have to sign up for driving the space shuttle. Understand that you are at risk, but determine what you need to do to match the challenge." For Fred, this meant making a personal investment on his own time conducting research and doing analysis to make sure he was up to the task. It also meant being willing to learn in the midst of performing.

Fred advises anyone seeking to gain leadership bandwidth to *build strategic thinking capability and knowledge of the broader business world,* particularly international business. This includes staying abreast of trends across a broad spectrum of industries, not just your own. "You can learn a lot by looking at how other industries handle things, and you can make comparisons and customize to your situation."

He acknowledges that his toughest challenge in building leadership bandwidth was in enhancing his communication skills. "You have to be able to speak to multiple audiences, including the front line, suppliers, board members, employees, colleagues, and customers to be on solid footing." He maintains that being knowledgeable gives you the confidence to move quickly when decisions are needed, and to be able to communicate those decisions effectively. Fred believes that as a leader with bandwidth, you don't have to be expert in a given area, but you do have to be knowledgeable enough to be able to effectively integrate information at a high level and be conversant in a variety of contexts. "You have to be knowledgeable enough to be able to customize responses to specific organizational challenges."

Then there is the notion of charisma. A good deal of press has been dedicated to the topic of charismatic leaders. But is having charisma important to getting leadership bandwidth? Fred is quite clear on where he stands on this one. *"Charisma may get you in the door, but it's credibility that keeps you there."* In Fred's view, charisma is vastly overrated as a leadership attribute. He believes that *executive presence* is important in gaining leadership bandwidth, but it shouldn't be confused with charisma. Executive presence is having the credibility that is grounded in capability, confidence, and caring for others. He says, "I've seen people who were charismatic, confident, and caring, but who lacked capability. I've also seen people who were capable and confident but who didn't care about their organizational stakeholders. In either case, these leaders simply don't have staying power."

25. "DEVELOP A FRAMEWORK THAT SUPPORTS TEAM VERSUS ME"

■ ■ ■

Greg Boal is president and CIO of AmerUs Capital Management, one of America's largest institutional fund managers. Greg describes himself as having been quite technically proficient earlier in his career, an attribute that was rewarded with increasingly greater responsibility. He says, "As a technical expert, I was a one-man show. But I realized fairly early on that the technical proficiency that had scored me the early wins had to be supplanted by other competencies as I garnered greater organizational bandwidth. I realized that I had to get out of my comfort zone of hard-driving individual achiever. I had to stop thinking I could do it all myself." Greg learned that not only did he need to manage himself differently, he also needed to communicate differently as his sphere of influence increased, and he had to change the way he touched the organization.

Greg explains that as a technical expert, his communications tended to be based on one-to-one interaction with colleagues, and they were very focused on the specific objectives he had established for a project or task. As the leader of an entire organization, however, his *communications have to be broader and more general.* "Today," he says, "I set broad goals, and I ask the team to establish a plan for executing against them. I don't set the specific objectives anymore." He observes that while he has less personal control, the upside is that he has more bench strength, he gets more buy-in, and he gets more substance when he puts ownership on the team. The team benefits from the cross-pollination that occurs, and together they own the successes and the failures.

Somewhat paradoxically, Greg says that developing a framework that supports "team versus me" required that he spend considerable time with each individual helping him or her build a solid professional identity that can be taken into a team environment. People are less likely to lose their individuality and are more capable of merging their interests with those of others when they are on a solid foundation as individuals. They are also more willing to take risks. It's really a shift from self-trust to trust in others. One of the reasons Greg feels so strongly about supplying this level of support to the up-and-coming leaders in his organization is that these ingredients were there for him when he was coming up. "I had bosses who invested time with me and who expressed confidence in me, and that made me more confident and strong." While Greg extols the virtues of high-performance teamwork, it's important to recognize that, at the end of the day, everyone is still an individual, and they want to hear how they did and what contributions they made. He suggests that a team environment that values and affirms individual differences and individual contributions to a larger shared purpose has the right balance.

Still another shift that Greg had to make was to realize the *importance of staying close to the team.* "As an individual contributor and technical expert, I could afford to remain at some distance from others, but being distant would not serve me well now." Greg explains that he had an opportunity to locate his office several floors above the members of his executive team, but he refused. "It was just too important," he says, "that I co-locate with those I influence every day. I did not want to be an absent leader." Greg believes that 95 percent of organizational members want to be led somewhere. "People migrate to those people they want to follow, and they want to follow those who create an organizational identity that's worthy. A fully present leader helps to create and reinforce that worthy identity." Greg explains that he holds "skip meetings" with staff at lower levels of the organization with or without the manager in the room. He says, "I learn a lot from these meetings, and through them I am able to develop a loyalty factor that would otherwise be difficult to do. I believe that as a leader, I have to be seen, and I have to be among those I lead."

26. "USE THE POWER OF YOUR PERSONALITY TO MAKE PEOPLE FEEL IMPORTANT"

■ ■ ■

It may sound a little strange coming from the deputy chief of the U.S. Army Medical Service Corps, but **Colonel Lisa Weatherington** is pulling no punches when she says that to be an effective leader, you must have a certain grace and charm and a personality that people admire. The Medical Service Corps oversees the work of 10,000 active duty Army personnel, Army National Guard, and Army reservists stationed all over the world.

Lisa shares that while she has always been a "people person," the idea took on added meaning as she came up the military ranks and garnered leadership bandwidth. She believes that *charisma is a critical attribute for success as a leader.* But exactly what does she mean by the term *charisma*? For Lisa, it's simple. She says, "Charisma is using the power of your personality to inspire others." She is able to observe it in leaders who make others feel important by acknowledging their contributions, and she sees it when leaders show a sincere interest in fostering the success of those they lead. Charisma is also very apparent in leaders who are ethical and who hold themselves to high standards. And leaders who are optimistic are those with charisma.

Lisa says, "My boss is a general, and we have very similar personalities. We're not the slightest bit weak, but we want to do the right things for people. We want to be the kind of people others will want to follow." *Want* to follow? That's right. She goes on to say that in her world, as tough as that world can be when her country is at war, the generals she knows have no tolerance for leaders who don't care about people. Those who misuse their power by diminishing others simply don't get promoted. She adds that generals also don't have tolerance for those who don't have what it takes to build teams.

So a leader who wants to develop more bandwidth has to *move beyond his or her technical skills and be a team builder.* Lisa explains, "To build an effective team, a leader must first and foremost have credibility. You bring credibility when you have good professional qualifications for the work you do and when you set an example of exemplary conduct for others." And that's not all. Lisa asserts that the best team builders possess the skills to relate with people, no matter what their rank. They never make anyone feel inferior. Moreover, top-notch team builders don't overuse their authority. Lisa says, "I get to work with the best of the best, so I don't need to overuse the authority of my position."

Another factor in successfully gaining leadership bandwidth is the ability of a leader to *optimize the power of networks.* Lisa has realized that as she has taken on broader organizational responsibility, networks are more important than ever. "I used to hang back in the corner, but now I really work the room." She has made it her business to meet people at all levels—and to get to know them. "The result," she says, "is that people want me on their team. I'm in the job I have today because I was invited in to it." Lisa goes on to say that networks have helped her do her work more effectively. "I can call and get expertise and advice from my network contacts at any time. It helps me be smarter in my job. After all, we all need information to do our jobs well."

Lisa observes that *leaders with bandwidth never burn their bridges.* She has seen people make this mistake on their way up, and they forfeit their opportunity to be considered for key positions. "It's important to always try to understand others' perspectives. It's okay to disagree, but it's not okay to be combative or argumentative." She advises that if you disagree with others, above all be respectful. And be sure that your position has merit. People respect others who do the homework to build their case rather than simply react at an emotional level.

27. "SEEK OUT MULTIPLE STRETCH ASSIGNMENTS TO CREATE BANDWIDTH"

■ ■ ■

Joe Mauro is vice president of operations for Wayne Water Systems, a manufacturer of water pumps and systems for residential applications, such as pools and spas and sump pumps. Since joining the company in 1991, he's had opportunities to work in engineering, manufacturing, sales and marketing, and plant management. He attributes the leadership bandwidth he has today to having had multiple cross-functional experiences.

Joe says that as a result of taking on several stretch assignments, he learned how misguided he was in thinking that manufacturing operations were the center of the universe. During a stint in sales and marketing, for example, he honed his communication skills and learned about the customer's perspective. He explains that all of his organizational assignments were deliberately designed as cross-functional developmental experiences with the goal of broadening his knowledge of the business.

In Joe's mind, *getting bandwidth is about broadening your knowledge*—gathering more information about your business as well as other businesses that you can use to gauge the overall health of your company. "There's a real danger," he says, "with groupthink, especially with very well-established companies. Without new ideas that challenge the status quo, a company can get very stale, and people can get complacent. The overall result is a system that becomes choked on itself and incapable of growth."

One important thing he says he learned is that functional area managers who aren't exposed to other areas of the company really do have tunnel vision. For example, engineers tend to talk too much and are too revealing in front of customers. Similarly, sales and marketing people really don't understand inventory-control issues. So a key value of acquiring cross-functional experience as a core strategy for building leadership bandwidth is the ability to understand the impact of a concept on the overall business, from design, development, manufacturing, quality control, marketing and sales, and profitability.

Joe believes that getting an advanced degree in business was another key factor in his developing bandwidth. While earning his MBA, he was in an environment in which he could interact with others and learn about real-world scenarios about companies other than his own. "You can relate other people's experiences to your context and make comparisons to what you're doing."

To develop critical-thinking skills and a global perspective, Joe suggests reading trade publications and major business publications. He adds that it's important to critically evaluate what you read and not just accept everything as truth just because someone wrote it. In his view, reading broadly helps you develop the skill of critical thinking. "I was at one time a plagiarist of sorts. I just regurgitated what I'd read, following things closely, but not really thinking for myself." He believes that you've got to be able to write your own story, meaning you've got to create customized solutions. To do that, you've got to be able think critically.

He offers offshore manufacturing as a case in point. Many issues have to be grappled with, including cultural issues, fostering acceptance of offshore manufacturing with existing employees, and overcoming the limitations of an overly narrow point of view. Even if you don't manufacture anything offshore, you're still in a global sourcing and servicing environment, and you've got to understand what it's about and be able to deal with it.

Finally, Joe advises that *developing effective presentation skills* is important to broad-based leadership success. "If you don't have the ability to effectively communicate your ideas, you won't earn the respect of others. It's just that simple." You can start with small presentations, such as those you might deliver at trade shows or with individual customers, and work your way up from there. But do whatever it takes to acquire the skills and the poise to deliver your ideas smoothly and confidently.

28. "LEARN TO CREATE CLARITY OUT OF COMPLEXITY"

■ ■ ■

As the senior vice president and general manager for Mattel's Worldwide Barbie Collectibles business, **Nancy Zwiers** had leadership bandwidth few ever dream of. Prior to this senior-level leadership role, she held the reins as senior vice president of worldwide marketing of the Barbie brand, so she knew Barbie inside and out. Nancy explains that in a consumer-driven business such as toys, the focus of management and the path to the top of the company is brand management.

Nancy relates that developing more bandwidth as a leader required her to *shed certain practices to make room for more responsibility.* What that meant in practical terms was that with every shift in responsibility, she had to change her delegation strategy. She also had to be crystal clear about what her company was paying her to do. "I realized that I was being paid for my leadership, direction setting, creativity, and decision making as opposed to the amount of time I spent on the job on tangible deliverables that I personally produced." She suggests that an individual seeking leadership bandwidth should ask the following questions: "Am I clear in setting direction? Am I making good decisions for the business? Am I creative? Am I fostering creativity in others?"

Nancy fervently believes that *critical thinking is the most salable asset of a leader with bandwidth.* The ability to synthesize complex information to make good decisions was what propelled her to the top of her organization—to that place where the leadership pyramid narrows considerably. She observes that her less successful colleagues were simply unable to create clarity out of complexity. "You've got to be able to look at data and make decisions with less-than-perfect information, and that means being willing to assume some personal risk in the process." Nancy suggests that *synthesis is the ability to take complex information and translate it into a point of view.* In her experience, many people get so tied up in the details that they can't see through them to get a point of view. She believes that this all comes down to having the courage to make decisions in the absence of certainty. She offers an illustrative story about an early assignment at Mattel that summoned her courage.

"I was the director of Mack (Mattel's magic nursery doll brand) and it was the peak holiday selling season when it became clear that we had excess inventory in both our warehouses and retail outlets. There was the threat of 'carryover' after the holiday season, which in the toy industry is deadly. The company president mandated that we do a promotion that would fix the problem. It was already mid-November, and we had less than four weeks to plan and execute a promotion. The circumstances called for a totally unconventional approach, with no time to second-guess, conduct analysis, or indulge in self-doubt. In a mere two weeks, we put together a television commercial that included an 800 number for customers to call to get instructions on how to buy one doll and get one free. They would buy one doll in a retail store, and we would ship them a second doll from the warehouse, thus reducing inventory in both. What was really risky about this was that we had no experience managing an 800 number, and we had no idea how customers would behave. It was essentially a high-risk proposition with little margin for error, and I knew I was putting my career on the line." The promotion was hugely successful, and the brand was salvaged for another year. The success of the promotion put Nancy Zwiers on the map and made her a star at Mattel.

Nancy suggests that *being sensitive to the opportunities that no one else sees is another factor in garnering leadership bandwidth.* Following her resounding success with the Mack promotion, she moved on to the Barbie brand, which was the lifeblood of Mattel, generating more than 50 percent of the company's profits. Barbie was the Mattel CEO's baby, and she was very involved with decision making on the Barbie brand. Nancy relates, "I wanted more responsibility and more authority, but I knew I couldn't directly challenge the CEO's ownership of Barbie. I saw, on the other hand, an area of the Barbie business, Barbie Collectibles, which I thought had high potential but was underleveraged. It was low-hanging fruit, so I asked for and got authority over this piece of the business. When I took it over, it had a revenue of $6 million compared to $1 billion for Barbie. I thought, 'No one cares about this, so let me show you.' It was my proving ground. In three years we grew the Barbie Collectibles business to $175 million, doubling it every year. There was, as I had suspected, pent-up demand that no one else saw. Everyone owned a Barbie, but not everyone owned Barbie Collectibles."

29. "REINVENT YOUR BRAND TO GAIN LEADERSHIP BANDWIDTH"

■ ■ ■

Richard DiMarzo is senior vice president, wealth management advisor and portfolio management director with Citigroup Smith Barney. Richard and his team manage $450 million in assets on the private client side and $1.5 billion in assets on the institutional client side. But that's not where he started. For the first dozen years that he worked with his firm, Richard was in the highly tactical position of managing bonds for individual client portfolios. He observes, "I was doing things on a very microlevel."

Richard explains that in his business, moving up and getting more bandwidth is about moving away from a particular base as you take on larger client portfolios. It's also about developing the capabilities of a team so they can think and act in alignment with you. And it's about broadening your knowledge of the investment business and all markets even if you're not the one making all the investment decisions for clients' portfolios. But there's even more to it. Richard realized that as he took on broader investment responsibility, he had to reinvent himself and his brand.

As a bonds expert, Richard worked with a team of investment professionals "in the back room." "I was known as the bonds guy—a very conservative person managing the most conservative part of a portfolio. I was seen as this boring guy dealing with boring bonds sitting in the background." When he was offered the opportunity to shift his role and develop his own book of business, he knew he needed a serious overhaul of his image. And it had to start from the inside out. He says, "I had to see myself differently, and I had to be able to convince others. You can become so pigeon-holed and branded in a particular way, it can be tough to break away."

Richard hired an executive coach to guide him in making the critical shifts, including symbolic changes as well as changes in how he conducted himself in the business. He faced some obstacles right away. "There were confrontations with colleagues and with clients who were initially put off by my taking on a bigger role. There were even obstacles I had to overcome to get a proper executive office, now that I was no longer the bonds guy in the back room." Richard persevered, and with the discipline and integrity that he maintains has always characterized his work, he won the confidence of colleagues and clients.

Richard says, "I don't select bonds anymore. I went from hands-on management to directing bonds management. I have analysts working for me, and now I direct the functional area. I spend my time leading the effort to create wealth for clients. I direct the bonds side, but I also assist in managing the other equity-based assets in client portfolios." He says that developing layers of support to manage the increasing complexity was critically important to his garnering bandwidth. But that move was not without risk. As he puts it, "There's a risk in that you're passing a client to a junior associate to directly manage. If you can't do that, you can't get bandwidth. You have to believe in your people, and you have to believe that you've got the ability to grow yourself and your business to a new level."

In addition to seeing the need to build a team that could manage the additional complexity of more clients with more net worth, Richard realized that he needed to enhance his interpersonal skills and his understanding of people and their circumstances. He observes, "I now need to foster organizational morale, help others develop leadership skills, and help advisors build skills for developing new business. I have to be willing to entrust others with significant responsibility without micromanaging them in the process."

Above all, Richard maintains, a leader with bandwidth is an individual who has clear and visible values and who models personal integrity. He sums it all up by saying, "You are a shepherd and a champion for organization-wide behavior. Don't lie, don't cheat, don't steal, and if you make a mistake, own it and make it right."

30. "ASK FOR ASSIGNMENTS IN AREAS OUTSIDE OF YOUR CORE EXPERTISE"

■ ■ ■

Marci Johnson has worked for Boeing and its divested business for 22 years, and during that time she's had four careers. She's now the executive director of sales and marketing for SPIRIT AeroSystems, the airplane components manufacturing division Boeing sold in 2005. Sales and marketing is an area that's pretty far removed from where she was when she started her career. Her story is a distinct twist on getting organizational bandwidth.

Marci worked in finance for the first eight years she was with Boeing, but then she became restless for a change. So she did what few people in finance would ever do. She asked for a job in manufacturing operations. What inspired her bold action? "I got involved in Boeing's Expo Program [Expo is short for executive potential], and I crafted a development program that had me spending time with operations managers. I got to follow them around, and I discovered that I was really fascinated with manufacturing. So I asked for an operations management role. The hiring manager told me that was too big of a stretch, so he gave me a job as business manager, which my finance background qualified me quite nicely for. Eight months later, after I'd proven myself, I got my first factory management role." Marci acquired some real leadership bandwidth traction in that role, an accomplishment she doesn't take lightly. She explains, "In a company the size of Boeing, it's easy to get lost in the shuffle unless you're willing to advocate for yourself. As a matter of fact, I've not had jobs that were simply handed to me. I've asked for what I've gotten every step of the way. Either a job was created for me, or a place was created within an existing job for me."

Following her stint in manufacturing operations management, Marci spent almost a year doing e-business development as a stretch assignment. When her boss left to take another assignment, she took over his program management role, and in the process obtained some real leadership bandwidth traction. She was still in that role when Boeing sold her division. When she landed at SPIRIT, she told the new CEO that she wanted to work in sales and marketing. After all, her program management role had involved internal business development.

What was Marci's strategy for getting the kind of visibility that's enabled her to pursue four careers within the same organization? She shares that early in her career she established goals that set the tone for her future. But in her view, what was more important to creating a sustainable advantage and real bandwidth was her performance. She believes that crossing functions has kept her on her toes and enhanced her performance. While that notion may seem counterintuitive, she points out that many people get a new job in a field they already know well and where their success is virtually assured. "But," she says, "I didn't have the expertise, so I had to get on a steep learning curve to be successful. I didn't have the option to take anything for granted. I was curious, I asked a lot of questions, and I listened well. I think I performed better as a result."

Marci advises that it's a good idea to take on broad stretch assignments that will develop you outside of your core expertise. She maintains that she's acquired the most bandwidth and her performance has been at its best when she's taken on assignments for which she's had very few of the traditional qualifications. For Marci, it comes down to identifying the people who know the things you want to learn, and then asking for the opportunity to work with them.

Finally, Marci offers that it's important to *recognize that everything doesn't have to be a sprint.* She adds, "If you're always intense at work, you're going to crash and burn at some point, most likely at a time when you can least afford it. If you don't have any reserves when you most need them, you don't appear to be someone who can manage yourself through the ups and downs. You have no bandwidth."

31. "MAINTAIN A STRATEGIC FOCUS IN EVERYTHING YOU DO"

■ ■ ■

Vicki Bertoch acquired serious leadership bandwidth when the computer services firm where she was a midlevel manager was acquired by Affiliated Computer Services, a Fortune 500 company that employs more than 50,000 individuals. She was given the job of vice president for site operations at ACS, a job that shifted her from managing contracts and business development to providing executive-level operations oversight for 200 employees covering two states.

Vicki says her ambition and drive and her willingness to assume risk enabled her to get traction in the merged organization. As a leader in a large firm, *you have to find ways to manage the world you're in but also be able to represent your skills and capacities to those at the top* of the organization. So what does she suggest a leader who wants to develop more bandwidth do to attract that visibility? In Vicki's experience, *taking on challenges that others don't want to take on*—you know, the ones that are not at all glamorous—and being successful with them can give you a lot of visibility in a large firm. She illustrates this point with a story: "There was a large contract we were bidding on. The business development and positioning for the contract involved a lot of minion-level work, like sitting at a booth at health fairs. When the key person quit, I stepped up. It was boring work, but not only did we win the contract, we got a lot of public attention, and I was recognized in the process."

Vicki believes it's important to *volunteer your talent even if you don't see immediately how it's going to benefit you.* It may be an opportunity to support peers, but she insists that *the importance of managing peer relationships well can't be overstated for a leader who wants bandwidth.* She observes, "Having good relationships with peers is critical in senior-level roles. Whenever you are being looked at for promotion, your peers are polled for their opinions about you. Naturally, you can't have a manipulative agenda when supporting your peers. It has to be about creating win-wins. But when you help others, it benefits you." This kind of collaboration requires some sacrifice on the part of a leader in service to the broader organization, but Vicki believes it is well worth the effort.

Maintaining a strategic focus is of particular importance for a leader with bandwidth. As Vicki puts it, "My job is to figure out what we need to be doing next year, not today." But a strategic focus also involves developing people who work most closely with the leader. Vicki fervently believes that she needs to always be two people deep in her succession plan. She says, "You never want to be captured by an employee whose departure leaves a gaping hole in your organization. Good succession planning and leader development can address that." Vicki believes that maintaining a strategic view means supporting people to move in many different directions in the organization. She exclaims, "I prepare people to slingshot right past me."

In Vicki's view, *a leader with bandwidth is personally invested in the company's bottom line and delivers results with bottom-line impact.* She observes that leaders who don't link division-level initiatives to the bottom line lose their credibility in the organization, and, as a result, they forfeit their flexibility to self-manage their own careers. For her, success in this area comes down to having the capacity to make decisions and handle authority. She has to answer some tough questions, such as, "What will it take to win the business? Can we make money for the company with this business? Can we keep our promises?" Putting it bluntly she says, "Plan or go home."

Finally, Vicki cautions that a leader has to be willing to *hang tough when it's necessary, even at the risk of being unpopular.* Hanging tough doesn't mean that a leader is off the hook for garnering the support and commitment of the team. That's not always an easy thing to do, especially when you've made a decision that doesn't sit well with everybody. "But," she says, "I am clear with my team about what kind of input I need. Sometimes, I just want input for a decision I need to make, and at other times, I want shared ownership and decision making." She reiterates that it's important that a leader not miscommunicate or mislead people about the limits of their decision-making authority.

PART 5

MANAGING COMPLEXITY
AND 24/7 STRESS
SECRETS FOR STAYING SANE WITH A FULL PLATE

∎ ∎ ∎

Complexity seems to be synonymous with organizational life as we know it today. It comes in many packages, and it is a full-risk, fast-forward proposition. Sometimes, it is wrought by a catastrophic event that unleashes chaos and confusion. At other times, it is the product of a high-stakes environment. Then, there is the complexity that is manufactured in the organization when people overreact to normal events. Whatever the source, leaders who have the capability to manage through complexity deliver results without leaving casualties behind, and they earn the respect of others in the organization.

Interestingly, no simple formula exists for managing complexity. Multiple strategies are effective. What's important is that the leader be able to read the environment and deliver the right responses for the circumstances. Moreover, while being able to respond nimbly in the heat of a crisis is critical, it's often the thoughtful planning and scenario development well ahead of a crisis that set the stage for the most effective actions.

Leaders who manage complexity well also manage themselves well. When confronting complexity, they don't cave in, and they do not allow themselves to be consumed by their circumstances. In fact, being able to observe a situation without being caught up emotionally is a critical factor in managing some forms of complexity. Moreover, having a handle on the critical few pieces of information well ahead of the necessity to make time-pressured decisions can make a life-saving difference in outcomes.

Effectively managing complexity often extends beyond the boundaries of the organization, requiring political astuteness and finessed communication to external stakeholders and interested parties. Communication lapses can rapidly escalate the complexity of a situation and erode a leader's ability to influence outcomes. What's clear is that much

71

of what shows up as complexity can, in fact, be anticipated, including what needs to be communicated and to whom.

The leaders who've shared their experiences on the following pages offer illuminating and captivatingly simple strategies for managing complexity that comes in many packages.

32. "GET INVOLVED"

■ ■ ■

Commercial construction is a complex operation. **Joe Duvall** should know. He's the division manager for Kitchell Contractors' Nevada division. Joe oversees construction projects for health care facilities, office buildings, retail space, and medical specialties. At any given time, Joe has 10 to 15 construction projects ranging from $1 million to more than $80 million on the docket. That's a lot of lumber and nails to keep track of. Yet, Joe, who's been with Kitchell for more than 21 years, brings what others have come to appreciate as a cool and calm demeanor to his role. So how does he manage all that complexity? Safety issues to manage, construction costs, scheduling, hiring highly qualified and responsible people to do the work, and, oh yes, keeping the customer happy—that's just to name a few of the things he must keep his eye on.

Joe doesn't hesitate when asked how he juggles so many balls at one time without dropping any. He says, quite simply, "I take ownership of the things I work on. That's so they never get away from me." He quickly adds, "I can't manage by ignorance or by not focusing. I get involved." By getting involved, he keeps the mission-critical things right in front of him, and he keeps things moving and on schedule. Behavioral science can attest to the power of *knowing* over not knowing. People do find it easier to manage themselves, even in highly stressful situations, when they know what they are dealing with. Joe Duvall puts this principle into practice every day.

Joe is quick to admit that he can't possibly manage every detail himself, and that there is a delicate balance he must strike between being involved and being overinvolved. The consequences of being overinvolved are numerous, including communicating a lack of trust in others, being consumed by details, and limiting what else he can take on in his role. And that leads us to his second big secret for managing complexity and 24/7 stress. He creates *shared ownership* of the work and the key deliverables within his team. He says, "Team decision making really does work." He believes that it is important for a leader to delegate effectively and then to ask the right questions to ensure that things are on track and being executed well. He does this by holding brief daily meetings, regular extended meetings, and separate meetings with project leaders.

Joe grows increasingly animated as he explains, "It's too late when a situation has run its course without your involvement. There are just too many things that can go awry with subcontractors, owners, architects—the interests and concerns of all these stakeholders must be managed well to complete a project on time and within budget. It never works to put your head in the sand. You can't just hand things off." Joe's words take on added importance when one recognizes that in the commercial construction industry, a good profit margin is in the 2 percent range. There's just not a lot of margin for error if you want to be competitive.

As a final note, Joe says he fervently believes that managing complexity and 24/7 stress is made possible by ensuring that everything he and his team does is in alignment with the company's core values. Joe appreciates that values guide behavior in circumstances when a building code or a company procedure manual doesn't serve up the necessary direction. He insists that he sleeps well at night as a result.

33. "CREATE SCENARIOS AND PLAN YOUR ACTIONS BEFORE THE DAY YOU NEED TO EXECUTE THEM"

■ ■ ■

Eldon Cotton has spent more than 35 years working in the utility industry, most of that time with the Los Angeles Department of Water and Power, the largest municipal electric utility company in the United States. Currently, he works with the Northern California Power Agency on special projects. As the assistant general manager for power with the LA utility, Eldon was responsible for the work of 7,500 employees. The sheer size and scope of Eldon's arena makes it a highly complex environment, notwithstanding the highly technical systems involved.

In a complex environment such as a large municipal electric utility company, Eldon maintains that it can be easy to get lost in a sea of details.

As a result, he says it's important to be *crystal clear about what constitutes a successful operation and translate that into clearly defined roles* that each team member must play. "Clear thinking must precede clear verbal and written communications. If your people are confused, you as a leader need to examine the original thought process as well as the communications." In his view, confusion is a symptom that you haven't planned and communicated well.

He goes on to say that before choosing a path of action, the leader must define the problem, set objectives, establish alternative courses of action, make a decision, and clearly communicate a plan. The leader then must be accessible to reinforce the objectives and support assessment and course corrections based on new information. This sounds simple enough, but Eldon asserts that as a public servant in a highly charged environment (no pun intended), a leader is in the public fishbowl. He says it's important that you always not only *do* the right thing but that you also *appear to do* the right thing. Thus, managing impressions becomes an essential part of the job of a leader in a complex environment.

What about circumstances where people's lives and safety may be jeopardized because of downed power lines in an earthquake or other natural disaster? Eldon says, "In a life or death situation, you'd better have *gradations of action* that are well thought through ahead of time. You must anticipate what can possibly go wrong and scrutinize your options before the fact." He goes on to say that there's quite a lot of thinking that goes into creating "what-if scenarios" and courses of action. "Then," he adds, "it's important that everyone is very well trained and knows what their roles are."

The importance of this advice becomes more apparent when you consider the fact that in an emergency, a leader may not have time to call someone higher up or consult a handbook. *"You use what you know and have committed to memory,"* Eldon says. "An emergency is no time to hold meetings and build consensus. You don't have that luxury; you have to act." Thus it is critical in an emergency situation in a complex environment that people have the *authority to act*.

Finally, whenever a major incident occurs, it is paramount that a thorough review and debriefing take place. Eldon stresses the importance of this process. "You have to learn what part of your system or your process failed or if human performance was impaired or inadequately prepared. You've got to close the loop, not just to review what happened, but also to evaluate the quality of decision making and problem solving." It's important that this process be conducted in a timely fashion, before the details become fuzzy and everyone's memory fades. Eldon says, "Use what you learn to improve your processes, your systems, your personnel training, and your communications."

34. "MANAGE THE CRITICAL FEW PIECES OF INFORMATION"

■ ■ ■

Neil Parker knows about fast-forward complexity in a way that few people ever do. Now a captain for the 737 jetliner and instructor and FAA evaluator for Delta Air Lines, Neil was a Marine Corps major and jet fighter pilot who saw Persian Gulf War duty. His story about managing complexity takes him back to the day in August of 1983 that he vividly recalls as though it were yesterday.

Neil had just taken off in the two-seat A-4 training jet he was flying solo when, at 750 feet off the ground, the plane's engine exploded. He says, "I was very cognizant of the criticality of my situation, but everything was seemingly occurring in such slow motion, I felt like I was in thick motor oil." Neil pauses to explain the phenomenon called "temporal distortion." He says, "When you're in a life-threatening situation, your adrenaline speeds up your thought process, but it feels like everything is occurring in slow motion." He goes on to say, "I was looking up through the top of the airplane's canopy, but I was looking at the ground. I realized in that split second that the airplane had rolled over into an upside-down position. I looked at my instruments and realized that the engine gauge was reading hot, and the engine speed was spiraling down. I could see that the engine was not functioning, and I knew I was in deep trouble. I was close to the ground, and I knew that safely ejecting from the plane with it in an upside-down position was impossible."

At this point, Neil explains the so-called "ejection envelope." "The ejection envelope is based on a chart that I had committed to memory while in training. My instructor told me that memorizing that chart might one day save my life." Neil explains that the chart essentially shows the operational envelope for ejection under different circumstances. In other words, under what circumstances can the pilot eject safely? He says, "This was just about the worst-case scenario I could possibly imagine. But at that moment I understood that while everything's important, there were only a few critically important things I had to manage." So what did he do next?

"I had lost my hydraulics, but I was able to correct the banking of the plane by manually using both the stick and the rudder. When the scene in front of me went from brown to blue—in other words, when I went from looking at the earth to looking at the sky—I pulled the ejection handle between my legs." Neil believes that the plane had already begun to descend when he pulled his ejection handle. "When I pulled the handle, I sat there for what seemed like an eternity before anything happened, and I thought, Now what? Then I heard the back seat go, and I was still sitting there. All of a sudden my field of vision filled with red. I knew that this was the color of the flame from the rocket on my seat, and a moment later I was out of the plane. Now I was in the air stream, with a violent 200 knots of air buffeting me. I was tumbling through the air and thinking that I didn't want to see the ground coming up, so I closed my eyes. Then chaos turned to quiet as the ejection sequence ended and my seat pulled away from me and my parachute opened. I opened my eyes and saw my airplane hit the ground about 1,000 yards in front of me. Then, in what could have been no more than five seconds since my parachute had been exploded open by a small grenade-like device, I hit the ground."

Neil's story is riveting in and of itself, but he maintains there were compelling lessons in it for him, and he believes those lessons can benefit other leaders. He offers the following strategies for those whose roles involve managing complexity:

- *Determine if you have time.* Many times a leader is faced with a decision but has the time to do the due diligence. In this case, rushing a decision may not be a smart thing to do. At other times, waiting can be deleterious.
- *Ask if you can give yourself more time.* Is there something you can do immediately, as in stemming the flow of blood from an open wound, while you consider your other options?

- *Use your expertise and the critical information right in front of you.* When the circumstances are critical, you have to act, and you have to act based on what you already know and the information that is immediately accessible.
- *Know what's important to know.* It's important to know in advance what the critical few pieces of information are that will enable you to resolve a critical situation quickly and safely.
- *Treat it as a circumstance.* Stay focused on your environment and don't allow your emotions to blind you to what's really important.

Finally, Neil observes that it's important that a leader steadfastly *resist the tendency to become complacent.* "Things are changing all the time, complex environments become even more so, and being on a continuous learning curve is part of what it takes to maintain one's effectiveness. To know what's important to know, you have to continuously assess your environment in noncritical circumstances and add to your experience and expertise. *Don't settle for being merely proficient.* Make mastery your lifelong aim."

35. "ANTICIPATE WHAT CAN GO WRONG AND HAVE A COMMUNICATIONS STRATEGY"

■ ■ ■

The fighting of wildfires is filled with mystique, and it is filled with danger. It's class-one complexity with very little margin for error. **Tony Kern** knows firsthand. A U.S. Air Force lieutenant colonel and B-1 bomber pilot turned Air Force Academy instructor, Tony left the military in 2000 to take the job of director of national aviation for the U.S. Department of Agriculture's Forest Service. The responsibility for fighting wildfires rests with the Forest Service.

Tony explains that for at least 25 years, wildfires have been fought with World War II vintage air tanker planes that have been retrofitted. Not that they were the only weapon in the arsenal. Of the 1,000 aircraft used in fighting wildfires, 750 are helicopters, but the public's perception is that of an air tanker dropping fire retardant. He says, "The singular view by the public was that of an all-American flying hero fighting fires, and no one did anything to correct that perception." That false perception complicated matters a lot when the wings of two air tanker planes came off during a firefighting mission, costing several lives when they crashed. The events that followed offer an illuminating model in managing complexity.

"The first thing we did," Tony explains, "is ground the planes. Our first priority was to get people out of harm's way and to slow the process down." In his view, it's easy to become paralyzed by complexity, so *slowing the process down is an important initial step.* "We then established two task forces: one to manage the public reaction and a second to focus on the immediate technical problems."

A number of things had not been anticipated in the disaster scenario planning by the Forest Service, including the intense public and media interest, and the attention of Congress. Tony explains that the public needed reassurance that there was adequate wildfire fighting protection despite the grounding of the air tanker planes. The public also needed reassurance about the efficacy of the helicopters. Helicopters are, in fact, much safer and more efficient in fighting wildfires than are air tanker planes. They can replenish their supplies without having to land at an airport, and they can hover over a fire to ensure that the retardant is properly placed. Tony asserts that a disaster response plan that includes a *communications strategy* is of critical importance in managing a crisis. Not having a communications strategy can pull vital resources away from the response effort, and unnecessary chaos and confusion can result. Moreover, *a response plan should be simulated ahead of time.* Tony adds that communications can be well managed and serve the mutual interests of the organization and a concerned public, and they can serve to build trust. On the other hand, communications that are poorly managed are likely to result in an emotionally charged public reaction that can spiral beyond a leader's ability to influence.

Tony observes that in a complex situation a leader has to make decisions in the absence of clear consensus. "A crisis calls for situational leadership, and sometimes you make a decision that can cost you your job. It takes a level of confidence and courage to do that." So what advice does he have for others who might face a complex situation to manage?

- *Get the high-risk situation under control as quickly as possible.* Stabilize the situation and buy the time you need to get a clearer picture of what's going on.
- *Bring together both experts and confidants.* Each group plays distinct roles in a complex environment. *Confidants* play important roles as trusted advisors and sounding boards when a leader's brain is in hyperdrive. They can provide an unbiased perspective and help a leader think through the options. *Experts,* on the other hand, ensure that a leader accesses the best available technical information to inform decision making. A *maven* is a special kind of expert who knows where to find the technical resources when they are most needed. Mavens can be extremely helpful in managing complexity, especially when there are unforeseen variables.
- *Manage the experts.* Experts, who are accustomed to being at the top of their fields, can be difficult to work with. They often come with biases they are reluctant to relinquish. They need to understand that they are working as part of a team in an environment that has distinct challenges. A process needs to be put in place that pulls out the best thinking from the group as a whole.
- *Normalize the headwork.* Often, a complex situation takes weeks or months to resolve. After the initial sprint that's required to stabilize a crisis, the situation becomes more of a marathon. A schedule needs to be put into place that enables people to add value but that doesn't burn them out.
- *Annotate the process.* There will be questions and there will be critics, so a record of the process and of the decisions made will be invaluable. There is also the need to review previously made plans and adjust them in light of the learning from the current reality. Moreover, as a final-phase effort, annotating the process gives people a sense of completion.

As a result of the air tanker plane crashes, new standards for airworthiness were put into effect by the National Aviation Program, and 50 percent of the planes that were grounded have been put back into service.

36. "MANAGING COMPLEXITY IS ABOUT MANAGING YOUR ENVIRONMENT"

■ ■ ■

Willie Smith is the director of acquisition management for the U.S. Federal Highway Administration. As a senior executive and chief contracting officer, Willie and his organization manage $1 billion in federal highway contracts at any given time. And that's just business as usual. When you layer on the compounded effects of hurricanes and other natural disasters requiring rapid response, the job becomes even more complex.

In Willie's view, the role of the contracting officer is to ensure the integrity of the contracting process—its fairness and equity. As he sees it, this is where the rubber hits the road with the Federal Highway Administration. Willie believes that it's important to build integrity into the process, starting with the hiring of people into the organization. For him, attributes such as training, experience, and a demonstrated commitment to stewardship all serve to ensure that taxpayers' interests are well served. He says, "It's important that I put myself into a taxpayer's shoes."

Willie believes that doing his job well requires *a keen awareness of the volatility of the environment,* including the public, the agency, the taxpayer, Congress, and the media. Moreover, because highways have a heavy federal-aid-program component, the environment includes the state transportation departments of each of the 50 states plus Washington, D.C., and Puerto Rico. He says, "Managing complexity is equal to managing your environment."

His experience managing complexity has repeatedly shown him the importance of a number of leader behaviors:

■ *Be proactive.* You need to develop anticipatory skills because you cannot afford to be constantly reacting to what's coming at you. When you are able to envision the future and plan for contingencies, you are less likely to be surprised down the road, and you can handle things with increased confidence and flexibility.

■ *Do what you like to do.* When you enjoy your work, you tend to see opportunities instead of problems in front of you. You tackle them with energy and enthusiasm. Willie says he is reminded of a saying he heard a long time ago: "Find a job that you love, and you'll never have to work a day in your life."

- *Play to your strengths.* This is the other side of doing what you like to do. When you play to your natural strengths, you can balance complexity with "effort and ease." Moreover, you garner self-confidence along the way as you stretch into new skills and succeed.

- *Resist falling into the trap created by embracing other people's anxieties.* You've no doubt experienced the loss of energy and morale that can result from being around anxious, stressed-out people. Willie believes you have to steadfastly resist reducing yourself to the lowest common denominator around you. Instead, he advises those charged with managing complexity to maintain their focus and intensity, to look for the opportunities instead of the problems, and to keep an optimistic outlook.

- *Maintain your situational awareness.* Don't just focus on how things are today; anticipate how things are likely to be tomorrow. This is really about developing the strategic skills that enable you to identify the future implications of today's actions, examine the trends that will create future demands, and read the internal and external politics that are going to affect your work down the road.

- *Foster an organizational structure that creates situational awareness.* The leader isn't the only one who needs to have situational awareness. Willie suggests that a leader can foster it through such things as maintaining open organizational communication at all levels, delegating responsibility, and creating soft landings when people make mistakes.

- *Create and communicate three or four signature themes.* When managing complexity, it's important for a leader to have a few critical communication pieces so people "stay on message." When the core messages are clear, people are more likely to embrace them and act on them with enthusiasm, purpose, and focus.

- *Manage your ego.* Willie asserts that if your ego is in conflict with the mission, you end up fighting every battle, big or small, and elevating your stress. So know where you need to engage— don't take every hill in front of you.

■ *Maintain a balance between your work and life.* By taking care of yourself outside of work you are more able to handle the day-to-day work-induced stress that comes with the package of managing complexity.

37. "IT'S LIKE HERDING CATS"

■ ■ ■

University of Windsor President **Ross Paul,** PhD, believes there is a widespread misconception that there is a difference between the private-sector and higher education. He points out that in the Knowledge Age, private-sector companies are hiring highly trained professionals with deep subject matter expertise, and, as a result, those companies have to be managed more like universities. "When managing professionals," Ross says, "it's important to recognize that their first loyalty is to their discipline, not to the organization." He thinks that the goal, whether you're in an academic leadership role or a business leadership role, is to create the conditions where entrepreneurship can thrive. As he puts it, "You're managing people who have more expertise than you do. It's like herding cats. They are at various stages of their careers, have varied backgrounds and subject matter expertise, and they have their individual career aspirations." Ross believes that the secret to leading professionals is appreciating their passions and personal aspirations and finding ways to align those with the mission of the organization.

Ross explains that in decades past, the job of a university president was that of a moral authority. It was prestigious, and it was easy. Now it's quite complex and not at all unlike the shift that occurred with paternalistic companies that dominated the first half of the 20th century. Now the job of leadership in any complex organization includes labor relations, development of new markets, government relations, public relations, stakeholder relations, and much more. And all of it is exacerbated by the pace of change. Ross notes, "We live in a pressurized world, with information overload and instant decision making. People are worrying about the pace and how to manage themselves and their accountabilities." Then there are issues of ethics, fair treatment, and diversity. These represent advancements, but they also add to the complexity. So how does Ross propose that a leader manage through complexity?

Have a vision and stay focused on where you're heading, not where you are. Staying focused on where things are rather than where you're heading can produce a lot of stress in the organization. People become defensive, competitive, and resentful. If you can allow people to produce at a pace that matches them, they'll have all their energy aimed in the desired direction and little or none of it directed in counterproductive ways.

Follow a personal strategy. Engage in pursuits that deviate from a subject matter or discipline. Read novels and things outside of your field. Take seminars in new subject matter areas. Doing these things broadens your perspective, and having a broader perspective enhances your ability to manage complexity. In addition, maintain quality personal relationships that provide support and affirmation. "You're more than your job, and relationships help to keep that in perspective."

Maintain a diverse skills and experience mix on your team. In Ross's view, you want people who are hard to manage. Having people who challenge you will create a stronger, more resilient team. Be willing to hear the bad news along with the good. It's incredibly easy to become isolated when you're leading in a complex environment, and you can get shut off from the very information you need to ensure that the organization is on the right course. Having a diverse team and engaging in frequent informal interactions will help you stay honest in this regard.

Know when to enter and when to exit. In Ross's opinion, a leader makes his or her most significant accomplishments in five to seven years. By the tenth year, he believes that a leader's liabilities become more pronounced. While it may be difficult to validate these time frames scientifically, his point is that a leader in charge of a complex environment needs to do the introspection and get the feedback that can guide the decision about when and how to exit gracefully.

38. "HAVE A SIMPLE, CRISP VISION THAT TAPS INTO PEOPLE'S PASSIONS"

■ ■ ■

As abbot of the Portsmouth Abbey and headmaster of the Portsmouth Abbey School, **Father Mark Serna** needed a unique take on managing complexity. Mark, as he prefers to be called, recently retired from the Benedictine monastery post he'd held for 14 years. He's now serving as a pastor in the diocese of Las Vegas.

In the monastery where Mark lived and worked for many years, boundary issues made his environment a complex one to lead. He says, "For five of the years I led the monastery, I was also the headmaster of the boarding school. I was the equivalent of a board president as well as the CEO. I was the headmaster and the headmaster's boss simultaneously, and this created significant governance boundary issues. I lived where I worked, and I had to be accessible 24/7. Not only that, I was involved intensely in the lives of the employees of the school. The school employed lay personnel as well as monks from the monastery. There were multiple levels on which I related: employer, priest, and colleague. I was a spiritual leader who also raised money, provided budget and financial oversight, managed building projects, hired and fired staff, and created a vision.

"Being the headmaster of the school was in and of itself complex, but there was a pervasive underlying tension in my role as abbot of the monastery. It's no secret that religious orders are not attracting the number of people they used to. The number of people choosing a life of spiritual contemplation and service is steadily shrinking. And that's not a problem you can solve by putting an ad in the paper to recruit monks. Nonetheless, there was this underlying community stress about the need to recruit new blood, and as the leader, I carried that with me."

Mark says that he devised what he believes were successful strategies for managing the complexity he confronted in his dual roles.

■ *Have a simple, crisp vision that taps into people's passions.* It's not enough to have good ideas. A leader must convey personal conviction and passion based on a set of core values. He defines it as the power of presence, and, in his mind, it is a power that is called forth in a leader. When a leader can cut through the complexity with a simple message that resonates with others, *their* passion for service is called forth.

- *Delegate authority in a convincing way.* It's important that you know the limits of what you can personally accomplish, and then be willing to convey trust in others. It's been Mark's experience that people want real responsibility. They don't want to be told they are trusted and then feel micromanaged around what they've been delegated.

- *Understand that you are not your job.* As Mark puts it, "The person you are is not identified by or exhausted by the job you do. It's a formula for disaster when you pin your identity on a role. You need a space you can step back into—a center or foundation that is more essential."

- *Have a spiritual practice that grounds you.* Although he is a priest, and his spiritual practice is rooted in Christianity, Mark says that a spiritual practice can be any one of a variety of things. The important thing, he notes, is that whatever your spiritual practice is, it should enable you to tap into a deeper sense of your being.

- *Establish friendships and pursue interests outside of work.* Pursue friendships that provide a safe space and a sounding board without any conditions or ties to your professional role identity. These are the kind of friendships where you can really let your hair down and just be yourself, without pretense. Then, Mark advises, seek out opportunities in the form of extracurricular interests to feed the spirit and ignite the imagination. You'll find that you will be more resourceful as a leader managing complexity when you are able to harness a richer imagination.

- *Identify someone who will tell you the truth.* You need someone who will give you honest feedback—to unabashedly tell you how he or she sees things. Having such a trusted advisor can keep you from feeling isolated, because many people are afraid to be candid with a leader, especially if there is bad news. Look to your trusted advisor to keep you honest and in touch. Such a truth teller can be an internal or external resource, but it should be someone who can view the organization and you as a leader.

■ *Don't allow success or the vision of success to deplete you.* When things are going well, it's easy to fall into the trap of overcommitment and loosening of personal boundaries. But it can snowball because you simply add to the complexity you're already managing. Mark advocates doing a careful self-assessment before accepting any role in a highly complex environment. He cautions against yielding too quickly to a seductive offer. Rather, he advises, carefully consider if the role is a good match for your strengths and if the organization's structure is healthy.

39. "DON'T ALLOW 'MANUFACTURED COMPLEXITY' TO OVERWHELM YOUR ORGANIZATION"

■ ■ ■

Pablo Sobrino has a distinctive opinion about organizational complexity. He believes most of it is *manufactured.* A career government leader, he's the regional executive director of the Department of Canadian Heritage Arts and Culture Programming for the Canadian government in British Columbia, Alberta, and the Yukon. His organization oversees museums, programs to promote multiculturalism, and Canada's official languages.

Pablo believes that manufactured complexity is often an outgrowth of people having an overinflated sense of the importance of their jobs. "People create crises where there aren't any. After all, if no one's dying, and the building isn't burning, you have time to consider your options when a challenge is presented." By way of example, he offers that employees can go into a panic whenever the minister has a question. "No one stops to ask, 'How urgent is the minister's need for an answer?'" Pablo says that when he encounters manufactured complexity, he goes right to the source and asks, "Who generated the request? What's really important, and what's merely urgent?" He says, "It's important to objectively sift and sort the issues; otherwise, it's a churn, and all we end up doing is fighting fires." Oftentimes, the churn shows up in the conflicts between the competing priorities. Once you become clear about the priorities, it's far easier to keep the churn to a minimum.

Pablo observes that manufactured complexity can also occur when dysfunctional bosses who have workaholic tendencies create crises with their incessant demands. Pablo is firm in his resolve to lead by setting a positive example for his organization in this regard. He says that he endeavors to respect boundaries in meetings and on people's personal time. He says he starts and ends meetings on time, and he resists the temptation to send e-mail or call employees after normal work hours. He adds, "I may compose some e-mail in the evenings, but I don't send them until the following morning because I don't want to send a conflicting message to my employees."

What tips does Pablo have for other leaders about what it takes to effectively manage complexity, whether it is manufactured or real?

Take responsibility for managing accountabilities. By being on top of things, you're in more control and you can prevent complexity in the form of manufactured crises from showing up. Not paying attention, on the other hand, can lead to crises creeping up insidiously.

Put systems in place that will influence behavior. Pablo offers the example of using the business plan that outlines the organization's direction to identify the tools and skills needed to achieve the outcomes. He observes that a typical business plan is not a living document. A good one, on the other hand, engages all employees and addresses all organizational systems and processes. Pablo asserts that he's a strong believer in processes for getting clear on priorities and organizing the work.

Protect employees from needless demands. Pablo assumes the role of buffer and negotiator for his employees to ensure that the demands made on them are reasonable. He also believes that when they make mistakes, *he* should assume responsibility. He says, "My employees act on my behalf, so the buck stops with me. Employees trust that I will stand behind them, and they are committed to doing the best job they can do. They've got more energy to focus on the right things when I help them to manage the demands." It comes down to a leader being willing to separate the priorities from the background noise.

Pablo also has some advice for leaders on how to manage themselves personally in the midst of complexity.

Honor personal boundaries. Pablo believes that the best leaders exercise self-care. They are clear about the priorities for their work and lives and ensure that they honor those boundaries. In his experience, a leader who does this is less likely to react from a stressed place and is more resilient.

Exercise self-discipline in personal reactions. Monitoring your personal reactions as a leader can prevent you from moving into a reactive mode. If you allow yourself to be at the effect of circumstances, you'll get caught up in the current. For Pablo, getting emotional distance is key. When he missteps, he looks for the learning and then moves on because he believes that dwelling on a failure diminishes his power.

Help your boss manage complexity. Be mindful of the complexity you may be creating up the organization with inflammatory communications and actions. Pablo maintains that putting complexity up the line is a powerful tool not to be misused. When you help your boss manage complexity, you aid and abet the boss's success and consequently your own.

40. "MANAGE THE 20 PERCENT THAT DRIVES 80 PERCENT OF THE WORK"

■ ■ ■

Ellston White had hung his hat at Boeing for 25 years and was nearing retirement when he was asked to join SPIRIT AeroSystems, the division Boeing sold in 2005. Skeeter, as he's known to family, friends, and colleagues, agreed to join the fledging organization, which had to peel itself away from its former dependency on Ma Boeing and establish itself as an entrepreneurial start-up. Things looked more than a little overwhelming when he took on the reins as CIO of SPIRIT. He notes, "We were 60 heads down from where we'd been at Boeing. And there we were, a skeletal crew facing more than 1,700 software applications that had to be transitioned."

Skeeter relates that the number one concern of people in his new organization was the workload and the number of concurrent projects. Added to that was his concern that his new information technology organization be viewed as an integral part of the new business, not just as a supplier. After all, information technology is ripe for outsourcing in any business, so it's Skeeter's commitment that his organization's services be competitively priced and effectively delivered. Acknowledging that the threat of outsourcing is a source of pressure for his people, he's projected more than $80 million in IT cost savings to SPIRIT over the next five years.

Total chaos, which is how Skeeter describes the situation on day one at SPIRIT, requires a vision and being purposeful about getting there. He observes, "We had a ton of projects facing us, we had to get our budgets in line, and we had to make a serious paradigm shift. For the first time, we had to worry about how much capital we had in the bank." He asserts that this required a disciplined focus on getting the right people on the team and then breaking down the barriers between people. For him that has translated into his spending a lot of time on the floor, being visible, and touching people personally. He notes, "I don't have the answers. I have a vision, and I have the objectives."

Skeeter points out that because SPIRIT is no longer a business unit within Boeing, it has had to scale up as an organization to an enterprise. And that means he has had to learn to manage himself differently to handle a new level of complexity. He says he needed to get smarter about some things, including changing his focus. "I'm a technologist at heart. I love to roll up my sleeves and dig into the problems. I needed to learn what being a CIO in a complex environment is really about. It's about strategy, not tactics." He goes on to say that he now understands that he is the person who sets the pace, creates the tone, and energizes the environment. He adds, "I have to keep my eye on the ball, or people will take their eyes off of it."

In Skeeter's experience, 20 percent of the issues drive 80 percent of the work, so in a complex environment it's important to manage the critical few issues well. He believes that it's a matter of understanding what the business is trying to achieve and then identifying the core deliverables that will drive the business. He advises starting small and defining a critical path. Then engage people in the work of planning and executing a solution—one step at a time.

Building the muscle for managing complexity going forward requires taking a backward look at how you got to the finish line. Skeeter observes, "People are amazed at the magnitude of their accomplishments when you do that. When you show people that they've got some mileage and confidence, it's not as scary going forward."

PART 6

MANAGING UP
MANEUVERS THAT WIN WHEN YOU NEED
TO LEAD THOSE ABOVE YOU

■ ■ ■

Managing up can be best described as the art and science of influencing, developing, and communicating with those up the organizational ladder. The capacity for managing up can mean the difference between a rapidly advancing and a stalled career, a healthy and dysfunctional relationship with one's boss, and effectiveness and ineffectiveness in delivering results. But very few leaders ever get even a rudimentary road map on how to manage up. They stumble and fall, sometimes failing outright, because of the sheer lack of any explicit guidance.

Those who have succeeded in the game of managing up and whose stories you'll read in this part have identified the need to develop astute observational skills about their bosses' contexts. They've learned that investing in their bosses' success delivers success to their own doorsteps. Counterintuitive as it may seem, they understand that by giving up a measure of control and parking their egos, they dramatically expand their ability to influence a host of outcomes.

Fundamentally, managing up is about creating mutual respect and trust that can be leveraged for shared success. A leader's willingness to be guided and influenced by those he or she wishes to influence is critical, as is adapting to stylistic differences. Successfully managing up requires nuanced communication and a finessed approach. For example, a leader who successfully manages up never tells his or her boss that the boss is dead wrong or lacks good judgment. Instead, the leader might take on the role of a trusted advisor, using powerful questions to influence the boss's thinking.

Leaders who effectively manage up are those whose unshakable credibility has earned them the right to influence in all directions in the organization. They don't squander their credibility by shooting from the hip or carelessly applying their influence. In fact, knowing *what* to influence is as important as *how.*

41. "COMMUNICATE, COMMUNICATE, COMMUNICATE"

■ ■ ■

Dorothy Buckanin has had plenty of experience navigating the sometimes challenging landscape of upward communications. After an early stint in the private sector, she joined the U.S. Department of Transportation's Federal Aviation Administration, where she has worked for 26 years. In her role as division manager for aviation weather and surveillance at the FAA's William J. Hughes Technical Center in Atlantic City, New Jersey, she oversees as many as 30 system engineering projects at any given time. Typical of the projects her team works with are those aimed at improving and enhancing runway status lighting at airports around the country. Her environment is complex, and managing upward communications is critical to her success and the success of those on her team. When you consider that Dorothy is one of several division managers reporting to a technical center director, the number of overall projects that the director has to know about can approach a hundred.

"The most important thing in managing up in a highly complex technical environment," Dorothy says, "is to *never spring surprises.* You must pass information that is mission-critical up the line in a timely manner. After all, your boss doesn't see what you see. He or she sits in a different seat and has a different perspective." Dorothy explains that a small problem can quickly escalate and become politically charged, so it's vital that you keep the boss in the loop and that you make accurate, fact-based observations.

She adds that jargon is in abundant use in the world she works in. Technical experts, in their day-to-day interactions with each other, make their communications more efficient by using shorthand references or acronyms when referring to various aspects of their projects. "But the higher up you go in the organization, the less focused technically organizational leaders are, and they may be altogether unfamiliar with the jargon floating around. If you want others to understand your message, you've got to constantly edit yourself and *communicate in plain English.* In short, you need to make sure that what you say could be used in a press release to the general public." This may seem obvious, but jargon gets used rather unconsciously and indiscriminately. How many times have you been the recipient of a message filled with alphabet soup, and you just nodded your head or mumbled in response because you were too intimidated or too embarrassed to acknowledge your ignorance? Well, bosses are no different. They're human, and if they don't get it they just might not say so.

Dorothy says that in managing upward communications, you must connect your observations to the organization's strategic goals. *"Link to your boss's goals,* and you will have all his or her listening faculties tuned in to you. By doing this, you also help your boss manage his or her communications up and across the organization effectively."

Finally, Dorothy advises, *"make your boss look good.* You never want to point the finger of blame at those above you when things don't go as planned. It's not constructive or useful. Instead, take the initiative to straighten out the problem. You must ensure that you are consistently effective even if those above you are not always contributing to solutions. Then make absolutely sure that you communicate your actions and the results. This is about assuming leadership without authority." Being a leader in the absence of designated authority does carry some risk that others will perceive you as stepping out-of-bounds, but Dorothy is confident that getting results is what she's supposed to do. And, as a seasoned leader, she believes she uses her discretion wisely and where it will add the most value to her organization. "At the end of the day," she adds, *"don't forget to share the credit* for a mission accomplished with others, including the boss. When you make your boss look good, you look good, and you are seen as being on a winning team." In her book, this is success plus.

42. "UNDERSTAND YOUR BOSS"

■ ■ ■

Cathy Woolley is no stranger to managing up. A seasoned human resources manager, her take is that you can't do your job unless you're managing up. Cathy, who recently made the shift from full-time corporate life to human resources consultant, was the senior vice president for human resources for more than 15 years for the Hutensky Group, a commercial real estate developer based in Hartford, Connecticut.

When managing up, Cathy says it's critical that you *understand the person you are working for:* what his or her goals are and what motivates the person. "It's very easy to help someone succeed if you know what's important to him or her and what he or she is trying to accomplish." This includes understanding what his or her expectations for you are. "Ask him or her to paint a picture of what good performance in your job looks like today and 6 to 12 months from now. Ask also what made people unsuccessful in the role in the past. When you know what expectations for success look like and what ineffective performance looks like, you can fill in the gap."

Knowing your boss includes understanding what's important to your boss. This comes down to the basics, such as knowing your boss's preferred work style. If your boss prefers to talk with you later in the day, don't barge in with something you want to influence the boss about at 8 AM. Similarly, a boss who always acts with a sense of urgency requires a different approach than the boss whose pace is slower and more calculated. Cathy suggests that this is more complex when you consider that you not only need to understand your boss but also the person or persons he or she needs to manage up with. *"You're not just managing your relationship with your boss; you're managing his or her other relationships as well."*

Cathy observes that *sometimes it takes more than one voice* in the storm to effectively manage up. "If you have colleagues who can support your initiative—if you can marshal them as a resource—you can be more influential." And that isn't all. You can expand a boss's horizons by exposing him or her to new content and new ideas. Sometimes, it's as simple as getting the boss in front of the team. "The boss can get a whole new perspective by interacting with the entire team and be more readily influenced as a result." Cathy acknowledges that this can be tricky at times for you don't want to create the impression with the boss that people are ganging up or that you need a coalition to get the boss's attention, so pick the issues carefully that you want to influence in this way.

At times, you can and should take initiative and let the outcomes speak for themselves. *"Don't ask for permission.* Great outcomes can sometimes be far more convincing than simply trying to talk your way through something." Cathy adds that when you're managing up, you're always walking a tightrope. "You need a well-thought-out, planned approach to managing up. It's important to consider what *you* want from the relationship with your boss." After all, it isn't a one-way street, and you owe it to yourself to balance the relationship.

Finally, Cathy observes that some bosses simply can't be managed perhaps because of a misalignment of goals or a serious mismatch in styles. This can become quite painful and could signal the need to move on to create a more satisfying and mutually beneficial relationship.

43. "TAKE ON AN ADVISORY ROLE"

■ ■ ■

Shel Holtz is an expert in business communication. Now the owner of his own communications consulting firm and author of several books on the subject, he's held a number of senior-level communications roles in companies such as Mattel. And he's had a lot of first-person experience in the art of managing up.

Shel shares that he once had a boss who was the head of the company's investor relations and corporate communications. "While the man was clearly an expert in investment, he was unqualified for the responsibilities of corporate communications. I knew more than my boss did, but this boss was not the kind of guy who could admit what he didn't know." Figuring out how to manage through this tangled web represents Shel's biggest success secret for managing up: *Get over needing to have the credit, and be willing to give it to someone higher up who may in reality not deserve it.* Shel says you've got to check your ego at the door on this one, but you'll score some big wins if you do.

He advises that *getting an understanding of your boss's context can be an important step in managing up.* In all likelihood, you report to someone who has multiple other direct reports, each with his or her legion of responsibilities and direct reports. As a result, your boss may tend to experience knee-jerk reactions to things. The simple fact is that your boss may not understand the circumstances as deeply as you do, so your job is to bring down the boss without bringing down his or her feelings.

Shel illustrates this last point with a story. "We had a company-wide reorganization within a company I was working in, and a key player was let go. There was a general announcement about the individual's exit that was very cordial, but when it made the local newspaper, the headline read, 'So Long Pal.' Well, my boss was livid. I was directed to call the newspaper and say that we wouldn't be talking with them in the future. Now I knew we couldn't do that. No business can survive without a relationship with its local newspaper. But I refrained from outright criticizing my boss. I took on the role of advisor and suggested that we consider the implications of a decision to cut off communication with the newspaper. I was careful not to be patronizing, merely respectful and curious. By respectfully pointing him down the path, he arrived at a conclusion on his own."

Shel maintains that it's important to *play to the boss's ego when managing up.* In other words, play directly to the boss's need to be in control, to be right, and to be successful. One strategy that has worked wonders for Shel is letting the boss make small changes that don't alter the outcome of the work product, but that allow the boss to take ownership of it. This is vital when you want the boss to sell your ideas up the organization. The more the boss owns it, the better he or she will be at selling it.

Shel insists that even when a boss is being really difficult, you can turn things around. But your being confrontational won't score you any points. Think about it. A company president doesn't have to entertain any opposition. You've got to use tact and diplomacy or what is sometimes referred to as "legislative leadership." It's about using influencing skills to appeal to the boss's need for control, results, image, or whatever else is driving him or her.

Another strategy that has worked for Shel is to *listen to the boss's problem and then offer a tool that represents a solution.* You should not focus on the tool itself, but rather on the benefits the tool can provide. In other words, don't try to sell your boss on a blog; sell him or her instead on the benefits of using the Internet to stay in touch with customers. Then measure the results of the tools you offer. If the tools you suggest deliver tangible, measurable benefits, the boss will be more likely to accept your next proposal.

Finally, Shel advises that it's important to *stay in touch without overwhelming your boss.* Remember, you're just one constituent; there are many others. Give your boss regular, succinct communications that focus on results. In so doing, you will make your boss's job of communicating with others easier, and you will be rewarded when you go in to sell your ideas.

44. "BE WILLING TO SEEK GUIDANCE, AND YOU'LL BE ALLOWED TO GUIDE"

■ ■ ■

As CFO of Broadway National Bank in San Antonio, **Chris Bannwolf** has multiple bosses. He reports directly to the person who is chairman and CEO, but he is also accountable to the president of the bank as well as to the vice chairman of the board. This threesome represents his most important group of constituents. Then there is the full board of directors and the board audit committee that he is accountable to. He admits that he has a lot of bosses to manage, and it does get complicated at times. But, given that he's been the CFO since 1997, he concedes that he has landed on some strategies that work in managing multiple and complex relationships at the top of the organization.

Chris insists that it is of utmost importance when managing up to *be sensitive to personalities.* Each of his three primary boss constituents holds the highest ethical standards, and is sincere and honest. However, one is very detailed in his orientation, one is overly general, and the third falls somewhere in the middle but asks a lot of questions. Chris says, "When I'm communicating or selling my ideas, I must tailor my approach to match the personality I'm dealing with." He adds that it's important to try to anticipate concerns and questions. His advice is be prepared, be factual, and be flexible. "It's a two-way street, so you have to let go of the need for control and anticipate that others might have different ideas. When this happens, back off a little; you don't want to appear to be stubborn."

It's natural that those you are attempting to influence will have their own ideas, but you can use this to your advantage. Chris advises that you *find the things that are easy for you to give in on*—the things that really aren't that important to the success of your idea. Be willing to concede on these things, and, in the process, you'll enable those you're trying to influence to take some ownership for your proposal. They're more likely to agree to something they have taken some ownership of.

Then Chris advises that you need to *respect the roles of those you want to influence.* In his case, the three men he's primarily accountable to have a wealth of experience and expertise, and he respects what they bring to the table. And the bottom line is that people are more willing to be influenced by those who demonstrate respect and who are themselves worthy of respect. "Seek the guidance of those you wish to influence. They appreciate those who appreciate them. There's mutuality, and they are more likely to be willing to learn from those who are willing to learn from them." Chris points out that in practical terms, these individuals can't operate in a vacuum, and there are things that others see that they can't see. They need feedback on what's going on in the rest of the organization and where resources are needed so they can make good strategic decisions.

Even with these strategies, you still will not always be successful in selling your ideas, at least initially. If at first you don't succeed, Chris suggests that it can be effective to *recast your message.* Capture additional data or reframe your information in a manner that more closely aligns with the thinking of those you want to influence. But, Chris cautions, it's important to pick your battles. "Don't make everything a big deal, because you don't want them to see trouble, stubbornness, or arrogance every time they see *you* coming."

Finally, Chris suggests that *using tasteful, well-placed humor* makes any situation lighter and more personal. "Business is business, but at the end of the day, you're working with people. It's important to have good rapport and be pleasant to work with. Things go more smoothly when people are enjoying themselves." Chris adds that a measure of light-hearted self-deprecation can help. "When you are willing to expose your own flaws with humor, it's a subtle invitation to others to do the same."

45.
"DON'T JUST KNOW YOUR FUNCTION; KNOW THE BUSINESS"

■ ■ ■

"When you are in human resources, people expect you to be an expert in organizational communication," says **Dale Reeson,** and she should know. Dale is the group director for international human resources for Ryder System, Inc. She's responsible for all the company's human resources functions in Canada, Europe, Asia, and Latin America. From where she sits, she manages up, and she facilitates others to manage up.

The first thing she tells a new manager is *"Don't just know your function, know the business inside out.* You'll quickly establish credibility with your management when you do that." She suggests that shadowing, asking questions, and doing research are all great ways to learn about the business outside of one's own function. "Then," she advises, "take what you've learned and figure out how to work with your manager to boost his or her success, your success, and the success of the business."

If you want to exert influence above, *you should pick the areas where you can be the most influential and where you have the most credibility.* For example, if you currently are working with someone whose primary focus is on bottom-line growth, show him or her how your idea will help to grow the business. Dale asserts that managing up is not about profiling or posturing with a boss in an attempt to get ahead. She quips, "It's about the steak, not the sizzle." She's clear that it's about being in alignment with the boss on what is needed for success. "When you're in the game and your actions are in alignment with your boss's strategy, your value to the organization will be apparent. Your intention can't simply be to advance your career by carefully managing your boss. If you do, it's highly likely that 'unnatural acts' will follow." So what are some of the other natural acts she suggests?

Be a sounding board for your boss. This is a great way to build a relationship, but you must be sincere. Dale advises that it's critical to be a good listener. She adds that you should not try to interpret, but that you should ask good, respectful questions to ascertain what you heard. By honoring these principles, your boss will come to trust and rely on you. "But," she says, *you must establish ground rules.* Be a sounding board, but resist the temptation to misuse the relationship by overrevealing information you have gleaned from others confidentially." It's gossip, pure and simple, and indulging it will come back to bite you in the form of distrust by the boss and by others.

Be strong and confident in who you are. Know yourself well enough to know what you can offer as a servant leader. Then step back and release yourself from the need to own the ideas. In Dale's experience, the success of an idea often hinges on its coming from the top down. If you try to own it, it may not have the same future it would have coming from the top.

Don't ever abuse your boss's trust. Dale can tell you that when other people notice that you've honed a great relationship with your boss, they will invariably prevail upon you to do their bidding. Don't do it. It doesn't help them, and it's a detestable issue for you to deal with. Moreover, doing other people's bidding reduces your credibility in the long run. You can be viewed as a "minion" (a low-level servant who does what others demand), and, in the process, you lose your power to influence. It's better, Dale says, to facilitate others to get the results they seek on their own.

Be an independent thinker. Dale shares that when she was working in a previous organization, her boss began to rely on her to carry out her boss's objectives. "Life was good, or so it seemed. One day, though, I saw that I was carrying the ball for my boss and doing her bidding. I realized that by being overaligned with her, I was like a duck on a shooting target, ready to be pulled down when she was." Dale's advice is that you don't simply want to be your boss's errand runner. If you are seen as merely a go-between, you have no real power. You've got to demonstrate your ability to think and to champion your ideas.

Build peer relationships. Building peer relationships is critical, because so many organizations today are matrixed, and positional power is history. Everything is intertwined, and you influence more than you control. When you are able to work effectively with peers, you garner the skills to influence with credibility at all levels. Moreover, being in the loop with peers means that you stay on your toes with respect to the overall business, and we know that that counts for a lot with the boss.

46. "IDENTIFY THE SYNERGIES"

■ ■ ■

Jack Healy has made his career in nonprofit organizational leadership. In his current role as president and CEO of the United Way of Greater New Haven, he has a complex array of stakeholders he must effectively manage up, including board members, donors, and business leaders in the community. He likes to think of managing up as creating an environment around him that authorizes him to go forward. As he sees it, many relationships must be managed to get the kind of authority he needs to do his job well.

Jack's first piece of advice for those who want to score wins in managing up is to *reframe what you're doing in a way that resonates with others and their needs*. Jack shares a story to illustrate this important point. "Every year we have a need during the annual fundraising campaign for extra manpower. Traditionally, area companies sent us 'loaned executives' as a way to meet a community need while providing their up-and-coming leaders with a broader experience. It's gotten tougher for companies to support us in this way because of the squeeze on talent and the forced efficiency following restructuring and downsizing. The question for us was how could we continue to access a valuable resource but do it in a way that met the needs of area businesses? We proposed that they send some of their new hires to our First Professional Step Program. Our commitment was to give them training in important subjects such as sales management, account management, and public speaking in return for their giving us some of their time and talent on the campaign. It was a win-win scenario. We enhanced companies' talent assets, and the participants made a contribution to their community."

Jack advises that it's also important to *create synergies*. In other words, create a partnership that enables each party to make their best contribution while managing their liabilities. He shares a story about his boss and himself when he was vice president of his current organization. He describes his former boss as someone who is a master of execution. He describes himself, on the other hand, as a strategy maker who is also a "hopeless systems thinker." Jack relates that in 2001, the organization was faced with a dilemma that was unprecedented for the organization.

"Historically, we'd been very successful with our fundraising, but there was a shift that was occurring with donor behavior. Increasingly, donors were expressing their desire to direct their United Way dollars to one or more specifically named organizations. It was becoming more difficult for us as a United Way organization to fund all the community needs because of the donor-designation process. So I advised my boss that we needed to do a needs assessment and identify the critical needs in the community. I laid out a big-picture scenario, but to make it real, I took her to meet with some other United Way organizational leaders and also with the developer of the needs-assessment methodology. In this way, she could visualize a step-by-step process for executing an evolutionary versus a radical change. She was won over immediately, and we went forward with the community\needs assessment."

Jack goes on to relate that as a result of the needs assessment, his United Way organization changed its marketing message from "One gift for all causes" to "Here's how we're impacting the community." Along with the change in marketing strategy, a change was initiated in the way community agencies were evaluated and funded by the United Way. It boiled down to simply this: going forward, agencies would be funded for delivering specific service outcomes, not for doing good work. Jack shares that this process has tightened up the funding process considerably, and now he and his organization are looking at evolving the evaluation and funding process to identifying community-wide outcomes instead of individual-agency service outcomes.

Jack believes that a leader who wants to effectively manage up should find ways to feature the person above him or her when there is success. He says, "Showcase him or her as the inspiration behind the success." He admits that this is totally antithetical to the notion of self-promotion, but it builds relationship equity. Sharing the limelight with your boss builds trust, empowers *you* to ask for support, and enables you to make important connections. Jack's take is that what you give you get back in full measure. He's quick to add that you absolutely cannot be manipulative with your boss. You can't have a hidden agenda that creates a set of conditions for your generosity.

47. "EMPLOY STAKEHOLDER ANALYSIS TO EFFECTIVELY MANAGE UP"

■ ■ ■

John Wiltshire is vice president of learning and development for MetLife Inc.'s professional services organization and his role regularly involves selling ideas and proposals to company executives. John maintains that understanding who the stakeholders are is critical to successfully managing up. These individuals pave the way for resources, and they are the senior champions for change in the organization. He believes that employing stakeholder analysis has contributed significantly to his success in managing up.

John defines stakeholder analysis as the process by which he determines what his stakeholders' concerns are and what the levers are that will move them from the positions they're in to where he wants to influence them to be. He's adamant that the process is not about manipulation but about "validating the position of stakeholders." Validating stakeholders' positions is about understanding and respecting where they are currently and then overcoming their discomfort by providing what they most need. John says, "I use influence management to determine what someone needs, and then I will tailor discussion and communication to influence him or her in a particular way. One style of influence does not fit all. One person may want data or analysis, while another may want to focus on process. Still others may be concerned about relationships or having the right people in place for an initiative." For John, it comes down to delivering a distinctive value proposition that addresses each individual's hot-button issues. His experience is that when he employs stakeholder analysis, he has a better chance of selling his ideas and having them roll out successfully.

John cautions that you have to treat every concern expressed by a stakeholder as valid, whether it's empirical or merely anecdotal. After all, it is valid for the person who holds the concern. He maintains that it's also important to nurture the relationship. "Just because everyone has bought in doesn't mean that everyone has the same level of acceptance. You have to know what you're managing to." Nurturing the relationship includes regular communication on plans and actions and getting stakeholder feedback.

Effectively managing up requires a high level of personal integrity and a willingness to stand courageously for what you believe in. John relates that he's had situations in the past where he's not felt comfortable with a decision made by senior leaders. "Someone might have wanted to shortcut a process to produce a short-term gain. Sometimes, though, to get where you need to be, you have to be willing to take a hit—that is, be willing to have other people be upset with you." John admits that making courageous decisions could feel like it's at the expense of your career. "Courage always involves risk and seeing the long view." But in John's view, people tend to exaggerate the risk—to imagine the worst. He says that he tries to imagine the best and worst outcomes, knowing that the real truth lies somewhere in the middle. He advises that it's equally important to check your assumptions. It's easy to ascribe erroneous assumptions to others, and, in so doing, inflate the perceived risk of courageous communication.

PART 7

LESSONS LEARNED FROM BAD BOSSES
NOW YOU KNOW EXACTLY WHAT *NOT* TO DO

■ ■ ■

Just about everyone has had a bad-boss experience, and many of us have had a succession of bad bosses. The fact that such individuals have a profoundly destructive impact is a brutal truth of organizational life, but just what makes for a bad boss? What are the attitudes and behavior that rattle people's confidence and diminish their effectiveness? And how can bad bosses be so oblivious to their impact on those around them? These are all important questions, and the leaders you'll meet on the following pages offer some blunt truths in response.

What's both confounding and interesting is that the people you'll meet here feel they have benefited personally from working for bad bosses. They may have graduated from the school of hard knocks, but they maintain they learned more about how to be effective leaders as a result of working for bad bosses than they ever learned from working for good ones. It should come as no surprise, then, that several of the leaders I interviewed for this part said they felt privileged to have worked for bad bosses.

The admittedly sympathetic conclusion of most is that bad bosses don't start out trying to mess up. They aren't bad people at the core, at least in the majority of circumstances. But somewhere along the way they acquire a highly distorted view of what it takes to deliver results, often misusing their authority and placing their self-interests above those of others or the organization. Everyone around them sees them quite clearly for who they are, despite the emotional toll their behavior extracts. Predictably, most bad bosses don't have staying power. They create organizational meltdowns that eventually erode their power base and drive them out, or they simply don't deliver results because they've never figured out that you can't coerce and demoralize people into making their best contributions.

Perhaps what is most compelling is that those who have worked for bad bosses have a fierce resolve to be a different kind of leader. They understand at a heart level what no leadership course could ever teach— what *not* to do if they want to engage the allegiance and commitment of others in their organizations. You'll be inspired by the stories of the leaders in this part. They tell it like it is, and they pull no punches when it comes to giving advice on how not to be a bad boss.

48.

"DON'T ASK IF
YOU DON'T WANT
TO HEAR THE MESSAGE"

■ ■ ■

Kostas Christopoulos feels fortunate to have had some bad bosses along the way because there's nothing like the clarity of vision and purpose that comes from observing what doesn't work for a leader. Kostas, who is based in Vancouver, British Columbia, is director of sales and marketing for Sutton Place Hotels, a five-star luxury-hotel chain. Kostas has been in the hospitality and travel industry for 17 years.

In his estimation, poor leaders can show up anywhere. They are just not attuned to what it takes to be effective. He shares an illustrative story of leader ineffectiveness while working in a different organization. "The business I was working in had been acquired, and the parent company had appointed a new president. The executive team, of which I was a member, was brought to a retreat. The president, who had clearly gotten some early signals that all was not well, asked for feedback from the team about his leadership. Some more cautious team members remained quiet, but others responded with suggestions about his opportunities to improve his effectiveness.

Unfortunately, the president didn't receive the feedback well. "He took it personally, and shortly after the retreat, he started to take shots at people; he became condescending. He went from bad to worse." Kostas explains that what was really hard for everyone was realizing that while the feedback had been constructive and given in good faith, he didn't seem to trust its validity or the people who had given it. "What's worse, within four weeks of the retreat, all the behaviors he had received feedback about were in full evidence."

The impact of a leader's unwillingness or inability to implement feedback can have an enormous impact on others. "People withdraw when they feel shot down by a leader. There's a negative undertone—an unproductive energy—that prevails as people try to sort out their negative feelings. Worse still, there is an atmosphere that can only be characterized as distrustful, and this leads to communications that are transactional.

People just go through the motions, appearing to be engaged, when, in fact, there are no major inroads being made in creating a vibrant culture and a competitive business strategy." He adds that the leader has no credibility in these circumstances. Ultimately, Kostas says that two good executives resigned, and not long thereafter, the president was forced to step down.

Kostas believes his experience observing ineffective leadership has offered him valuable instruction about what *not* to do:

- *Don't ask for feedback you're not willing to hear and act on.* When you ask for feedback, you increase the expectations on the part of others that you will do something with it.
- *Don't discount the importance of others' perceptions.* While the perceptions others hold may conflict with the view you have of yourself, it's important to realize that their perceptions are valid for them. If you've gotten what seems to be disparate feedback from different constituents, it may be that you are interacting with each group differently.
- *Don't shoot the messenger.* One of the worst things a leader can do is take out reprisals of any kind against those who challenge him or her with feedback, particularly when that feedback has been invited or requested. People will feel terribly betrayed, and you'll be even worse off than if you had just ignored the feedback.
- *Don't discount feedback that's not eloquently presented.* Not everyone packages their messages in the most articulate manner, and sometimes the emotional overtones come through. Don't dismiss the feedback that comes with emotional strings on the package. Instead, look for the core message.
- *Don't wait until it's too late to make a course correction.* There is, as happened with the ill-fated company president Kostas describes, a point of no return when you've lost so much credibility and the trust is so low, you simply can't be effective.

Kostas believes that many leaders derail by overly relying on their business acumen at the expense of relational skills. "Their business acumen may be what got them a top-level role, but it's not what will keep them there." Moreover, a leader who overvalues position and authority can't get much leverage in the organization. They need the bench strength on their team. As Kostas says, "You need strong people to run a successful business, and strong people expect to have a voice."

What's the most instructive thing for Kostas about his experience with bad bosses? He says that's easy to answer. "It's not about the leader's power; it's about how effectively others are empowered."

49. "THE TEAM BEHIND YOU IS YOUR BIGGEST PRIORITY"

■ ■ ■

Pamela Hines says she has been privileged to have more bad bosses in her career than good ones. Why does she feel so privileged? She says her bad bosses have been the basis of some of her most important learning, and that learning has made her a better leader. Pamela is the vice president and director of Value Based Six Sigma at ITT Industries' Space System Division in Rochester, New York. The company manufactures high-tech products used in the defense industry, fluid technology products such as pumps, and electronic components. She's been with the company for about a year, having worked for most of the previous 26 years at a Fortune 500 manufacturing company.

Pamela's assessment of bad-boss behavior starts with what she has observed to be a *tendency to jump to conclusions,* often because the boss wasn't listening or just didn't feel the need to gather input before reaching a conclusion. She says that when a manager is guilty of reaching conclusions without the benefit of others' input, people can feel badly treated. "Moreover," she continues, "those managers who don't understand differences in communication approach or work style, and who treat everybody as though they're the same, can do a lot of damage." For example, someone who is more introverted in his or her style may need time to reflect and think before offering input. Then again, someone who is more intuitive may offer insights based on his or her considerable experience and expertise but that are not based on immediately available data.

Pamela shares an illustrative story about a manager's jumping to conclusions: "I was in a senior-level role, and my manager didn't like something I had done. He left me a voice-mail message in which he was screaming at me. In listening to this one-sided, highly reactive and emotional communication, I was instantly demoralized. I knew from that experience that if I have a problem with someone, I need to have the difficult conversation face-to-face. And I have to seek to understand rather than form premature conclusions."

The most damaging behavior by far that Pamela says she has witnessed is managers who place their *self-interests above the organization's interests*. She fervently believes that managers whose foremost concern is their bonus or retirement can't be effective. She says she's seen such self-interested individuals make short-term decisions that are damaging to the company in the long run. She adds, "I've learned that I have to let go of my selfish interests. It's not always easy, but it's important for the organization's viability."

Similarly, Pamela says that she has observed managers who *focus on organizational politics to the exclusion of the work.* "They profile themselves, and they posture in meetings with top brass. They spend a lot of time interacting with those in the corner office, but they lack substance because they are not focused on the work that will drive the organization's success." Pamela insists that for a leader to be effective, it's critical that his or her focus be on the work. She says, "If I am a person of character and substance, you'll see it in my work." In her view, your accomplishments—your contributions to the organization—shout more clearly what you're about than any amount of posturing ever could. "I have to be more than the name and title on my business card. I have to honor my values and demonstrate my commitment to excellence in my work."

And then there are the *bosses who don't share credit with others.* Not sharing credit seems to line up with the tendency to place self-interests above the interests of others. The bosses in question are those who steal the limelight, claim other people's ideas as their own, and take the credit when things go well. Pamela offers that experiencing this behavior first-hand has instilled in her one of her most important lessons as a leader— that *the team behind a leader is the leader's highest priority.* "When you fully invest in your team, team members will follow you now and in the future. They will take the hill for you," she says.

50. "IT'S NOT ABOUT THE RESULTS, BUT HOW YOU GET THE RESULTS"

■ ■ ■

Marlow Hicks is director of North America operations for Almatis, Inc., the Little Rock, Arkansas, company that was originally a division of Alcoa. The company manufactures aluminum, abrasives, ceramics, and materials such as electrical insulators. Marlow shares his experience of working for a bad boss when he was the plant manager for a production division with a major chemical manufacturing company. "The plant was in serious trouble when I took it over, but that was the least of my worries. The vice president I reported to could only be described as a micromanager. He called me every single day over a year's period of time to ask about daily production. He focused constantly on the negative, never seeing anything good about people or the work they were doing. He fundamentally didn't trust people or their abilities to get the job done. He would upstage and embarrass people in meetings by looking for small problems to pick on people about. He always had to be right, even when he wasn't. In fact, if his mind was already made up about something, new facts or information couldn't influence him. Nothing was ever good enough for this man. He couldn't acknowledge people for doing a good job. Instead, he'd say, 'But you've got other problems that need attention.' To make matters even worse, he had a habit of cursing at people."

Marlow shares that there was a trickle-down effect of his boss's bad behavior. "My direct reports observed what got rewarded in the company: intimidation, roughshod behavior, and disrespect, and they concluded that that's what it took to be successful. They began to emulate the behavior they observed in my boss. So not only did I have my personal situation to deal with, I had the fallout from it to manage as well." Marlow explains that he realized that his direct reports were fearful and that they were simply trying to do what they thought was wanted. "I coached my people to think for themselves, to identify what was going to create sustainable success, and to ignore the background noise. I told them that it's not just getting results that matters; it's *how* you get the results."

In Marlow's experience, people want to follow those who are honest, direct, and other-focused, and who demonstrate caring. "You have to demonstrate that you care about your team—that it's not just about the money." Marlow believes that people want their leader to be interested in their well-being, their development, and their ability to get ahead. They want to know that a leader cares about their work/life balance. As he puts it, "People will run a sprint for you as long as it's a two-way street, and this means flexibility both ways, not just when it's important for the business."

"You've got to give people the opportunity to perform. Give clear direction on the objectives, not *how* to get things done. Let them figure out the how. They'll be far more creative if they are given the opportunity to help you, the leader, work out the plan for executing on the objectives." According to Marlow, he explains to his people that how they are going to get to the end result is not his concern on a day-to-day basis. What is his concern is getting his people the things they need to be able to execute. "It's also my job to remove obstacles to their success." Marlow is quick to add that while he doesn't want to interfere with people on developing the "how" of execution on objectives, there is no compromise on the expectation of honesty and integrity in achieving objectives.

He cautions that a leader should never criticize people in public. "Take it offline if you have critical feedback. Always maintain people's dignity in public." He says it's also critically important that a leader acknowledge people, even if it's for the effort they've made. "People can get down in a hurry if you only focus on the negative. And when people are down, it's hard for them to summon the energy to perform, and they can't play to their strengths. So a leader has to focus on what they do well, and what's needed at the end."

Marlow says that his most important lesson from working for a bad boss was realizing that he didn't have to be disempowered in the process. "You can and should identify what kind of leader you want to be and find a culture where what you bring to the table is valued."

51. "DON'T BE SEDUCED BY YOUR POWER OR POSITION"

■ ■ ■

Doug Blonsky runs one of the world's most famous public places. A landscape architect by background, he's the president of the Central Park Conservancy and the administrator for New York's Central Park. Central Park attracts more than 25 million visitors from around the world each year, making it the most visited public space in the world. Noteworthy about Doug and the organization he leads is that 85 percent of the Central Park budget comes from donations and 15 percent comes from fees for service from the City of New York. It's a masterful public-private partnership, with Doug reporting to a nonprofit board of directors for the Conservancy and to the New York City Parks Commissioner. On the subject of the Conservancy, Doug quips, "We get people to invest in their backyards."

Doug believes he's a more effective leader today because of what he's learned over the years working with ineffective bosses. He's experienced bad bosses whose singular focus on one facet of organizational leadership left big gaps in other important areas. He's also experienced bosses who were overly demanding and controlling, often resorting to interfering with the work of others and failing to invest in relationships throughout the organization. He says the impact of the behavior he's observed has included organization-wide distrust, soured relationships, and disgruntled management team members. Doug says he survived the tough-boss situations he found himself in because of his determination to make a difference and because he has always had a lot of social capital with employees and stakeholders. "Eventually and quite predictably," he says, "the dysfunctional organization under an ineffective leader has a meltdown, and a reshuffling of leadership is the result." He says that the lessons he's learned along the way have informed his approach to leadership, which he believes can be summed up as working with others to get results without trampling on people. Here's his sage advice:

Figure out how to work with everyone. Doug points out that in a complex organization with many different constituents and interest groups such as Central Park, a leader must forge relationships with all constituent groups. In his case, that includes board members, city officials, politicians, employees, donors, and park visitors. You can't afford even one bad relationship because you carry the angst around inside you, and it diminishes both your morale and your effectiveness.

Don't be seduced by your power or position. So you've got a highly visible role in an organization that has a global brand identity. That's no excuse for overusing your authority. Doug says, "Self-praise stinks!" He adds that overusing authority can create an explosive situation, as he's experienced at times in his career when working with ineffective leaders. Admitting that he's still a work in progress, he says that his employees use humor as a way to gently remind him to stay grounded and not be in persona.

Create shared ownership. Doug advises that you've got to let people do things their way, even if they fail. By investing in their development and then giving them the latitude to do their jobs, you establish a safe space for them to be creative in generating solutions, and both the organization and the employees grow in the process. As a final note on the importance of overcoming the seduction of power and position, Doug maintains that a leader must share information about the organization's performance widely. When people know exactly what you're measuring and how they're doing on what you're measuring, you create broad ownership for your organizational strategy.

Know your strengths and your weaknesses. Your organization won't succeed on the basis of your personal strengths alone. Every leader has an Achilles' heel, so it's important to know your weaknesses and balance them by putting people around you whose strengths balance your weaknesses. Doug insists that you can't allow yourself to feel threatened by strong, gifted people, because they only make you and your organization stronger. They do not take power away from you.

Have a passion for the work and the mission of your organization. Bring your own passion to work and surround yourself with people who share that passion. The energy will be in the right direction, and there is less likelihood that self-interests will overtake the landscape.

52. "LEAD AS IF YOU HAVE NO AUTHORITY"

■ ■ ■

Liz Gilliland is currently on leave from her role of assistant deputy minister of labor and citizen services in the Canadian province of British Columbia, but she's not far away. She's teaching at the University of Victoria's School of Public Administration where she hopes to inspire young leaders to enter government service.

Liz relates that she worked with an ineffective leader who was heading up a government agency. "She seemed to have the right intentions for getting outcomes, but this boss tended to blame others in an effort to get a handle on the overall situation when things weren't going according to plan." In Liz's view, an effective leader does not target individuals in an effort to discern what's wrong or burrow down into the details to find fault. She adds, "With this boss, it was always about *who* rather than *what.* She should have considered all the systemic issues that contributed to a failure to deliver outcomes, but she was incapable of systems thinking. Such systems thinking would have by necessity entailed examining intergovernmental relations, organizational communications, and internal processes and structures."

The impact of the bad-boss behavior Liz witnessed was demoralized staff who were not performing and not reaching targets amid a general feeling of unease. "There was professional politeness, but it was really a reign of terror. We became the organization that talks about, not with, people. There was divisiveness, suspiciousness, and no one was taking any risks. No one was stepping out and taking any initiative, and, as a result, performance stayed in the hole."

Liz explains that she had to figure out how to manage herself in her own role, inasmuch as she reported to the agency head. "I had to ask myself what was the moral thing to do, but also what was the smart thing to do. I had to strike a balance between being overly revealing and tight-lipped. I couldn't be my usual bluntly honest self." Liz goes on to say that while she was a buffer between the boss and others in the organization, she also didn't want to encourage people to hide. "I would report on things in a general way, being careful about how I communicated. I didn't want to misrepresent anything, but I also didn't want to duck the issues. It was really difficult." Liz concludes her story by relating that ultimately, the individual left the organization, and that she stepped up as the acting agency head for about a year.

Liz says the most important lesson she learned from working with this particular ineffective boss was to not look for the *who,* but to look for the *what* when there is a problem. She says it's important to look at what's at play and ask the questions that invite people to observe the whole system. She adds that the "who" part always gets dealt with by asking "what" questions. She says, "By not fixing blame, you create the space that invites people to step up and assume responsibility. People are energized by this process, and they can have a lot of fun with systems analysis." Liz notes that rarely does an organization rise or fall based on the actions of one or a few people. Problems are generally collectively owned. So there's little to be gained by finger-pointing.

Liz says she's also learned that leadership is really a dance and people sign your dance card by choice. "I've learned that as a leader I have to enroll people by sharing my hopes and aspirations—inviting them to dance with me. I've also learned that I have to enact what I am saying through engaging others in the work. For example, when I was preparing a briefing, I did it with a diagonal slice of the organization. I was meticulous about giving people the opportunity to be involved. I shared what I thought the problems were, but then I looked to others to create the solutions. I extended my trust and I believed in them, and they didn't let me down. They really rallied. My most important lesson from all of this is that you have to lead as if you have no authority."

53. "PRACTICE CONNECTIVE LEADERSHIP BY GETTING CLOSE TO PEOPLE AND ALLOWING THEM TO BE THEIR BEST SELVES"

■ ■ ■

Tom Knowlton got his career start in sales and marketing roles with Colgate-Palmolive and General Foods. Following a stint at Leo Burnett he joined Kellogg, where he had a meteoric rise to president and CEO of Kellogg Canada. In 1989, he became chairman and managing director of Kellogg Great Britain. In 1992, he was named president of Kellogg Europe and executive vice president of the Kellogg Company. In 1994, he became president of Kellogg North America. After leaving Kellogg in 2000, he served as dean of faculty in Ryerson University's School of Business until 2005. He currently sits on several corporate boards, including that of the Wrigley Company in Chicago.

Tom Knowlton's career would be the envy of anyone with ambition and attitude to lead a global company. What is most impressive about Tom isn't his impeccable credentials, but his commitment to leading with heart. Tom believes that working for an ineffective boss early in his career sensitized him to the power of leading through "connective leadership." Tom relates, "When I was at General Foods very early in my career, I had a boss who almost totally destroyed my confidence. He wasn't trustworthy, his ethics were not sound, and he demonstrated a complete lack of integrity in his communication. For example, we had dinner one evening, and he told me what a good job I was doing. A week later, I got a scathing performance evaluation. That's when I knew I couldn't trust him.

"I tried to understand what was behind this man's being such a bad boss. I had been hired into the company by someone else, and I had been made brand manager for Maxwell House Coffee within a year of joining the company. I began reporting to this individual following an organizational restructuring. My boss had not gotten brand management responsibility until he'd been with the company for 15 years. I really think he resented my having responsibility of this level at such a young age. I determined then that I wanted to be the kind of leader others respect and trust."

After Tom left his bad boss and received an assignment at Leo Burnett in which he had direct reports, he realized that he had good instincts for working with people. Inspired by his bad-boss experiences, he made relationships the cornerstone of his leadership approach. He shares that his success formula was to surround himself with the best people, to cast a powerful vision, and then to create an environment that enabled people to make their best contributions. "People told me that they loved working with me because they knew that they couldn't fail—that they could only learn," Tom says. He adds that he has always actively encouraged contrarians who would not simply say "Yes" to him. He says that he also created opportunities for people to connect through retreats and social gatherings. "The cumulative effects of things like this were profound in terms of the allegiance people gave me. I determined that I wanted to get close to everyone who worked for me. I didn't let the thought of a possible future need to terminate someone get in the way of that," he shares. In Tom's experience, people are inspired and motivated in an environment where the top person gets close to them and allows them to be their best selves.

While the relationships the leader creates are the cornerstone for people's being able to deliver their best work, there's more to consider. In Tom's view, the leader must live the values of the organization every single day. "Everyone is looking at the top. A leader must hold the highest ethical standards and have the ability to articulate a credible vision. People want to know how you're going to get there, and what roles they will play to help you get there."

Tom believes that casting a vision that is both pragmatic and inspirational is the starting point in creating effective organizational strategy. He maintains that an organization can grow only by innovating, and that means crafting cutting-edge strategy. He's fervent in his belief that an organization can't cost-cut its way to prosperity; it can only cost-cut its way to loss of allegiance and momentum. Innovation, in his mind, is guided by vision, and the leader's imperative is to attract top-quality people and unleash human and financial resources through powerful and inspiring connections with people.

54. "DON'T BE AN ENERGY VAMPIRE"

■ ■ ■

John Peil, president of Eagle Ideas, a marketing and sales consulting firm in Asheville, North Carolina, has a long history of sales and marketing leadership roles. His bad-boss experience occurred on a job he held with a multinational petroleum company during what he describes as the early days of continuous quality improvement. His boss, the corporate vice president of operations, gave his blessing for the initiation of a quality improvement team. "But," John says, "the process quickly went afoul when the team didn't rubber-stamp the VP's personal agenda. He disbanded the team and threatened to fire all of us who had been involved. As a direct result, quality initiatives ceased at that company altogether. We were terribly disappointed. We'd been trained by Charles Deming's firm in continuous quality improvement, and we were poised to use what we'd learned to make a positive difference in the company." John further shares that, to make matters worse, his boss had an anger-management problem. "He criticized people, was dictatorial, and demonstrated continually that he didn't value people or their input. Most disturbing was his lack of integrity. I was asked to join him and another manager for dinner at a restaurant to discuss an upcoming downsizing. The bill for three people came to $250."

John went on to other more fulfilling leadership roles in his career, but he carried the lessons from his bad-boss experience with him. He says that his biggest lesson is that a leader has to take the high road of professionalism in every communication and in every action. He insists that a leader can't be credible if he or she engages in emotionally charged, angry communication. For John, the solution is simple. If you're a leader, you must manage your disruptive emotions. If you're on the receiving end of charged communication by a leader, you need to establish boundaries, and refuse to engage until things have cooled down. John relates that it's amazing what happens when you refuse to react—when you control your emotions and your reactions to others' emotions—rather than let them control you.

John maintains that it's imperative that a leader create an environment that fosters taking risks and making mistakes. In his view, organizational growth simply doesn't occur in the absence of creativity and empowerment. His bad-boss experience impressed upon him how overly critical bosses can squelch creativity in an organization. He also fervently believes that diversity on a team creates a context for varied perspectives that are the vanguard of innovation. He adds, "A leader has to be willing to challenge and to be challenged if innovation and growth are the goal."

In John's view, highly effective leaders elevate people's self-esteem. "No one takes risks when they're not feeling good about themselves. And an overly dictatorial leader simply doesn't appreciate that the value of the sum of the pieces is more than they could bring to the table themselves." John refers to such ineffective leaders as "energy vampires" because they drain people's creative energy and diminish their self-confidence. He quips, "Dictators and teams don't play in the same league."

Finally, John observes that effective leaders plan their goals and then stay the course. They don't get sidetracked or distracted by mood swings or the emotion of the day, in the manner he once observed his bad boss do. They look for what needs to be changed to grow the business, they create a vision, and then they engage others with their positive energy about the future. They do this by creating a platform of healthy dialogue to talk through what needs to be done to deliver the most-needed results.

PART 8

THE PARADOX OF SUCCESS
LEADER BEHAVIOR THAT
SCORES EARLY WINS BUT CREATES
TRAIN WRECKS IN HIGHER-LEVEL ROLES

■ ■ ■

It's compelling and seductive. Like Classic Coke, it's a success formula that's easy to love and hard to give up. The trouble is, as leaders take on higher-level leadership roles, the attitudes and behavior that served their success on the way up no longer serve them or their organizations. Sometimes leaders overplay an old success formula because they don't know a better way. At other times, they intentionally overuse it because they're convinced that what made them successful on their way up will serve their success going forward. They're dead wrong, of course, but they don't always recognize the fallacy in their thinking until an outcome of less-than-expected results forces a more honest appraisal.

The leader's mandate in a higher-level role is to recast the criteria for success given a new and changing landscape of players and responsibilities. But what are the behaviors that must supplant those that succeeded in prior roles? How does the leader make the necessary shifts? Who are the people who have the ability to influence these shifts? The leaders you'll meet here have benefited from the sage advice of mentors and coaches along the way and have been willing to examine their attitudes and behavior in light of new and changing responsibilities. They will be the first to admit that it isn't easy to let go of a cherished success formula, and doing so requires courage and discipline.

What makes it worthwhile for a leader to trade in an old success formula is the same ambition and attitude that scored the early wins. When there is a drive to succeed and a clear gap in performance accomplishments, you'll find a leader who's ready to listen.

55. "FROM ME TO WE"

■ ■ ■

Anne Renken knows from firsthand experience how behavior that contributes to early successes can derail even the most intrepid performer at higher-level roles. Anne is a veteran sales professional in the hospitality industry. She started as a sales representative with the Marriott Corporation 20 years ago. She steadily moved up the ranks and is now a regional director with Marriott's Global Sales Organization. In that role she leads a team of sales professionals serving Fortune 500 customer accounts.

She vividly recalls that her early successes were driven by a singular focus on meeting individual objectives and working independently of others. "It was a *me* focus in those days." She adds that when you are at a lower level, you're worried about moving up, so the tendency is to orient around your personal interests. And the reward system tends to be driven by individual achievement at a lower level, so there's no incentive to think about things differently.

Anne's experience shows that things clearly shift as you move up the organization. *"The equation changes from 'me' to 'we' and encompasses more individuals than just one's self.* You have to rely more on others to achieve a goal. The goal becomes a joint goal." With very large corporate accounts typical of those Anne and her team sell to and service, multilevel team members are needed to support them well.

Anne says that at a lower level, she was rather unconcerned about senior management and what they did in the organization, much less about what impact they could have on her. But, she adds, when you move up through the ranks, you have to interact more frequently with senior executives and you must learn the skills to *interact upward.* Many junior-level people are in awe of senior executives and are scared to interact with them. But being able to interact effectively with those up the organizational ladder is critical to moving up. In effect, *you must learn to partner with others higher up the ladder to move ahead.* Some senior executives make it easier on those who are up-and-coming by being more engaging and demonstrating interest in seeking the input of those at lower levels. But, Anne says, "Someone needs to grant permission to a lower-level person for him or her to be able to partner. It doesn't just happen by coincidence." Being willing to engage as a team player to solve a problem or tackle a tough customer challenge can make all the difference in attracting the attention of those in the corner office.

Anne believes she was fortunate because she met a lot of people over time who were willing to partner with her, grant her authority to act, and support her in her moving up. And in a sales organization that translates to larger accounts and a higher level of responsibility, including leading a high-performance team.

56. "FROM AGGRESSIVE TO PERSUASIVE"

■ ■ ■

Gary Benson is an up-and-coming leader who has a clear picture of how overreliance on old success formulas can be just as detrimental to an individual's career as it is for a business. Gary is the director of sales for sterilization and laboratory services at Ethox Corporation, a growing player in the medical-device sector of the health care industry whose home offices are in Buffalo, New York.

Gary is not a bashful guy, and he never was. He describes himself as having been an "anxious go-getter" when he started his career some 12 years ago. "I had customers to manage and technology to manage. And while I didn't have any direct reports early on, I was in charge of training new hires. I was given a lot of freedom to execute my own plans. I handheld new hires, often just out of college, and helped them learn lab techniques, industry practices, federal government regulations—the whole nine yards. I transformed them from newbies into professionals. I was clearly operating as a technical expert in those days, and I was recognized for that. What's more, I was quite the independent thinker. I had my own way of doing things, and no one complained because I had great outcomes." Just how good were the outcomes Gary delivered? "We were doing such a great job training lab technicians, we had a talent pool that was the envy of other employers. And guess what? They stole people away from us by paying them a whole lot more than we could afford to pay them."

Gary explains, "Early in my career I was a bit egotistical. I was more aggressive than I was assertive—I was the proverbial bull in the china shop. Those things seemed to bolster my success in those days. My aggressiveness helped me to create stretch assignments that developed me, and I took on a lot of responsibility." Gary hasn't lost his competitive edge since then. He insists that he's still as driven to succeed as ever, and that he's a work in progress when it comes to managing his competitive tendencies when working with others. "But," he says, "I'm more sensitive now to the fact that my competitiveness can get in the way of my success, particularly if I close myself off to others' ideas while in hot pursuit of my own."

Gary has also realized that his earlier bullishness and the ease with which he was able to get his young recruits to do things on his terms have had to give way to a more persuasive rather than directive style. "I've learned the hard way that I must work to gain the trust of others and their permission to influence them rather than to simply assert my point of view. I've had to keep my independent streak in check. I've also had to learn to compromise and to pick my battles more carefully. I've learned that to be successful I have to be less bullish and more deliberate and calculated in my approach to people."

Gary says that his unwavering drive to succeed has meant that he's always had a tendency to get too entrenched in the day-to-day details. "I've had a need to involve myself so that I can assure successful outcomes. But that just doesn't work anymore; it's not a success formula. I now realize that I have to be able to manage on a more global level. I can't afford to be so hands-on." What has helped Gary make this important shift? He says that what's helped the most is hiring great people, ensuring that expectations are communicated early on, and then letting them run with it. "I've learned that when I authorize and empower people, they are much more likely to 'scale up' their performance and meet and exceed expectations."

Gary's biggest challenge has always been dealing with circumstances in which a lot of restrictions are placed on him. He says that his independent streak just rails against being controlled, but he now realizes that that he has to manage both his attitude and his mouth in those circumstances. "I'm likely to assert my opinions too loudly, and when I do that, I lose social capital and the ability to influence. After all, you can't influence people's discretionary effort or their loyalty using the force of your will." Gary says he's still learning how to rewrite his success formula, but he's clear that as an organizational leader who wants to succeed in today's environment, he must exchange his fierce independence for interdependence—the finessed skill of creating a shared vision and getting things done with others.

57. "FROM TACTICAL TO STRATEGIC"

■ ■ ■

When Boeing sold its commercial airplane parts manufacturing division early in 2005, it was as though it had just launched a rocket. The division was sold largely intact, with a manufacturing process, one very big customer (Boeing itself), and a highly experienced employee base. As **Janet Eaton** describes it, "Mama Boeing was no longer commanding the ship when it landed squarely in Wichita, Kansas, as the new entity SPIRIT." Janet, a former Boeing manager, is now the manager for the leadership and organizational development group at SPIRIT AeroSystems. She has responsibility for developing and executing a host of programs to develop current and future leaders, including succession planning, performance management, individual and team coaching, leadership training, and human talent structuring. She has first-person experience with the paradox of success. "We're living it in real time every day," she says.

As Janet describes it, being a part of the new company carries all the benefits of not being accountable to a corporate parent but all the risks of being an entrepreneurial start-up organization. That's where it gets tricky. "On day one of the new company's existence, the average age of our employees was 48, there had been no major new hiring in several years, and the average length of employment was 15 to 20 years. We had all grown up in the Boeing culture, and we were still acting like Boeing employees, doing all the things that made us successful there." The big disconnect was that most of the management group jumped two or three levels in responsibility when they took over the reins at SPIRIT.

Janet explains that in the Boeing culture, success was determined largely by how well a manager was able to execute against strategies created by others. Quality, cost, delivery, safety, and morale were the important success criteria for effective execution. She says, "We had only one customer, and delivery was the driver." She goes on to explain that at Mama Boeing, everything was streamlined, and there were clearly defined processes and systems for everything from manufacturing to employee development. "We knew how to please our one and only customer. Sure there were challenges, but we understood the landscape. We could see it clearly because we had a fairly short-range view, and our work was largely tactical."

Janet paints an entirely different picture of what success in the new company looks like. "Today," she says, "we're running a company, not simply operating a division. We have to have a long-term strategy for diversifying our customer base and creating a value proposition. It's also quite clear that we have to create a corporate identity separate from Boeing, with its own vision and mission. There were clear road maps for us at Boeing, but today we have to find our own way among a myriad of choices." And that's not all. The term *business acumen* has taken on a whole new meaning for Janet and the managers she supports. "We have to understand global markets, not just a product line, and our executives have to be decisive and be able to move quickly in a highly competitive marketplace. Our midlevel managers, on the other hand, have to be effective translators of corporate strategy, and that means creating altogether new manufacturing processes and systems as new markets create demand."

Janet adds that so-called "soft skills" have never been more important to effective leadership. She says, "Our managers' skills and experience do not represent a match for some of the challenges of the new territory we're facing, so it's critical that they listen well and are willing to learn and be influenced by others. What we knew before no longer serves us in our new circumstances. We've been shuttled out of our former comfort zone, and to be successful, we must be willing to accept that we're no longer the experts we were in the Boeing environment. We must be willing to hire and use the expertise we don't have." Janet concludes that it takes a winning spirit to win at SPIRIT.

58. "FROM PERSONAL OWNERSHIP TO SHARED OWNERSHIP"

■ ■ ■

Steve Ives is president and CEO of the Merrimack Valley YMCA, one of the top 100 of the thousand or so YMCAs across the United States. He started his career in the nonprofit world of the YMCA as a part-time lifeguard. He then became a program director and after that moved up quickly in the organization. He relates that a neighboring Y was financially troubled, so his Y entered into a management agreement to turn the organization around and reduce its debt. Steve was named assistant executive director, and six months later, he was named executive director. He led the merged organization for the next eight years, more than tripling the size of the operation during that period. As Steve puts it, "Things were going along swimmingly. My charismatic leadership style had won the trust of the board, staff, and community early on. They saw me as this guy who turned things from desperate to thriving. I was the superstar, and I really enjoyed that status."

Steve goes on to explain that he proposed a capital campaign to the board to upgrade facilities to accommodate an increasing number of members. "They agreed to it without really thinking much about it. No one questioned me on the idea, and I now realize that it was because they were afraid to question me or to say no. They wanted to keep me, and they figured that to do that they had to agree to things that would keep me challenged. Moreover, because the board had become quite dependent on me, the members had sort of faded into the background. As a result, they did not take on any ownership of the capital campaign. We actually had a couple of people resign from the board within six months of joining it because they didn't feel there was anything for them to do. Still, I didn't quite get what was happening.

"After two years, with me running the show entirely, we had raised about $2 million towards the goal of $3.4 million, and we were winding down the campaign. It was clear that the organization was in a downturn cycle because we had grown too large for the community to support. To complicate matters, a fitness center opened up next door that offered $15 a month in fees, so we had members leaving to grab a better deal. I was faced with the prospect of having to reduce the number of staff in the face of diminishing revenues. And while we had done well with the capital campaign, it was necessary to adjust the facility expansion in light of less-than-expected capital campaign results.

"About that time I got an opportunity to pursue the CEO role in another New England Y. Well, to put it bluntly, my board was frantic. The board president threatened me with reprisal if I took the other job. I pulled out of the running for the other job, but then my board president and vice president resigned. The board insisted that I sign a contract, and when I refused, they fired me a week later. In less than two years, I had gone from superstar to unemployed."

Steve ended up taking the job of CEO for the other New England YMCA organization—the role he's in today. But he brought plenty of learning about the paradox of success with him from his previous role. He says, "*The bottom-line learning for me is that a turnaround is really about an individual leader, but long-term sustainability is about a team.* I didn't shift my own gears after the turnaround. I didn't properly develop the board, and the consequence was that I wasn't able to use the volunteer talent that was right in front of me. Moreover, I was unable to find a way to get the board to take ownership for the things a board should take ownership of. The truth of the matter was that the board was at a safe distance where everyone was comfortable, including me."

Steve says he now realizes that he and his board were in collusion to keep him in the superstar role. "I was seduced by my turnaround success and by my ability to woo people to my way of thinking, and it ended becoming a trap for me. I was unable to create shared ownership, but I was also unable to leave without there being a total meltdown. It was a mistake for me to allow things to revolve around me so completely. And in the end, I realized that I couldn't talk my way out of something I had behaved my way into."

Steve now understands the fine line between micromanagement and shared ownership. A board needs to have responsibility for vision, organizational direction, and policy, but it shouldn't be involved in day-to-day operations, staffing issues, facility management issues, and the like. There's a natural tension—involved but not overinvolved. And Steve understands a whole lot more about himself and the paradox of his own success. He shares that he has been able to develop a great staff and board team in his new CEO role, and everyone is thriving. "The board members were clear when they hired me that they wanted a CEO who was more participative and inclusive than my predecessor and who could also rally the community. What's neat about this is that I still get to use the 'woo' factor and play to my charismatic strengths in winning the support of the community; but at home, I keep it in check."

How has Steve accomplished the shift from charismatic leadership to shared leadership? He explains that he brought in an executive coach to develop the skills of the entire team. "I needed to do this because the team members didn't know how to say no to me, and I knew that was dangerous." Steve says that today he's no longer standing at the bully pulpit, selling his personal agenda. The entire team has ownership, and it's awesome.

59. "FROM DELIVERING RESULTS TO FACILITATING RESULTS"

■ ■ ■

Steve Cox is the director of global complaint management for Hospira, Inc. His organization, formerly a division of Abbott Laboratories, manufactures medical devices and generic drugs. Steve is a veteran quality-control professional, having held a number of senior-management roles in health care companies.

Steve explains that his early successes were the result of a singular focus on short-term goals. "I went after the low-hanging fruit in pursuit of my own self-interests." As a young leader he learned that going after the low-hanging fruit, however, could set up a team to expect that everything will be easy. This functional versus strategic focus can prevent the members of a team from seeing the bigger picture. He also says that he learned a lot about recognition and reward and how his short-term focus had resulted in his reinforcing the wrong behavior in his team. "I used to reward people for putting out fires instead of delivering longer term, more profitable successes." He chuckles as he adds, "Your team is a reflection of you as a leader. If you are always acting in a particular way, that's what people emulate. I was a firefighter, and I was rewarded for that. I was so tactical, and I thought that made me successful. I was wrong."

Steve says he can't overemphasize the importance of having a mentor or coach to help in overcoming the paradox of success as a leader. "When I derailed, my mentor would figuratively smack me and say, 'What were you thinking?'" Even so, Steve admits that it took a few failures for the importance of a strategic versus tactical focus to really sink in.

Steve explains that while he looked for guidance and direction from his boss when he was a junior-level leader, holding that expectation today would be counterproductive in a senior-level role. He now looks to his boss as a sounding board who can add to his perspective but not make decisions for him or direct him. Steve also recognizes the need to manage the relationship with his boss, and that's something he didn't have a grasp on early in his leadership career. "The thing that helped me the most was to understand my boss's style and what that individual needs from me. I realized that it's not a one-size-fits-all approach." He adds that early on, he figured others would either be like him or they would adapt to his style. He now knows that he has responsibility for adapting his style to others. It's a shift out of self-focus into other focus.

Roughness in communication is tolerated in younger leaders at lower levels of responsibility, but it's a formula for derailment in higher-level roles. Steve says that at higher levels of leadership responsibility, communications are more nuanced, and "influence management skills" are critically important. Steve pauses and then adds, "They taught me all this accounting stuff in college, but they taught me nothing about people skills. When it finally hit me how important this stuff is, it was an epiphany."

Steve points to another aspect of his junior-level success that no longer serves him. "Early on, because I was trying to demonstrate that I was worthy of promotion, I focused on personally delivering results. Later, I had to come to grips with the fact that what's more important is the process for generating results—the how, who, and what. I had to learn how to facilitate versus drive to get the results at all costs. I had to learn what behavior on my part would lead to the best results. It's about the tone a leader sets and the relationships the leader establishes. You don't want to leave a trail of dead bodies behind you."

This reminds Steve of an experience he had as a leader in a former high-profile company. "There was an employee survey, and the results were abysmal. In response to the survey, the vice president said, 'The results aren't too bad based on the fact that we're operating in a predatory environment.' In his mind the diminished employee morale was justifiable." Steve says this experience helped him frame what kind of company he wanted to work for. As he puts it, "Early on, I would have said, 'What a great business model or what a cool product.' Now I want to be able to say, 'What a cool culture.' I now have the crystal-clear clarity that it's about the work, but it's also about the environment the work is done in."

60. "FROM LOCAL TO GLOBAL PLANS AND ACTIONS"

■ ■ ■

Shirley Kreutzfeldt has worked for Abbott in North Chicago for 31 years. Today, she is the director of compliance services for Abbott's Global Pharmaceutical Operations, but she remembers well the shifts in thinking and behavior that were required when she moved from being a manager of a single team to being a manager of managers.

As a front-line manager Shirley was directly involved in problem-solving specific issues that were within her realm of technical expertise and job parameters. "When you're dealing with technical issues within a defined area of responsibility, what needs to be done is very clear. It's pretty hands-on work." Being too hands-on, however, can be a derailing factor when you step up to be a manager of managers. Such a manager needs to focus on a different set of problems—those of a broader organizational nature. Because this leader can often see problems others can't see—his or her perspective is different—he or she must shift the focus of problem solving. A manager of managers also is expected to have more outwardly directed influence as opposed to focusing on directing the work other team members are doing.

In Shirley's experience, it takes more effort to create a context for people in higher-level leadership roles than it did as a first-level manager. "The challenge for the leader is to raise awareness without raising resistance, and this challenge is magnified when the leader's span of influence is global and multicultural dynamics are introduced." For Shirley, it's about understanding what people value and then presenting information in a way that's sensitive to their context.

As a first-level manager, Shirley was not so keenly aware of the organizational issues impacting her area. She didn't have the broader organizational perspective that she subsequently discovered was absolutely essential in higher-level roles. "At a higher-level leadership role, it's incumbent upon you as a leader to seek out information regarding the broader organizational strategy and how it impacts your area of responsibility. You have to be a source of information for your part of the organization. What I discovered, however, is that just how to do this was not explicitly stated. I stumbled upon it along the way."

Another area that Shirley says she had to learn to manage differently as a manager of managers is how she spends her time. One obvious shift was that of moving from coaching individual contributors to coaching managers, but there's more. She says she had to get used to developing work assignments for others in areas that she'd never performed in. "I had to learn to value others' expertise over my own. This can be difficult if you've been viewed and rewarded as a technical expert. You no longer have the detailed day-to-day knowledge that you once had. You've got to accept that and appreciate what others bring to the table." Having made the shift, Shirley is convinced that both she and her organization are better off. "When you entrust and empower others, they feel better about what they're doing, and they deliver better results."

Shirley is quick to add that a manager of managers can't totally neglect the need to evolve his or her own technical expertise. With limited or obsolete technical knowledge, she believes that such a manager will likely find that the speed of decision making in a critical situation may be impacted. Moreover, the manager may be compromised in his or her ability to evaluate the ideas presented by others.

As a manager of managers, Shirley realized that she needed to communicate differently. As a front-line manager, it was mostly about one-to-one and small-group communication. But as a divisional-level manager, her communication needed to be tailored to larger forums. "While front-line communication tends to focus on the work at hand, higher-level communication tends to focus on where we stand on the issues and where we're heading. It's a level of communication that's broadly interpretive versus descriptive or analytical." Shirley discovered that while it is fairly easy to convey messages with energy and passion in one-to-one and small-group communications, it's a different animal for the higher-level manager. "At a higher level, being believable requires more energy. On the other hand, the weight of what you say is greater, and you've got to be sensitive to that. Clarity is important, as is creating the right context in your communications."

Shirley has found that setting up communication forums to share information across organizational functions increases efficiency, seeds ideas for innovation, and fosters organizational networks. "If a leader at a higher level doesn't do this, he or she becomes the bottleneck to the flow of information in the organization. Fostering broad-based communication is critical for building strategic awareness and developing people's decision-making capacity."

Handling delegation represented another learning curve for Shirley as she took on higher-level leadership responsibility. "As I moved up, I made the assumption that I needed to be hands-off. I realized that I needed to consider other people's styles of communicating and working, their level of expertise, and the criticality of situations where I needed to delegate responsibility. What I learned was that I needed to think through the whole assignment, including what the responsibility for communicating outcomes was as well as who else at higher levels might be involved. I learned that it's important to identify what delegation means in each particular assignment."

Finally, Shirley explains that she learned that a manager of managers must focus on building cross-functional relationships with peers from multiple disciplines. "You can do things as part of cross-functional groups that you could never do on your own." She also learned how important it is to manage the relationships with those in leadership roles above you, especially the relationship with your boss. "As a higher-level leader, you need to be able to ask your boss to help you create opportunities to represent your ideas across the organization. You want support to gain visibility and contacts." Shirley insists that this isn't just about advancing your career, it's about influencing organizational strategy impacting the bottom line.

61. "FROM SELF-INTERESTS TO SHARED INTERESTS"

■ ■ ■

At 33 years of age, **Terry Bellamy** is the youngest mayor in the history of the state of North Carolina, and she's the first African American woman to be elected mayor of the city of Asheville. She was just 27 when she was elected to her previous role as a member of the Asheville City Council. While Terry would be the first to acknowledge that as a young political leader she is learning in real time, she also has been around long enough to have made some shifts in her success strategy.

Terry explains that she got her start as a public servant working with various nonprofit organizations in her native Asheville. "I've always been a doer," she says, "but then I got to participate in Leadership Asheville, a city government–sponsored leadership development program that develops individuals to serve in public service roles." That's when she shifted her focus to "building good relationships by helping people succeed." When she started working in the public sector, she had a more narrow focus—a focus on the present and what could be done in the moment to correct a problem. As she's matured and taken on broader public-sector responsibility, her focus is now on supporting the development of policies that are broad-brush, not keystroke. "We need to paint the picture in vivid colors so everyone can see it." This is about economic development, affordable housing, education—and a vision that is so far out that it's forever. She realizes that the more narrowly focused, tactical approach she took as a very young leader won't serve her highest and best purposes now. She maintains that politicians in general need to get a bigger vision that's inclusive of the whole, not just their political bases.

Terry has had to shift how she communicates about the issues. "There was a time when I would bring issues to the forefront based on a message of disparities. It was a negative way to approach things, and I've learned that you can't succeed on a bad slant. What's really important is to find common ground that goes beyond the mere fact of socioeconomic disparities." She has also had to learn how to compromise—

to understand the need for give-and-take, adding that early on she had a decided tendency to be emphatic. Terry insists that she never compromises on her core values, but she does seek to build consensus on a path forward. In a similar vein, she shares that she works in the center of things these days, neither to the left nor to the right. "I've had to learn to embrace others' perspectives. After all, they can often improve on my ideas." Terry says that while she previously would have been more likely to act on her own ideas, she fully appreciates the value today of using her role to pull public and private interests together.

Pointing to the generation of younger political leaders who are emerging at all levels of government, Terry says that she sees more bipartisan approaches replacing the traditional scrapping between political leaders from different parties. "The under-40 group understands that pulling parties together to get things done is what's really important. Policies that work have investment from both sides of the fence." For Terry, it comes down to having the heart to serve.

PART 9

GOING AGAINST THE GRAIN
SECRETS FOR SUCCEEDING WITH CHALLENGING THE STATUS QUO

■ ■ ■

The seeds of great ideas are often sown by mavericks, those whose perspectives extend beyond the boundaries of conventional thinking. These people issue the rallying cry for a different approach or a better way. But challenging the status quo isn't easy, nor is it risk-free. Courage and tenacity are requisite qualities for the leader who goes against the grain, but that's not all. What elevates the message to a level that commands attention? What succeeds and what fails in getting an idea accepted? The answers to these questions and more have inspired the leaders you will meet in this part. Each leader who contributed his or her ideas here has grappled with how to manage himself or herself and how to manage the organizational context to ensure that good ideas get a voice and that no one shoots the messenger.

What is both surprising and illuminating is the fact that mavericks don't generally get labeled as mavericks. Sure, they have edgy ideas that challenge conventional wisdom, but the way they go about challenging that conventional wisdom seems less unconventional than the ideas themselves. That's because they have a knack for finding a way to work within the system to move their ideas forward. They understand that they don't get new ideas adopted by trampling on those they wish to influence. Instead, they forge the relationships that will entertain their ideas, and they strategize on how to work within the existing context. In other words, they make the most of the opportunities to use relationships and existing systems to change mind-sets.

Leaders who successfully challenge the status quo understand something else as well, and this may be the single most important factor in their success. They understand that they don't have all the ideas or even the best ideas. They make a point of using their relationships and the system as a whole to draw out the best ideas from everyone. Indeed, they foster a cultural context that supports everyone to challenge conventional thinking to grow the business or solve an important problem.

62. "MANAGE BUT DON'T TRY TO ELIMINATE RISK"

■ ■ ■

As a senior vice president of Marsh @WorkSolutions, a division of Marsh & McLennan Companies, Inc., **Bill Weyers** and his employer are in the business of managing risk. So why, then, would he own and fly a 60-year-old airplane? After all, many people believe flying in small planes, yet alone one that is 60 years old, is downright risky and dangerous. In Bill's view, those who are not intimately familiar with something have a tendency to either *overestimate or underestimate the risk associated with it.* Bill maintains that he's much more comfortable landing his plane on a grassy runway than merging his car into traffic on a busy interstate. He characterizes himself as *an informed risk taker.* He adds that for those who wish to provide leadership in their organizations, the parallel is clear: *"You can't lead by staying on the ground!"*

Bill defines going against the grain quite simply as "the willingness to vocalize and put your convictions out there for the purpose of improving the circumstances of colleagues and the business." Yes, such willingness requires courage because speaking up isn't always the safest choice. Many people are just more comfortable maintaining the status quo. They may feel powerless about their circumstances, but they are unwilling or unable to take a stand for what they believe.

Bill emphatically believes that if you are going to be a leader, you must be willing to *assume risk in your endeavors.* "You can manage risk but you can never totally eliminate it. If you are not willing to risk, there is no forward movement, and without forward movement, there is no progress. This is true for individuals, and it's true for organizations."

Bill advises those venturing into this arena for the first time that *taking small steps can be highly effective.* "You don't have to go all the way to the edge and put yourself at extreme risk. It may be that you simply need to try something different." He emphasizes that it's important to *work within the system while stretching at the same time.* "People mistakenly believe that leadership is all about big actions. The real truth is that *it's about a lot of little actions executed with clarity and consis-*

tency." Bill believes that you stretch by growing your skills, acting without always asking for permission, and being willing to make mistakes. "If you're stretching, you're going to screw up from time to time. You have to be prepared for that and be willing to celebrate the learning."

So how does a leader who wants to bring others along effectively change minds? Bill suggests a few simple strategies:

Create an environment that invites people to take some manageable risks. Begin by asking the questions that challenge long-held assumptions, such as, "Do we really believe that? What is the evidence that supports the assumptions being made?" Then put a new idea on the table and invite others to question it. It's like rebuilding a muscle that's atrophied. In Bill's estimation, corporate America has overmanaged people to such an extent that an environment has been created that is rather unfriendly to those who challenge convention. "People shouldn't have to put their livelihoods at stake to speak with conviction about what they think can be done to improve the business." A leader is an instigator, but he or she isn't the only one who should be challenging the status quo. "As a leader, you are responsible for creating an environment that allows others to flourish, and that includes being willing to have your own views challenged. "

Establish the expectations for a respectful process. Communicate your intentions to stir things up and then walk your talk by actively creating a spirited dialogue. Bill cautions, however, that if anything is really off-limits, say so. And make it clear that you are not inviting chaos. Demand decorum and respect. "When you create an environment that supports going against the grain, you establish a creative tension that's good for the business. By keeping things stirred up, you keep people on their toes—and stretching."

Create shared ownership. Bill observes that it's just human nature to value one's own ideas over those of others. Moreover, we humans are more likely to act on what we personally believe in versus what we are asked to buy into, so it's critical that a leader create shared ownership when challenging the status quo. A leader can do this by identifying common objectives, i.e., finding out what everyone wants. As Bill puts it, "When there's something at stake for everyone at the table, courageous actions multiply."

Actively seek diverse points of view. You may have to ask and then ask again, because people will naturally be suspect at the outset that the request for input is just giving lip service to participation. You have to demonstrate that you really mean it by first asking and then fostering a process that draws out the ideas.

Resist the initial tendency to evaluate or judge new or different ideas. Ensure that all the ideas get heard, and then invite the questions that challenge the assumptions. Good ideas can stand tough scrutiny, but it's important that they don't get squelched too early.

Create outcomes by acting on the most promising ideas. Creating shared ownership also means designing an action field for testing the veracity of ideas. If unconventional ideas get heard but they never get acted on, people will give up, figuring it's just not worth the effort.

Recognize and reward those who offer divergent views. Celebrate those who courageously go against the grain, and always, always share the credit.

63. "LEARN ON THE GO—WITHOUT A ROAD MAP"

■ ■ ■

Ethan Strimling is young man with a big heart and a level of maturity that belies his 38 years of age. He's serving his second term as a state senator in the Maine legislature. He's also the executive director of Portland West, a social-service agency serving kids at risk and low-income and immigrant families. He's held the top job there for the past nine years. This former New York City resident and Harvard-educated leader has a lot to say about going against the grain. But what strikes one immediately upon meeting Ethan Strimling is his modesty about his personal accomplishments. Instead of focusing on himself, he prefers to focus on the organizational and legislative constituents he serves. It's then that the maverick in him is fully illuminated.

Ethan says, "It's radical to think that 100 percent of the kids in our community could graduate from high school, that 100 percent of the adult population could be gainfully employed, and that everyone could have a permanent home. And it's absurd that we put kids in prison and expect them to come out as whole human beings, with different attitudes and behavior than when we sent them there in the first place." But Ethan is quick to point out that he doesn't think he's alone in having a vision of something better. "I believe," he says, "that most people have the hope that this vision could be realized, but they don't feel they have a voice, or maybe they just don't see the options in front of them."

While Ethan is reluctant to think of himself or his organization as being in the social-action business, he agrees that he is in the business of helping to change minds and move people to action, whether it's in the state legislature or back home at Portland West. In Ethan's mind, the first and most important thing leaders who want to challenge the status quo should do is to *ask questions and then listen.* "People know a lot, and it's important to draw out of them what they already know and what they care about. When we don't listen, we create unnatural divides that are not productive. When I sit down with someone from a different political party, for example, what's really clear almost from the outset is that we really do want the same things. We just have different paths for getting there."

Ethan suggests that it's also critically important to *illuminate the core values.* When you identify the core values that people share, you begin to create a dialogue—a shared understanding—and you break away from the turf issues or partisan lines. "The social fabric really is strong at the core. We have to help people reconnect to that. When people feel isolated, they feel as though they are being talked at. It's important to turn every meeting into an opportunity to listen." Ethan admits that sometimes this is tough and he gets derailed by talking too much. But he comes full circle when he reminds himself that people only move forward together when they create a dialogue that is rooted in a shared purpose.

He's also had to learn how to channel himself into the problems that he is asked to influence and help to solve. Whether it's in his organization or in the legislative chambers, he can find himself being thrown into circumstances that he doesn't feel prepared to address. So what does he recommend that a leader do at times like these? "You have to develop your understanding of the problem or issue and gather the resources around you. Most important, you have to be willing to jump in when you're not ready and deal with the traffic that's coming." He adds that the most successful people he's known are those who take what's in front of them and do their very best with it. They learn on the go—there's no road map. "It's an attitude of optimism and a willingness to jump in. You can't be scared of losing, because if you are, you're not going to take risks, and you're not going to survive."

Ethan remarks that no matter what, you never get everything you want when you challenge the status quo, but you do get *some* of what you want. He believes that that's what happens when you balance your self-interests with the interests of others.

64. "BREAK THE RULES THAT WEAKEN AND CONSTRAIN"

■ ■ ■

Irv Katz is the chancellor of a university, and he's proud of the fact that the institution of higher learning he leads is a model of unconventionality. He was part of the group of academicians who founded the International University of Professional Studies in the late 1980s. The school, which has no traditional brick-and-mortar classrooms and laboratories, offers graduate degrees in what he calls a "student-friendly" learning environment. But wait, we're getting ahead of ourselves. Irv's own story of adult learning is instructive.

Irv Katz obtained his undergraduate and graduate degrees, including a PhD in psychology, from traditional universities. "When I was a student," he says, "institutions of higher learning were scary places. There was incredible pressure, and fear and intimidation were the norm." For at least ten years after he completed his doctoral work, he had recurring nightmares about not completing a course or about a professor taking a dislike to him.

After holding a number of key academic appointments, including the chairmanship of a university psychology department, Irv decided that he wanted to be involved in an educational setting that conformed and adapted to the student and where faculty would bring applied knowledge as well as academic knowledge. Instead of sitting in large classrooms grinding through a prescribed curriculum, students would work with mentors who would guide them to the proper resources to fit their learning needs. This is the operating model for IUPS, where Irv Katz has served as chancellor since 1994.

No doubt, Irv and his colleagues challenged the status quo when they founded IUPS. "We were a threat to the traditional university system and to the accrediting bodies that review them." So what are the factors that have made IUPS the thriving institution of higher learning that it is today? What has enabled Irv and his colleagues to successfully challenge the status quo? Irv explains that, for starters, if you're unconventional and you have the kind of visibility that a university has, you'll get opposition, guaranteed. You'll be scrutinized by the media, other universities, legislative bodies, legal entities, and, of course, the media. But the most important success factor, hands down, is that you *appeal to your target audience.* In this case, the target audience was comprised of adult learners who were hungry for a collaborative learning experience. Irv says this is the way many innovative ideas have been able to rise above the negating opinions of those holding the keys to conventional wisdom.

Secondly, Irv advises, those who challenge the status quo must have a *mission that resonates and touches a chord.* The mission of IUPS is to elevate the consciousness of the planet. There's nothing bashful about that mission statement, and it connects deeply at the heart of concern for many people who want to improve the world they live in through acts of service. It's daring, it's bold, and it's out of the box.

Those who succeed with challenging the status quo must be willing to *break the rules* but must also be *prepared to deal with the consequences of breaking them.* In the case of IUPS, breaking from convention meant breaking away from accrediting bodies that Irv and his colleagues believe can strangle the creativity in an educational system. "Accrediting bodies as well as other universities are threatened by the likes of IUPS." Why? Irv believes that distance learning programs are attracting large numbers of students, and the result is decreased enrollments elsewhere. IUPS also challenges the philosophy that forms the foundation of traditional learning institutions.

So there will be challenges and unwelcome scrutiny, and you need to be prepared for that. "You need to anticipate criticism, and you need to have resources to deal with a critical audience." Just how does the maverick go about this? For starters, *make sure that your communications are clean and clear.* Be factual, be honest, and be straightforward about who you are and what you do. Be just as clear about what you're not. Then *make sure your product or service is of the highest quality.* Let your work speak library volumes for you. One of the dangers of being on an innovative playing field is competitors who, in an effort to imitate what you're doing, end up diluting or misrepresenting your model. The integrity of your model is threatened when that happens, and you must be ready and willing to manage through that situation.

Finally, Irv Katz observes that those who are successful in challenging the status quo *maintain a community of practice.* A community of practice stretches everyone involved, keeps everyone on their toes, and raises the bar. It also provides the environment for continual learning and innovation. In other words, those who successfully challenge the status quo put in the very mechanisms that will prevent them from becoming the face of convention down the road.

65. "CREATE FEWER MESSES WITH A MORE METHODICAL APPROACH"

■ ■ ■

When **Cindy Reynolds** took over Commercial Communication Services in early 2001, the 20-year-old firm that sells business telephone systems, business networking, and structured cabling business wasn't growing. Six months later, 9/11 hit, after which the telecommunications industry really tanked. In the midst of all the chaos and confusion brought on by 9/11, the mind-set was, "We're going to live with what we have." After all, most people viewed telecommunications as fairly stable. The technology had been around a long time, and everybody was used to it. But starting in mid-2004, things began to shift. Advances in so-called "converged technology," in which computers and telephone systems are integrated, started to change the face of business communications. Cindy, who had exchanged a successful career in the automotive industry for her CEO role at Commercial Communications Services, knew that she had to shift her company out of a traditional mind-set about telecommunications for her business to survive and thrive.

Cindy believes that it is imperative when attempting to shift mind-sets that a leader have the *courage to say what he or she is going to do and then do what he or she says.* That sounds simple enough, but in Cindy's mind what's important is that this sets a tone that conveys a commitment to keeping promises—to employees and to customers.

Cindy also believes that when a major shift has occurred in technology, it may be advisable to *infuse a new and different talent set* rather than try to put all your efforts into changing existing mind-sets. In her case, she hired new talent to implement the converged technology part of the business. Some people with older skill sets left the company. Cindy notes that peer pressure can cause people to reevaluate what kind of value they are adding. But she doesn't think that changing mind-sets is simply about infusing new blood into the organization. She insists that a leader also needs to demonstrate an interest in and be willing to make an investment in people's development. For her, this means providing new tools and skills that broaden existing employees' perspectives and bring them out of their traditionally wired mind-sets.

In Cindy's experience, *shifting mind-sets requires leader credibility.* A leader earns credibility by demonstrating self-confidence and confidence in others, focusing on results, and having patience. She believes that many CEOs don't have the patience to earn credibility with their employees and they tend to overemphasize the power and status of their positions. This doesn't work for Cindy, who maintains that a leader has to manage his or her ego and be willing to be educated by others. "You don't change mind-sets by overusing authority or by the force of your personality. You earn the credibility to do it."

Cindy suggests that changing mind-sets requires that a leader *be willing to lead from the heart and not from the head.* For Cindy, this means that a leader must understand people and what they need to succeed. In her role, she has been forced to come from a different place because she simply didn't have the technology knowledge when she took the organizational reins. "It comes down to believing in your heart that people have the talent to give the organization what it needs." She says that, unlike a lot of CEOs, she doesn't get consumed by the bottom line, and she believes that this is a totally unconventional perspective. In her experience, when she focuses her energy on supporting people to be and do their best, the business results follow.

Cindy observes that when going against the grain, a leader must *create an environment in which everyone can contribute and be successful.* It's all about having very high standards—about supporting people to play a bigger game. Cindy believes that not having the company she leads revolve around her as the CEO is central to its success. "If I develop people's muscle for tackling new and unconventional things, people will be more confident in making decisions and executing plans."

Perhaps most unconventional of all, in Cindy's experience, is the notion that the leader doesn't have the answers. She suggests that a leader who wants to support others to go against the grain *builds a team and a structure and a process that supports making decisions that are good for the company overall.* In her mind, it's about building a team that enables others to develop as leaders who have their own views to contribute.

66. "BE ENTREPRENEURIAL ABOUT PRESERVING THE PAST"

■ ■ ■

As the executive vice president of the Biltmore Company, **Steve Miller** oversees the operations of the largest home in North America, the 8,000-acre Biltmore estate in Asheville, North Carolina. The Biltmore, which hosts more than 1 million visitors each year and has annual revenues of $115 million, also features a highly acclaimed winery, several restaurants and retail shops, a working farm, biking and horseback riding trails, and a five-star hotel. But what's most impressive is the fact that the estate, built by George Vanderbilt in the late 19th century as an oasis for his friends and colleagues, is still family owned. In many ways, going against the grain *is* the Biltmore story.

Steve Miller, who has worked for the Biltmore since his college days in the early 1970s when he cleaned stables and groomed thorough-bred horses, observes that private ownership of estate properties like the Biltmore is almost unheard of today. High operating costs for such large properties, not to mention staggering property taxes, have resulted in many being transferred to nonprofit foundations or the government. He adds, "It's been said that you can't take a private estate the size of the Biltmore and make it profitable as a business. We've been about challeng-ing that wisdom." Steve believes the Biltmore's success is a direct result of an entrepreneurial leadership philosophy that has been at the fore-front from the beginning. "George Vanderbilt envisioned a self-sustaining estate modeled after those he saw on his tours in France. In the late 1800s the estate was a working farm. Later, the first school of forestry was de-veloped on the property. Now tourism, a winery, a hotel, and licensed lifestyle products are the focus of the business." In Steve's view, going against the grain is really about adaptation—seeing the need to adapt well before adaptation is forced upon you.

The efforts of Steve and his colleagues to transform the Biltmore into a profitable family-owned business offer a model in unconventional thinking. A prime example of this is the estate's winery. "The Biltmore's establishing a winery business in western North Carolina represented out-of-the-box thinking for this region. Sure, we have the warm days and cool nighttime temperatures grapes need, but the area has high humid-ity, so we had to work with that. Now we're quite proud of the fact that the Biltmore estate wines win blind taste tests in California wine country."

Steve is so passionate about the Biltmore and its entrepreneurial vi-sion, he'd much rather talk about that than himself. But it's clear that it's the leadership behind the vision that is at the core of the business's suc-cess, so he agreed to share the principles that guide his leadership efforts.

Find the right talent. Steve maintains that going against the grain is made possible by constantly infusing fresh perspectives and new ideas into the system. He believes that a healthy balance between people who are talented at conceptualizing and designing and those who are great at organizing and executing is critical to getting the right mix of talent.

Get an attitude. For Steve Miller, this comes down to being willing to take a creative idea and figure out how you can make it work, not dwelling on why it won't work. "You just can't analyze everything to death. If you do, you can always find reasons to not pursue everything. You have to be willing to take risks." He believes that a healthy drive to achieve underscores his own capacity for going against the grain.

You don't have to do it all. The creative genius that sparks great new ideas doesn't grow out of only one person. Steve believes a leader who goes against the grain takes full advantage of the talent on hand by delegating and sharing ownership. In fact, he's seen many entrepreneurs fail because they have trouble sharing and delegating.

Focus on people and purpose. Steve observes that while this mission is not unusual in family-owned businesses, it is unconventional for publicly owned companies under constant scrutiny by stockholders and Wall Street. He believes family-owned businesses have an edge over publicly owned corporations. "Leadership in a family business is personal. It's about living your values and creating commitment in others. We strive to maintain a personal touch in every aspect of our business, from our guests to our employees." Steve says people and purpose are honored through things such as highly visible leadership and storytelling that keep the history and heart alive at the Biltmore.

Have a mission that goes beyond making money. Steve believes that an excessive focus on the bottom line is what causes many businesses to become stuck in old success formulas or trapped in trying to satisfy Wall Street. In his view, when you can move past the focus on the money, you have the flexibility you need to think out of the box. "It's counterintuitive to think that an organization committed to preservation like the Biltmore would be so entrepreneurial." But the real truth may be that the commitment to entrepreneurial thinking may be what ensures the continuing vitality of the organization.

67.

"HELP PEOPLE BE
THE BEST THEY CAN BE
WITH CRYSTAL-CLEAR
CLARITY EVERY DAY"

■ ■ ■

Richard Peddie takes a business approach to sports, and we're not talking about sitting in front of the television on Sunday afternoons. Sports *is* his business. Richard is the president and CEO of the Toronto Maple Leafs, the Toronto Raptors, and Maple Leaf Sports and Entertainment, Ltd. With annual sales of $1 billion, it's the most valuable sports franchise in all of Canada, and with 52 headline shows annually, it's the fourth largest concert arena in the world. As a global leader in sports and entertainment, it's no coincidence that the organization's mission is to create champions, and every aspect of hiring, training, evaluating, and promoting top talent is in accordance with a set of core values that speak to being the very best.

Richard was an unlikely candidate for the top job of leading the Raptors organization in 1997. He was the organization's first professionally trained manager, and he wasn't trained in sports. He came from the packaged-goods industry, having held senior-level roles at Colgate-Palmolive, General Foods, and Pillsbury. While Richard is quick to point out that other sports organizations apply rigorous business approaches, he believes that his organization is distinct in its industry. "Coming out of 19 years in the packaged-goods industry, [to me] the Raptors didn't look that sophisticated." The Maple Leafs organization bought the Raptors in 1998, and Richard became the president and CEO of the merged organizations. Richard believes he brought a level of business acumen that helped his organization become a global sports leader. So what are the principles that underlie the Toronto-based sports giant?

Richard says that, first and foremost, his organization is a meritocracy. "We bonus and promote based on merit. Not everyone is equal, but things are not cutthroat or out of control. We're also a learning organization. We train and promote our leaders from within. We actively corporate-engineer, and I'm not talking about downsizing. We plan cross-functional moves and promotions for our high-potential leader candidates. In fact, 70 percent of our current managers and directors have successors identified."

Richard points out that his is an industry that's generally not so disciplined as others. "There's no Procter & Gamble in sports. Our senior leaders are not rated like traditional company leaders are. So we mine other sports organizations to glean the best practices. We also benchmark against other successful companies that are our corporate partners. I've got the president of McDonald's Canada and Coke Canada coming in to talk to our junior leaders." He chuckles, adding that sports writers have a real problem with his organization being a business. "We're a brand with line extensions. Profitability is not what the media is interested in. It's how the teams perform."

So what does Richard Peddie think his organization does differently than other sports organizations? He lists several things that he thinks separates the men from the boys on the playing field, including:

- Being a vision- and values-based organization
- Having a strategic plan and an annual performance plan
- Conducting research on every constituency that utilizes the organization's sports and entertainment offerings
- Being close to the fans; in his mind, extraordinary service sells and resells
- Bringing rigorous business discipline to the table

Richard believes that it's imperative to put a really good management team in place, and that means developing young leaders right from the start. Going beyond participation in the company's leadership development program, young managers get to make regular presentations to the board. He explains that his organization goes quite junior with management participation. It's a terrific opportunity, but there's also pressure to perform. "They know that they need to have their act together, but they are rewarded for that." For example, a young beverage-service person will get invited to hear the McDonald's president speak.

Richard and his megasports organization are doing a lot of things right, even if they are not doing them in traditional sports organization fashion. The organization receives more than 20,000 employment applications every year, and there is less than 10 percent turnover among employees. What's next? Richard explains that his goals are to increase enterprise value from $1 billion to $2 billion (the purchase of a soccer team is under way), to execute superbly, grow people, and win those championships. He says that above all, he aims to help people be the best they can be with crystal-clear clarity every day. In summing up, he recalls that the word *fan* comes from the word *fanatic.*

68. "CREATE AN ORGANIZATIONAL CULTURE THAT CHALLENGES THE STATUS QUO"

■ ■ ■

When **Fedele Bauccio** cofounded the Bon Appetit Management Company in 1986, it was with an appreciation of the fact that the food-service industry was mature, and frankly, not doing very well. The fare served up in colleges, hospitals, and even corporate banquet rooms was by and large uninspired. But Fedele was convinced that he and his colleagues could change all that. Bon Appetit's business model was to customize to every location it served, use fresh food from local markets, and deliver uncompromising quality. He says his company rode the trend of Oracle, Silicon Valley, and Google, and in the process became a preferred brand by being entrepreneurial, turning on a dime, and producing and delivering a competitive product.

Fedele believes that the most important thing he did to challenge the conventional approach to food service was to create a culture of people who love to work with food, but who can also work without rules. He says, "We banned rules and rule books in our business. We knew we had to act differently, and that we had to treat people differently if we were to succeed in what had become a rather stodgy market." Bon Appetit's mantra was very attractive, and lots of people wanted to sign on to work in a culture with no rules, few props, no institutionalized tools and techniques, and an open invitation to act independently. But Fedele says that creating a culture of going against the grain required Bon Appetit to be very selective about those it hired. That's not been a problem. The company does absolutely no recruiting, and its turnover for both exempt and nonexempt employees is well below the norm in the industry (less than 20 percent compared to more than 90 percent).

Fedele attributes the company's success in attracting the brightest and most creatively independent staffers to the fact that Bon Appetit created a signpost in a cluttered market by focusing on the company's distinctiveness and building a solid brand. He says that achieving that distinctiveness meant that Bon Appetit not only had to be selective in its hiring but also in which organizations it took on as customers. "We had to refuse business that we felt wasn't good for us or the brand image we were trying to uphold." It was and continues to be a mind-set of thinking the opposite of what the industry is thinking, being highly focused, and being willing to sacrifice some business. In Fedele's view, what he and his colleagues did was create exclusivity. "Our approach works only in certain environments. We're positioned as the most expensive food-service operator, but we deliver the value to match what we charge."

So how does the company's culture get embedded when all but about 40 of the more than 13,000 employees work in customer locations? Fedele says that people set their own priorities, but they live the dream. The dream, as he describes it, is to be the premier on-site restaurant company known for culinary expertise and socially responsible business practices. This is about hiring the most creative talent, using fresh foods from local markets, and tending to the well-being of guests and the surrounding community. "Our people have a clear sense of direction and purpose. They are encouraged to be creative within a strong set of core values. We let them have the freedom to color outside the lines, to make a contribution, and to enjoy what they do every day." Fedele is fervent in his belief that a leader must be the steward of the company's brand and think in a very focused way, lest people get bored with the core values and drive the brand into chaos.

Fedele believes that people who succeed in a culture whose brand is all about challenging the status quo share certain attributes. The most important attribute is valuing individuality over conformity. He also believes that success depends on continually reaching and stretching, building community, not being rule-bound, and having an unwavering passion for the work. He's quick to add that individuality, while being the singularly most important attribute for success, must be channeled. People have to be able to work with a team. "In my organization, I don't have to be a traffic cop; peers hold each other accountable. My job is to communicate the core values and then be sure I live them."

PART 10

MANAGING PEER RELATIONSHIPS
ADVICE FROM SUCCESSFUL COLLABORATORS

■ ■ ■

Flattened organizational structures and the lightening-fast speed of business today have converged to make collaboration skills more important than ever in the success of individuals and organizations. Everyone must be more capable of collaborative leadership—at all levels of the organization. Indeed, a significant derailing factor for high-flying executives who ascended the organizational ladder on the merits of their business acumen is often the lack of ability to effectively influence peers. One thing is clear: sustained individual success depends more on what a leader can influence than on what he or she can control. Real clout in the organization is about garnering respect and cooperation from multiple stakeholders.

What successful collaborators have learned—and willingly share on the following pages—is that collaboration begins with checking one's ego at the door. When leaders are as willing to be influenced as they are willing to influence, the stage is set for the integration of multiple perspectives and a better outcome than any one person could have created alone. Successful collaborators stress that collaboration isn't about posturing or using sleight-of-hand manipulation to get one's way. Such feigned attempts at collaboration predictably backfire. An important psychological shift is critical for entering the collaborative space.

Those whose success hinges on effective collaboration insist that the benefits of multiple perspectives far outweigh the transient discomfort of giving up control. Moreover, creating win-wins has its own appeal: deeper and more satisfying interpersonal relationships and shared ownership for the work. For some, collaboration is the only way they can effectively manage their overloaded plates. Through collaborative partnerships, they find they can play full out to their strengths while rendering their liabilities irrelevant.

Collaboration is more than a requisite set of attitudes. It takes real skill to listen well and to integrate divergent perspectives. And it takes interpersonal savvy to manage through the creative conflict that effective collaboration involves. The very best collaborators actively foster collaborative organizational cultures in which both the requisite attitudes and skills are made explicit, and people are rewarded for the collaborative successes.

69. "UNDERSTAND AND ALIGN WITH THE GOALS OF THOSE YOU SEEK TO COLLABORATE WITH"

■ ■ ■

Becky Olejar is a consummate collaborator, and that's why her customers rely on her. Becky is a Standards for Excellence facilitator with Maritz, Inc., a decades-old company specializing in customer-satisfaction research and customer-support training and consulting. Automobile dealerships across the United States represent the company's largest customer category. Becky supports Cadillac dealers in their aim to keep their customers happy, because they know that having satisfied customers translates to increased sales and larger profits for their dealerships.

Becky works with dealership owners and sales teams to use the data gleaned from customer surveys to identify "targets for action—the attitudes and behavior that will enhance their customer service—and their customer-survey ratings. Becky says that her job requires a lot of collaborative skills. After all, she's not the boss, and sometimes the findings she has to share with her Cadillac dealership owners are not the most welcome information. "Everybody thinks they're doing an outstanding job already, so they're not prepared to hear anything that contradicts that." So how does she engage dealership owners in a collaborative process to enhance customer satisfaction? She offers the following tips and strategies, which she says have served her purposes in this as well as prior organizational leadership roles:

- *Understand and align with the goals of those you seek to collaborate with.* Collaboration is rooted in shared purpose.
- *Be willing to listen!* Becky asserts that this is by far the most critical skill for anyone aspiring to be an effective collaborator. When you listen with the intent to understand others, you create trust and forge the relationships that support collaborative outcomes.
- *Demonstrate an interest in others and their success.* Great collaborators know that it comes down to an acknowledgment that "We're in this together."

- *Contribute your ideas without being attached to them.* Collaboration is not about getting your way, but about integrating your ideas with the ideas of others.
- *Focus on the opportunities rather than on the problems.* With your eye on the ball in front of you, there is less likelihood that people will get bogged down in defensiveness and blaming.
- *Focus on the process rather than on the person or team.* Keep the discussion issue-based to prevent people from personalizing criticism.

Becky, who also has specialty training in organizational coaching, believes that coaching is a vital skill in collaboration. "When you bring genuine curiosity, a personal interest in others, and great questions to the table, people are more receptive to working with you and integrating your contributions."

One of Becky's overriding goals is to encourage employee involvement, or shared ownership of customer-satisfaction improvement opportunities. "Automobile dealerships can be pretty hierarchical, and dealers often want to maintain tight control over their operations. So it's a leap for them to move from a single leader mind-set to one that embraces shared leadership." In other words, they need to become collaborative leaders who foster effective internal collaboration.

Becky's approach to fostering collaborative leadership is to help dealership owners *identify the guiding principles for customer service and the critical boundaries that everyone must observe.* For example, there might be a boundary that no one takes a car for an overnight test drive. She also encourages dealership owners to communicate customer-survey findings to all employees and then encourages their collaborative input regarding service-enhancement opportunities. When everyone has a stake in the actions and the outcomes, success is virtually assured.

70. "COLLABORATION IS A CHOICE; IT'S NEVER FORCED"

■ ■ ■

Julie Cook is a financial center manager with Clarica Financial Services, a Canadian firm that provides insurance, investments, and financial-planning services. She co-manages the operation with a partner. The arrangement is unique among the organization's 80 branches. "It was a choice," Julie says, "and that's one of the cardinal rules for any collaboration. You can't force collaboration." The collaboration reflects what Julie describes as a deliberate move away from one person being "top dog" to a shared leadership model. The financial center that she and her colleague run employs more than 30 financial advisors and support staff, each of whom contributes to the success of the business.

Julie says that while collaboration is launched based on people's choosing to work in partnership with each other, other things enhance its likelihood of success. The first thing is respect, she says. It's about respect for each individual's skills and abilities as well as respect for personal and professional boundaries. It's also about trust, and that means having confidence in another's ability and making a full commitment to the process of working together. Effective collaboration is also enhanced by open communication. Open communication includes having a shared vision and an agreed-on strategy for accomplishing the goals as well as clearly defined accountabilities. "You have to be willing to ask for help—to be able to admit when you don't know something."

Effective collaboration requires that you be willing to let go of your ego needs for things such as power and control. "It's about sharing power, control, responsibilities—and the credit for a job well done," Julie says. She has observed firsthand the positive impact of collaboration in her organization: when leaders model collaboration, the impact ripples across the organization. Others follow the example set by leaders, and that impacts the bottom-line performance of the organization.

The biggest obstacle collaborators are likely to encounter as they work through the process is *strong divergent opinions.* Julie points out that in any collaborative endeavor there is diversity of backgrounds, experiences, expertise, and opinions. In fact, the best collaborations seem to thrive on the creative tension that results from such diversity. She strongly advises, however, that the first thing an aspiring collaborator has to be willing to do is to let go of having everything his or her way. "It's much like a marriage," she says, "and you have to be willing to make concessions and to compromise. It's about allowing everyone to enjoy success. No one person gets the trophy."

So what are her success tips and strategies for other would-be collaborators?

- *Look for a good skills mix.* While divergent thinking creates tension, it also generates the most creative outcomes. If everyone thinks alike, you're not going to get anything new or different.

- *Know what you're good at and what you're not.* Julie observes that while this sounds so basic, it's really about knowing when and how you can contribute to a collaborative effort. You don't have to be great at everything to effectively collaborate. After all, collaboration is about taking advantage of the rich diversity of skills, experience, and expertise in a group.

- *Support your collaborative partners publicly.* Julie believes that it's essential to show visible support for your partners whenever you represent the partnership in a public forum. If you have a disagreement, bring it to your partner or partners privately.

- *Be inspired and energetic.* Bring your enthusiasm to the table. If you bring halfhearted inspiration and energy, you will likely drag others down and usurp the collaborative process. If, however, you are having difficulty with something or someone, you should not swallow it nor feign enthusiasm. Far from it! You must work out whatever issue you may have with those you are collaborating with in a timely fashion so that you are able to contribute fully to the process.

- *Assume a learner's mind.* Be willing to be open to learning from others. Fundamentally, this is about being as willing to be influenced as you are to influence. The minute you decide that you know everything there is to know and that you don't have anything to learn from others, you cease to be a partner in a shared process.

- *Invest for the long term.* Collaboration is quick or easy. In fact, it's a more rigorous and demanding process than working solo. The payoff is in the long term.

71. "CREATE THE ENVIRONMENT THAT SUPPORTS COURAGEOUS CONVERSATIONS"

■ ■ ■

Tom Via works in a fast-paced, intensely competitive (if playful) environment. He's the vice president of merchandising and marketing for Toys "R" Us Canada. As a member of the senior executive team in his company, he has firsthand experience with what works and what derails successful peer relationships at the top. According to Tom, teams at the top have some distinctive characteristics. "We're the keepers of the organizational culture and values. We're observed by people at all levels every day. We're the role models and we're also the strategists in the business." From Tom's perspective, a team at the top must set the tone for effective collaboration throughout the organization.

Tom notes that one of the things that characterize a team at the top is a natural competitiveness. "It's important to channel the competitive energy, and we do that by creating a shared strategy for our business. We all have a competitive energy for accomplishing goals—for winning in the marketplace—and that's healthy. But we keep our eye on our shared business strategy. I have a copy of each of my colleague's objectives, and they have mine. We revisit these as a group on a regular basis to ensure that we are aligned as an organization and as a senior-level team." While behavior such as properly channeling competitive energy is important, Tom points out that effective collaboration is about mind-sets. At Toys "R" Us Canada, the company's core values drive collaborative conversations.

Tom fervently believes that it's courageous conversations that keep the collaborative spirit alive in his company. He defines a courageous conversation as an interaction between two or more people in which there is safety from reproach or reprisal. As he sees it, such conversations can be downright uncomfortable at times, but the safety factor takes out the fear factor. "Courageous conversations support tough feedback and bad news. We believe that we must listen to each other, because if we don't, we're missing opportunities to move our business forward."

Tom explains that communication is so important to effective collaboration at Toys "R" Us Canada that whenever there is a failure anywhere in the business, he and his colleagues look for the communication breakdown behind it. It's easy to see why this is an important focus. Poor communication can lead to conflict, and that can lead to failure to accomplish a goal. "It's a muscle we've worked hard to develop across the business, and it's a primary focus of our executive team." So what advice does he have for leaders who want to foster greater collaboration in their organizations?

- *Create safety.* Tom advises that safety is fundamentally about ensuring that there are no political ramifications for someone's input. With Tom's executive team, this means that someone's input will never be used outside the group in a hurtful way, only to accomplish a shared goal. But safety is also about honoring confidentiality of fellow collaborators, respecting diversity of thought, and demonstrating integrity in supporting agreements once they are reached.

- *Invest in individual development.* Effective collaboration still comes down to people being able to do their very best every day, so it's important to build individual skills and confidence to develop effective collaborators. Developing skills and confidence ensures that people's ideas stay relevant—that they stay on top of their game. They bring that to their collaborations, and, as Tom puts it, "We play beautiful music together."

- *Catch people when they fall.* Effective collaborators engender trust that they will be there when their colleagues misstep or fall. In Tom's experience, the best collaborators support their colleagues without expectation of reciprocity.

- *Engage in "downtime conversations."* Tom advises that those who want to be effective collaborators should engage in the type of informal, non-mission-critical conversations that build relationship equity. These informal interactions create the safety net and provide the lubrication for the tough conversations that are inevitable in any relationship. It's like building an emotional bank account from which you can make withdrawals from time to time.

72. "IT'S NOT ABOUT WINNING BUT ABOUT CREATING WIN-WINS"

■ ■ ■

Brian Sherwood runs one of the largest telephone companies in the United States. He oversees the services for 200,000 telephones, more than 60,000 mobile phones, and literally millions of minutes of talk time per day. But if you're wondering which of the Ma Bells Brian runs, hold on. His telephone company is owned by the Boeing Company.

Brian relates that success in his job depends on his ability to forge relationships with managers of business units across the company. This is not something he takes lightly. "It used to be that my area was one of a number of company-wide services known as shared services. People had to use our services then, but that's no longer the case." In what Brian describes as the shift to free-market competition, he and his team must now compete with outside vendors to secure the telephone contracts. "My internal customers have the same affordability issues as any business, and we have to be in 'armlock' with them to creatively evaluate their processes and recommend affordable solutions. We're all about creating win-wins." He readily agrees that even though he's a preferred provider, he doesn't always get the business. He does, however, have responsibility for the service interface with the Boeing Telephone Company for services secured from outside vendors. As he puts it, "I have to forge the collaborative relationships, whether I get the business or not." Does he have any misgivings about that? "Not at all," he says. "It's part of the territory." So what advice does Brian have for aspiring collaborators?

All the individual parts of a business must be successful for the organization as a whole to succeed. Brian's philosophy is, "Like the separate parts of a car working together, all of us are together smarter than any one of us." He says that if an issue comes up for which he doesn't have an answer, he reaches out to others without hesitation to get their insights. He says he's developed a ton of contacts over his years at Boeing, and those relationships have really paid off. "You know you're only one phone call away from getting an answer, even if the person you call doesn't have it. More likely than not, he or she knows someone who does know the answer." Brian attributes a great deal of his personal success to *having an extensive network* that he can access on a moment's notice.

Brian observes that *great collaborators maintain a positive attitude.* For him, this is about generating positive energy that invites people to approach him. He says, "People want you in their networks when you are a positive, forward-thinking person." Brian adds that while maintaining a positive attitude is critical, collaboration is also about *leading the way in communicating with others about their needs and how your capabilities can support their success.* He insists that you've got to create the opportunities for collaboration by constantly communicating your collaborative intentions and what you can offer.

As Brian looks back on the missteps he's had over the years, he can point to two things: failing to communicate frequently enough and failing to be proactive enough to understand people's needs. In his experience, when you fail to do these things, people create false assumptions about what you can and can't do for them. It all comes down to being willing to invest in relationships for the long term and nurturing those relationships through frequent interaction.

Brian asserts that it's important to *know your own limitations.* "Be honest about what you can and can't do. People will respect you more for being honest and for having clear boundaries. If you don't get squared up with your limitations and you overcommit and then don't deliver, your credibility goes to zero." Brian's observation is that words are nice, but it's your actions that will speak volumes about you. If you want people to believe you, the two have to be aligned.

On a related note, Brian advises that great collaborators own their mistakes. "Never attribute the failure of a proposed solution to others or to circumstances. It's your responsibility to own it even if the real truth is that others participated in or contributed to the failure." He notes that a customer doesn't care where or how the problem occurred; he or she just wants a solution at an affordable cost. Brian says his mantra is, "I own it, so let me see what I can do to correct the problem." He knows that in his company, he's a single point of contact and that his customers are looking to him for leadership. For this, he suggests you have to have broad shoulders.

73. "EMBRACE THAT THERE IS ENOUGH TO GO AROUND"

■ ■ ■

Kimberly Martin works in an organization whose very foundation is based on effective collaboration. She's the managing director of sales innovation for PricewaterhouseCoopers's Sales Strategy Group. In her job, she develops tools and programs that support effective business development and client-relationship management for the firm's client-service professionals. As she puts it, "I help the consultants working on the front line expand their client relationships and enhance the services they deliver." As a managing director, she reports to the partner who leads her group, and her peers are the 18 to 20 directors who also report to the group partner.

Working with smart people—that's where trouble can start and why it's so important to Kim that she effectively manage peer relationships. She explains, "We run into problems whenever people get competitive. The reality is that there's simply too much for any one person to manage alone. That's what drives the need for collaboration more than anything else. To be effective in this game, you've got to have everyone on the same page. Moreover, our organizational matrix structure requires active collaboration. We don't individually own anything; we all own it."

Recognizing that tensions can mount when individual control needs surface and when there is a mad grab for resources, Kim has created an operating philosophy for collaboration that she says has served her well in what by any measure is a complicated environment to work in. "First and foremost," she says, "understand and embrace that there is enough to go around. You can afford to let go of your need for control and still be successful." Secondly, Kim advises that aspiring collaborators need to eliminate the question "Who's right?" In her view, it's more important to look for common ground than to be right. The truth is that diverse opinions stir the pot and contribute to better outcomes.

Kim also advises that garnering self-confidence is a must for effective collaboration. Why? For her, it's simple. "When you have self-confidence, you are more able to let go of your need for control. You know then that you can still have great ideas and not need to own the outcomes." Self-confidence also means that you know what your strengths are and that you are willing to ask for help from your peers. In Kim's experience, giving and getting help from colleagues sets up reciprocal relationships that are good for clients, the business, and you.

Kim believes that while you don't have to like everyone to be an effective collaborator, if you can at least appreciate what people have to offer, you can forge effective relationships with them. She says that it's also important that you don't take yourself or your circumstances so seriously. Taking yourself too seriously plays out in overvaluing your own ideas or needing to exert excessive control. Lightening the mood with humor is a great way to not only take yourself less seriously, it also makes you more likable to work with.

Kim also has some advice on what can derail collaboration:

Disagreeing without demonstrating respect. This boils down to not trying to understand others' perceptions. You can be passionate about your ideas, but you have to be respectful of others who don't see what you see. Kim advises that when there is disagreement, it's a signal that you need to evaluate how well you're communicating and how well you are hearing out other people.

Communicating without validating understanding. You can't assume that just because you said it, others will understand what you said. Kim sees this tendency most often when people are attempting to communicate about things that are not so linear or that are emotionally charged. She says, "It's your responsibility to be clear, and that means accepting 100 percent responsibility for what you say. If others don't get it, it's time to look at yourself."

Failing to handle conflict. Kim advises that the responsible thing to do when there is a significant level of tension is to identify it and work through it as a team. Otherwise, things can fester, and work is negatively impacted. On the other hand, when there is minor tension, for example between two people, it can actually make matters worse to drag things out into the open and overuse the group process. In these circumstances, Kim says she's found that simply elevating her attention and being more conscientious in her communications has helped ameliorate minor conflicts. What's important, no matter what, is that conflict gets handled, even if it is handled by being extra-caring in managing the relationship.

74. "BRING HUMILITY AND DO YOUR HOMEWORK TO BE AN EFFECTIVE COLLABORATOR"

■ ■ ■

When he was just 26 years old, **André Bauer** was elected to the South Carolina House of Representatives. When he was 29, he was elected to the state senate, and when he was 33, he was elected lieutenant governor. He's the youngest state lieutenant governor in the United States. André doesn't believe that he's an exceptional person. In fact, he insists that he's not cut from the mold that many politicians are. He didn't come from a political family, and he didn't enjoy wealth or privilege growing up. He didn't even study political science in college. So when he decided to launch a political campaign to win a house seat in his state, he knew he needed to work harder to gain visibility and win the trust of voters. He walked door-to-door meeting constituents, and he set up roadside chats for commuters driving to work. He also sent every registered voter a birthday card. He maintains that his campaign was more about building relationships than it was about talking politics.

Since becoming an elected official, André has continued to forge relationships with constituents, house and senate members, and the experts he has assembled to work with him on key legislative projects, including his oversight of the Department of Aging in South Carolina.

André Bauer is high on the subject of collaboration, noting that it not only played a key role in his electoral success, but it continues to support his success in office. As chairman of the National Republican Lieutenant Governors Association, he's forged relationships with the lieutenant governors of all 50 states. And that, he says, has been good for helping his constituents make important business connections. He's also gleaned some great ideas based on initiatives in other states. For example, the lieutenant governor of Illinois spearheaded the Military Relief

Act. The act enables state taxpayers to donate money to offset salary losses when military reservists are called up for full-time duty. André wants to replicate that in South Carolina.

André observes that an important aspect of collaboration is the willingness to surround yourself with people who are smarter than you are. He says, "I'm the visible person to discuss and represent the issues, but I can't be well versed in everything, so it's important that I be able to tap into the expertise of others." André says he's not too proud to learn from other people. In fact, he thinks everyone he meets has something to teach him. He believes that effective collaboration stems from a sincere desire to be of service and to work in partnership with others to better the circumstances of his constituents. It's no surprise then that he believes humility is an important aspect of collaboration.

In any politically charged environment, whether a government or a private-sector organization, it's easy to derail as a collaborator by getting caught in the trap of overvaluing the influence of certain individuals, particularly those you spend a lot of time with. André cautions that when this happens it can cloud your perspective, and you can become biased without the benefit of all the relevant information. He advises including multiple perspectives to avoid being trapped in bias.

Making ineffective use of time is another way to get derailed. You can't be an expert on every issue. When you get spread too thinly, you can't adequately prepare for meetings, you offer less than thoughtful input, and you contribute to hasty or poorly-thought-out decisions. In André's view, an effective collaborator sorts and prioritizes the issues and does the homework to glean the knowledge that will support making intelligent contributions on the issues that really matter. And that's not all.

The prevailing view that many people have of politics and politicians is that things are forever caught up in partisan debates. But André paints a different picture of the real day-to-day world of lawmaking and state administration. He says success hinges on forging long-term relationships rooted in trust and mutual respect. He maintains that it's just as important in government as it is in any business context to appreciate different perspectives, to seek common ground, and to integrate your ideas with those of others.

75. "MAKE COLLABORATION AN ORGANIZATIONAL IMPERATIVE FOR SUCCESS"

■ ■ ■

Scientists are hardwired to be independent thinkers. Years of training develop both expertise and egos, and that's hard to overcome. But **Larry Chandler** maintains that scientists can't be successful in his organization if they don't develop the skills of collaboration. He should know. Larry is the associate area director for the U.S. Department of Agriculture's Northern Plains Area. His organization is a federal research arm for the USDA. Larry notes, "These days, there is a lot of emphasis on the impact of what we do and how well we're spending taxpayer dollars." He acknowledges that while collaborative skills are important factors in his organization's efficiency, being a leader in a research organization isn't easy. It's a little like herding cats.

Larry believes that he's been successful in developing a collaborative organizational culture because he understands how scientific types think. After all, he is one himself. He says the most important thing he does is find out up front what the passions and concerns of his new hires are. He adds, "I want to know what pushes their buttons." By understanding what matters to his employees, he can channel them into projects where they will make their best contributions. But that's not all.

Larry applies organizational resources to ensure that people develop the skills for effective collaboration with their scientist peers. He acknowledges that learning to become a "we versus me" person can represent a tough shift for professionals whose very identities have been built on a foundation of expertise. He is reminded of how he felt as a young scientist. "I just wanted to be left alone to do my work—that is, until I realized that collaboration actually helped make big leaps in science. That's when I retooled my own thinking." As a result of his own experience, he maintains that it's important to help people look at the benefits of working collaboratively and to personalize the incentives for doing so. He points out that monetary gain is simply not a motivator for some people.

In Larry's organization, individuals with strong egos do sometimes try to take over a process. As he puts it, "They're not there to listen or to work for the common good. The impact is that people don't trust them because they are so self-interested." To be successful at collaboration, individuals must embrace the needs and concerns of all stakeholder groups. True enough, but what about expertise? Isn't that what people are hired to bring to the table? Larry asserts that the answer to this is an unequivocal "Yes." "Everybody brings expertise and, thus, ego to the table; what's important is how it's managed. It's about blending self-interests with those of others. We all have ideas and opinions, and they are important to the success of any collaborative endeavor. The trick is to manage the tension that ensues when multiple experts get together in a productive way."

Larry Chandler maintains that as a leader, he must be clear in his communication that collaboration is essential for success at the USDA. "People who have a broad range of contacts and collaborators have a track record of success. Scientific awards may be given to individuals, but everyone understands that they don't achieve results on their own." Moreover, because scientists, like many other professional groups, don't want to be managed by bosses, collaboration represents an organizational imperative for reaping the benefits of their talent.

For the aspiring collaborator, Larry offers this advice:

- *Examples are helpful.* Seek out someone or a group that has accomplished something important and ask how he or she or they did it. Find out what worked and what didn't.
- *Get involved.* Find ways to get involved in a collaborative endeavor, preferably with others who are experienced with applying collaborative frameworks.
- *Keep an open mind.* Check out the possibilities for joining with others. You may be more than a little surprised. It could be one of the best things you've ever done for your career.
- *Find the value in disagreement.* There's gold to be mined when brilliant minds differ and then blend the best of everyone's point of view.
- *Put your self-interests aside.* Check your ego at the door, but bring your talent and your arsenal of ideas to the table.
- *Treat everyone with respect.* When you communicate that everyone has value, you'll find yourself on the receiving end of the same respect.

PART 11

LESSONS FROM MISSTEPS
AND SETBACKS
WHEN EXPERIENCE *IS* THE TEACHER

■ ■ ■

Just what is the value of a painful misstep or setback? If you believe the leaders who've shared their lessons learned on the following pages, a misstep or setback is worth its weight in gold. Not that any of them sought out such a lesson. Missteps and setbacks just plain happen when they are least expected and totally unwelcome. They can be more than unsettling; they can be life-altering. Indeed, some of the leaders who've shared their stories here were confronted with crises they say represented the wake-up call that turned them on their heels and pointed them in the direction of authentic leadership and physical and emotional well-being.

Despite the magnitude of the setbacks some of the leaders have experienced, they agree that they have a lot to be grateful for. Why would anyone feel gratitude in the wake of a leadership misstep or setback? To understand this is to appreciate the full extent of the cycle of crisis and renewal that a setback can represent. One leader interviewed for this part puts it simply, "Setbacks are comebacks."

Though not always the life-altering kind, missteps and setbacks seem to be commonplace in the organizational landscape. They are part of the package that comes with accepting the risk of leading in a high-stakes organizational environment. Certainly, some of the missteps and setbacks described on the following pages ensued when leaders accepted highly visible assignments with significant risk. Could they have seen the problems coming? Perhaps, but it's easy to become so consumed by the pressures of the work that a person can completely miss the clues in the environment to impending trouble. The misstep or setback is most likely to be the thing that stops the train and forces a shift in perspective.

The shift in perspective that illuminates a new path forward is truly the gift in missteps and setbacks.

76. "TAKE CARE TO MANAGE THE POLITICAL SIDE OF ANY NEW INITIATIVE"

■ ■ ■

Kathy Flora is convinced that missteps and setbacks have made her not only a better leader but a better person. One thing's for sure, they haven't dampened her spirit. Kathy, who is now the director of Coaching Services for CoachInc, shared her adventures and the bounty of learning that ensued from the missteps and setbacks she experienced in a former role.

Kathy was the vice president of a $20 million division at one of the top three human resources consulting firms in the United States. She had grown the division, a virtual suite of services offered through Internet and phone, from $4 million to $20 million in a mere 18 months. With her characteristic enthusiasm and energy, she tackled the challenges of staffing up to meet explosive demand, training and developing the five different business line leaders, and developing interactive online learning tools for a Web-enabled coaching and consulting model designed to be an adjunct to her firm's traditional outplacement functions. She says, "We had a wonderful product, and a generous and wonderfully collaborative development team. It was a blast going to work everyday. It was productivity plus, and it was the most fun I'd ever had in a job. I had a staff of 110, and my clients included the Fortune 100."

Kathy says she didn't see trouble coming until, well, it was too late. "I just didn't fully understand or appreciate the organizational politics, and I stepped on toes without realizing it." She explains that while she was the VP of a very profitable division, she had not grown up in the organization. "I was a contractor when I started," she says, "and I just didn't have the relationships and the social capital to pull this one off." So what happened?

Kathy explains, "While my division represented a cutting-edge approach to doing outplacement business, it represented a serious threat to the traditional way outplacement services were delivered—through brick-and-mortar facilities and face-to-face interaction." A bit bluntly she adds, "Corporate politics is all about territory and what you control; it's not simply about outcomes. Unfortunately, I got painted with a brush that didn't really fit me, but the truth is that other people perceived me as not caring about their traditional way of doing business, and they saw me as eating their lunch."

With the clarity of 20/20 hindsight, Kathy relates what she feels she would do differently if she could roll back the clock:

- *Spend more time up front learning who the critical stakeholders are and forging relationships with those individuals.* "I was naive about the fact that the end customer was not my only stakeholder."
- *Find ways to collaborate and create win-wins rather than focusing exclusively on blazing new trails.* "I hit the ground running and was all about doing rather than relating, and this was a big mistake."
- *Invest in identifying and selling system-wide solutions.* "As soon as we realized how profitable my division was going to be, we should have shifted from being a profit center (and therefore an internal competitor) to being a service center, with all the profits going to the regional offices. I saw the solution, but I was unable to sell it."
- *Ensure high-level corporate sponsorship at the outset of any innovative and potentially disruptive business model.* "A fundamental change in the organization's business model requires the highest level of sponsorship to ensure it can be implemented. Moreover, entrepreneurial initiatives need to be nurtured and protected, even if it means spinning them off from the traditional organizational realm."
- *Enroll someone who can be a personal mentor and champion to help identify and overcome blind spots and remove organizational obstacles.* "I was on the research and development side of the equation, not the operational side, and I didn't have the resources to integrate the business model we'd developed across the broader organization."
- *Don't invest so much personally in the job that you lose your health and your soul in the process.* "I was addicted to the project and what we were creating, and I couldn't even see that I had no boundaries. I remember days when I was at my computer for almost 24 hours at a time. That's just nuts!"

In the end it was decided that the virtual outplacement business would be replicated in each of the organization's regional offices, and Kathy was told to dissolve her team. What does she now believe would have represented better choices? "They could have spun off the division into a separate business entirely, or they could have leveraged top-down support to fully integrate the model into all the regional offices. In the latter case, my group could have functioned as a service center in the same way that human resources departments function in many organizations. The way they did it is more expensive and less efficient than it needed to be."

Kathy sums it all up by saying, "At the end of the day, what's important is to know your personal strengths and how you can play to them." And that is her biggest lesson of all.

77. "IT'S NEVER TOO LATE TO WAKE UP TO YOUR POTENTIAL"

■ ■ ■

The fact that **Walt Weatherington** is black is central to his story. He's now director of Emergency Preparedness and Continuity of Operations Plan (COOP) for the U.S. Department of Labor. His organization responds in the aftermath of natural disasters like Hurricane Katrina to ensure that working folks' lost income is replaced. But his story begins in Alabama where he was born and raised.

Walt attended segregated schools in Alabama, and, after high school, he enrolled in an all-black college in Florida. "From the beginning," he says, "I was always in the company of people who were like me, and I didn't see the need for anything different." After a short stint teaching school and earning his graduate degree in school administration, Walt entered the U.S. Army. Walt says he thought success in the military was about being technically proficient and doing his job "two times better than anyone else around." He admits that he was the quintessential "good soldier." He adds, "I was afraid to step on any toes, and so I adopted behavior that I deemed would keep me on the straight and narrow. I was dutiful, careful, and cautious." Walt says he now realizes that he fooled himself into thinking that he could succeed by simply doing his job and satisfying his boss. "Proficiency just isn't enough," he says, "and your boss isn't the only one you need to be concerned about."

When on duty, Walt maintained narrow lines of communication with his boss and his direct reports, and when off duty he hung out with black enlisted personnel who were beneath his officer rank. So Walt became invisible—just another fish in the pond. He was a good soldier, but he wasn't on anybody's list of military fast-trackers. "The military is about leadership, but I wasn't convincing," he says. "Instead, I developed a rationale for my behavior, and I kept myself safely tucked away in the corner."

Walt was keenly aware, however, that some of his black colleagues were moving out ahead of him. "Everyone knew who the fast-trackers were and could see that they managed themselves differently. They recognized the importance of relationships, and they did the things that would contribute to their success. I thought those who integrated their networks were guilty of brownnosing, but the real truth was they took risks. They asked the provocative questions that challenged the prevalent assumptions about how things should be done. They did their homework, and people listened."

Walt admits that he was simply too fearful to do the things he saw his more successful colleagues doing. Not only was he not a risk taker, he had done such a good job of making himself invisible, no one was there to foster him. He says, "I didn't ask, and no one offered." Is it any wonder, then, that Walt was in emotional pain throughout his military career?

Walt retired with the rank of major from the military in 1996. He worked with the private sector for a while and then joined the U.S. Department of Labor in 2001. That's when things changed for Walt. He proudly observes that he advanced further in four years with the Department of Labor than he did in his entire military career. That notwithstanding, he admits that when he joined the Department of Labor he still had some more lessons to learn. "I was still very rank-conscious; I thought rank equaled power. I quickly learned that while rank might have gotten some measure of cooperation in the military, I couldn't rely on it anymore. I had to learn to use myself differently. I finally realized firsthand how important relationships are to success, and I decided to do something about it." As his skills and confidence grew, his concern with rank diminished, and his success easily followed. He says, "I've stopped relying on the power of authority and started developing the power of presence."

Walt has been promoted in each of the four years since joining the Department of Labor, and he's now looking at opportunities in the government's senior executive service. He holds no resentment towards others about his past missteps and setbacks. He believes that he holds total responsibility for both his successes and his failures. These days, Walt is happier and more confident than he's ever been. He communicates comfortably at all levels of the organization, and he creates followership and gets results through relationships. Does he have any regrets about being a late bloomer? Without hesitation, he says, "It's never too late to wake up to your potential."

78. "MANAGE, BUT DON'T OVERMANAGE"

■ ■ ■

Steve Pisarcik, who is senior vice president for operations for Kitchell Contractors, oversees several commercial construction divisions spanning multiple states. Steve explains that during his lengthy career as a manager, he's made the mistake many times of stepping in with his employees and "helping too much." He offers, "It's easy for a leader to simply take over, whether it's a problem to be solved or a team that needs direction. I've had to learn the hard way to keep my mouth shut even when people are struggling." So what's wrong with helping people do their jobs, even if it's more help than they bargained for? Steve doesn't hesitate to respond that every time he's stepped in and taken control, people have gotten too comfortable. "They don't have to deal with the issues. They can be spectators rather than players." Are there consequences to this? You bet.

When people are let off the hook by a leader who simply assumes control for the hard stuff, people don't learn from their own experience. And when they don't learn, they don't develop the skills necessary to take on additional responsibility or advance their careers. From Steve's perspective, a leader then becomes an unwitting ally in holding people back. He further explains, "It could take months or years to resolve an important issue in the construction business. There are many nuances that must be learned and managed through direct experience." He acknowledges that there are going to be instances where people struggle; it's virtually guaranteed. A leader can be overly sympathetic and move into rescue mode. Alternately, a leader who's worried that performance outcomes could be at risk may feel compelled to step in to ensure a goal is accomplished on his or her terms. This problem can be particularly acute when a leader is overly concerned about his or her job security or has difficulty letting other people fail on the way to success.

Steve believes that when the leader takes over the work of a team, the team is essentially rendered powerless. Team members can become disgruntled and question why they are even in the conversation, believing now that meetings are a waste of time. Steve's learned that he must guide and facilitate the team's process and hold people accountable for their commitments without overusing authority. He is firm in his conviction that a leader doesn't do the work of the team. As he puts it, "Once you've placed the magnets on the refrigerator, they stick."

So while there are clear and compelling consequences for individuals and teams when they are overmanaged, what are the consequences for the leader who missteps in this way? Steve offers that the consequences of overmanaging for him have been numerous. "Overmanaging keeps me too grounded and looking in my rearview mirror rather than on the road in front of me. Moreover, I'm too entrenched in the details. I have to really fight this because my natural stylistic tendency is to overattend to details anyway. The upshot is that my efforts in other strategic areas vital to the organization's success are diluted."

So just how does a leader provide the necessary guidance without getting overinvolved and running the risk of taking on the work of the team? "First of all," Steve suggests, "when people are struggling, you need to hold back. Otherwise, they will drop responsibility like a hot potato." His motto is: "People need to grow, and I don't need to review, scrutinize, or bless everything." But there is more to it than simply knowing what *not* to do. Steve maintains that a leader needs to establish the strategic goal and outline the parameters for the deliverables. Then back off and let the strategy be developed and executed by the individual or the team.

He adds, "I need to monitor progress and hold people accountable—I'm not going to let something important dangle or die." So there is a clear distinction between backing off and abdicating leadership responsibility.

Steve has seen a lot of people in the world of work become comfortable working within a certain scope of responsibility that operates like a set point. They perform within the limits of their set point, and they expect pay increases over time based on their performance within that same set point. Now that's entitlement masquerading as job loyalty, and it can be deadly for an organization. Steve observes, "Over time, people who are entitled can become resistant to *any* change that pushes them even slightly out of their comfort zones." What he's learned from this "near-death" experience is that it's vital to establish the expectation for performance stretch from the very outset.

79. "SETBACKS ARE COMEBACKS"

■ ■ ■

Irene Pfeiffer impresses those who meet her for the first time as someone who is confident, optimistic, and grounded. She is all those things, but she insists it's because of what she's learned about herself through overcoming missteps and setbacks. Irene talks about her experience in a senior-level human resources executive role with Shell Canada.

Irene experienced a significant setback when she was told that she and her entire human resources group were to be downsized by Shell Canada. She says the first lesson to learn is to realize that in such a circumstance, it's not personal. "Don't flatter yourself; it's not about you," she adds. Sure, her first reaction was the altogether human one of feeling annoyed and indignant. She thought, How could they not recognize the value I bring to the table?

Irene indulged her negative reactions for a short time, but she realized pretty quickly that her best purposes would not be served by a negative attitude. Instead, she took a hard look at the lessons she could take away from her time at Shell Canada that would make her a better leader.

She observes unflinchingly that while you may be in a position to influence change, other people and the organization as a whole may not change at the same rate you do. When you assume that your pace of change will be matched by others, you may find your efforts backfiring on you and your change initiative set back. Moreover, you can't assume that the appearance of support from others represents real commitment.

Irene learned that a good leader not only takes on a position and does it well, but also knows when to exit. She says, "You have to look at the skills that are needed by the organization. Don't let your ego get in the way and then stay too long." Irene admits that she'd had a gut feeling prior to her layoff notice that she needed to move on. She says, "I'm not a maintainer, and the moment I got into a maintenance mode, I sought to change that, and that's when I got into trouble with my bosses. They weren't ready for my initiatives." She recognizes now that she is an innovator and an implementer, and that she is not able to contribute meaningfully to an organization that values stabilizers.

Why do leaders stay in positions beyond their ability to make a difference in an organization? For Irene, it comes down to ego needs—the need for recognition, the need for safety and security, the need for achievement. All these can get in the way of a leader's being able to exit a situation gracefully. She says, "Leadership is about knowing when to move in and when to move on. Moving in is far easier than moving on. You get all that internal chatter going on inside your head, and the next thing you know, the decision for your departure has been made for you."

Irene observes that it's important to simply be open to the learning that comes from setbacks. "Being open to possibilities isn't always easy, but it *is* a choice. It's the flip side of being a victim, because you do in fact have a choice about that, too." She says that as she's matured, she's made a commitment to taking a learning approach to the "white water," because, in her mind, sometimes you just don't get better unless there is some kind of crisis. That's when setbacks are comebacks.

80. "BEING A LEADER IS NOT ABOUT BEING 'ONE OF US,' BUT IT IS ABOUT CREATING INCLUSION"

■ ■ ■

As president and COO of LoJack, the highly successful manufacturer of radio-controlled tracking devices for motorized vehicles, **Rich Riley** admits that he was clueless about how to manage himself as a young, up-and-coming leader. He had a series of successful leadership roles before taking on the top job at LoJack, but he maintains that no one ever said, "Here's how to be a leader." He learned about leadership through the old-fashioned school of hard knocks.

Rich shares that in his 20s he assumed significant responsibility for managing a merger when the printing firm that employed him acquired another firm in New York. "I rolled up my sleeves, and I worked really hard. There were union issues, staffing issues, and a host of other things that required detailed attention. I thought that I needed to be a peer working on problems alongside others," Rich observes. Then one day he received a wake-up call. "I got very clear feedback that people didn't simply want me to be 'one of us.' They needed a leader with a clear vision and a road map for a credible future." Rich says that in that moment, he grasped for the first time the difference between being a manager and being a leader. "I grew up believing that I was no better than anyone else. I still believe that's true, but I now realize that a leader can demonstrate respect for others while holding a powerful vision."

Rich believes that the transition from manager to leader is very difficult, and many individuals in leadership roles are working with a flawed formula. "A lot of people believe they're successful because they are tough. They think that empathy for people is too soft for business." The real truth is that those who hold those views are not likely to be around long enough to see the long-term impact of their actions. After all, just about anyone can get results short term with tough actions like layoffs. Rich Riley's prescription for leading with success, born of his own missteps, is to have a vision and a framework for creating the wins.

It's important to hire the right people and then get out of their way. Rich observes, "People need support, they need accountability, but they also need be trusted to execute without being overmanaged."

Rich says, "I've been lucky; I don't pretend that I've accomplished anything great." He agrees that this is his way of keeping things in perspective and avoiding the trap of ego he has so often observed in others in leadership roles. While he may be modest about his past accomplishments, he is a man on a mission with LoJack. He believes that the organizational culture had become overly bureaucratic with too much top-down decision making by a few people. His view is that leadership is not about telling people what to do any more than it's about stepping in and helping too much. He maintains that what people need is a framework that will support good decision making.

To illustrate how he has applied these principles at LoJack, Rich shares the experience of establishing a strategic plan for the company. "It was a painful process, because people weren't used to having that level of input. And because they had a better view of their areas of responsibility than of anything else, they actively championed their personal agendas. Then some senior-level people thought that as a result of their broader scope of responsibility, they should have more say in a planning process. But the hard reality was that there were more opportunities than there were resources to address them, and we needed a framework to support decisions for the overall best directions for the company." Rich observes that what people learned in the strategic planning process was priceless. They learned to put the interests of the company above their personal interests and to evaluate opportunities based on projected return on investment. It was an analytical versus an emotional process. More important, they could communicate a solid business case for decisions because they were part of a process for creating a shared purpose.

81. "SUCCESS IS ABOUT THE WORK—AND THE NETWORKS"

■ ■ ■

As the Manufacturing Excellence manager for the Americas Business for the petroleum giant Exxon Mobil, **Jim Hallahan** is no stranger to big business. He's worked with Mobil and the merged Exxon Mobil since 1980. But what he's learned about himself as a leader through the guidance of missteps and setbacks can be instructive to leaders in any organization.

Jim shares that he got his first glimpse of himself as a less-than-perfect leader when he gathered feedback from his direct reports in the 1990s. He used a third party to help him gather the data because, as he puts it, "You never get it all when you ask directly. You're the boss, after all." He says he cringed a little going through the process, feeling as most people do, apprehensive about the outcome. He relates that what he learned was a bit sobering, but useful beyond measure. He found out that others thought he wasn't walking his talk. He gives the example of coaching. "I confused coaching with feedback. I thought that by giving feedback I was coaching. It didn't click with me that coaching was really a two-way developmental conversation. I was giving my direct reports the tools and asking them to coach their people, but I wasn't doing it with them."

Jim relates that he has a style that is extroverted and easily triggered by things happening in the environment. "People told me in the feedback process that I didn't really seem to be listening. How could I when I was so busy multitasking while they were trying to talk to me?" What he learned in the process is that it's the relationships a leader builds in the workplace that matter most, and those relationships are built with conversations. Listening is the cornerstone of conversation. He says that he now also understands that in relationships at work, it's not just what he wants that's important. It's also important to understand the needs and wants of others. "I ask the questions and really listen now to the answers about what people need to be able to deliver in their roles and what makes them tick."

Organizational politics has been another area of deep learning for Jim. He doesn't think he attended enough to politics early in his career. "I put more into doing the job and delivering strong business results." He knows that he had a choice about how to manage his job, but he admits that it was difficult for him to turn it on and off easily. "I was always on," he says, adding that he now realizes he could have taken some of that time to build networks. "I made an assumption that success was about the work, not the networks." Today he has a broader appreciation of the importance of being able to use one's influence to get things accomplished. "It isn't just about out-of-work social interactions or being one of the 'good ole boys.' It's about getting things done without using authority." His advice to others is that you have to have a strategy for moving up in the organization, and it has to include influencing skills as well as goal-driven performance.

And that's not all. Jim advises that in order to move up, it's important to have mentors who can guide you. He thinks his career would have advanced more rapidly if he'd had a mentor or coach to help him create a strategy and give him clues to the process of moving up. He explains that he learned some of the gamesmanship by watching others and trying to figure out what would work for him. Does he have misgivings? "Not at all," he says. "I could complain, but then when I take a step back I realize that my prior experiences have actually developed me better for assuming broader responsibility going forward. It's been more of a marathon than a sprint, but I'm okay with that."

82. "DON'T LET WINNING AT WORK MEAN LOSING AT LIFE"

■ ■ ■

Over the course of a career spanning more than 35 years, **Manville Smith** held key roles with the 3M Company, the Parker Pen Company, Right Management, and Spherion®. But it was in his role as president of Parker Pen that he learned what he considers to be the most important lesson of his lifetime, and he learned it only after experiencing a devastating personal setback. Manville says, "I was a 'caveman' during the early part of my career. I was incredibly focused on getting bottom-line results. I was overly demanding and superstressed-out personally. I trampled on people, and I admit it, but I couldn't seem to do anything differently at the time."

When Manville took the reins at Parker Pen, the company was in desperate need of a turnaround, having lost a huge market share to Cross. He quips, "We couldn't survive selling refills. It was a very difficult situation. I knew that if we didn't do something to correct the problem, the company would face bankruptcy." He explains that the manufacturing process relied on old, outmoded processes requiring massive human effort. There was no real automation, and it made the company highly uncompetitive. So, a decision was made to reduce the number of manufacturing facilities worldwide from 17 to 5 and to retool the remaining plants.

Manville explains that the company was in the middle of the restructuring process when one day while sitting in a board meeting, he felt ill. He woke up much later in a hospital room, unable to move one side of his body. At age 42, Manville Smith had had a severe stroke that left him paralyzed on one side of his body and unable to speak. It was a tragic blow to a man who, a day earlier, had been on top of his game, or so he'd thought. Manville says the stroke caused him to have an epiphany. He became acutely aware of how fragile human life really is. But he realized a whole lot more than that. He came to grips with the fact that being a leader is about more than money, and it's about more than power and position. "I'd become so inhuman in my dealings with people that I couldn't live with myself, and I made myself sick." Manville says he also realized that winning at work for him had literally translated into losing at life, and that's when he woke up. He exclaims, "It took me over 20 years to learn that leadership is not the exercise of authority, and you can't exercise leadership without followership."

What happened next surprised and humbled Manville in a way that he could never have imagined. "Parker Pen had had an antagonistic relationship with the employee unions, and here we were going through a restructuring, closing plants, and taking people's jobs away from them. But there was this huge outpouring of compassion and support from both the employees and the union representatives. I was humbled by the response from people, but I also realized for perhaps the first time how big a deal a restructuring entailing a loss of jobs is for people and their families." He tells of shutting down a plant in Spain. "In the town where the plant was located, people raised sheep and made pens. Sixty-eight families stood to be impacted by our decision to shut that plant down." Manville says that he got personally involved in helping employees figure out what they were going to do next to earn a living. "We helped people do things like buy a taxi cab or open a store." Not surprisingly, as the restructuring progressed, there were no strikes or other untoward events.

On a final note, Manville insists that a leader needs to *tell the truth, regardless.* "In my caveman days, I used to withhold information. I greatly underestimated people's capacity to accept change, and I defaulted on my duty to tell the truth. In so doing, I paid the high price of people's mistrust and their unwillingness to tell *me* the truth."

83. "TRUST YOUR INTUITION WHEN THINGS ARE TOUGH"

■ ■ ■

When **Gerard O'Toole,** executive chairman of the Nissan Ireland group of companies, acquired the franchise for Japan's Daewoo in 2000, he expected nothing but fast-forward profits. "We got off to a magnificent start," he says. After all, Daewoo was the 16th largest corporation in the world, with a massive shipbuilding and auto-manufacturing operation. Gerard explains that he had already signed a ten-year agreement when he discovered to his utter dismay that it wasn't worth the paper it was written on. Daewoo, it turns out, was in serious trouble and had declared bankruptcy. With the company in receivership, there were many more questions about the firm's viability than there were answers. Gerard goes on to explain, "I had 3,000 to 4,000 cars in stock, and people were wondering if the cars they had previously purchased were worth anything. Concerns about availability of parts and validity of warranties were on everyone's mind."

Gerard goes on to explain, "I had to look down the road. This was a global franchise, and my intuition was that it couldn't just evaporate."

Ford Motor Company considered purchasing the distressed company, but eventually walked away from the deal. General Motors ultimately bought Daewoo and put it under the name Chevrolet. It has since recovered. Gerard notes, "I could have liquidated some 15 months before GM purchased Daewoo. In some ways that would have been a clean solution, but it would have meant putting dealers out of business and firing staff. My gut kept telling me that there was enough history with Daewoo to support a turnaround."

What Gerard says he learned in this serious setback with his automobile enterprise is how important it is to stay the course when things are tough. "Respect and a high regard for the feelings and commitments of others are critical to long-term success in any business. My reaction came from within—it was intuitive." In Gerard's view, a full plate of human respect is essential, and you just don't go below a certain threshold of respectful behavior. He doesn't think he's essentially changed in the more than 30 years he's held the reins of the Nissan Ireland group of companies. "I treat people with respect—the way I'd like to be treated." It was that overriding conviction that turned him away from an expedient decision to liquidate the Daewoo line.

Gerard believes that being able to use intuition in business is an important leadership attribute. He cautions, "In the final analysis, you have to go with your instincts, because you can end up paralyzing yourself with analysis when confronting a problem." Gerard advocates that there are times when you simply must be able to act in the absence of data or despite what the data is telling you. It's his firm belief that successful companies are run by people who make it happen now. And while you can't ignore facts and analysis, which are the bedrock for good decisions, you've got to be able to act quickly when decisive action is called for. With the Daewoo setback, all the data at the time suggested that the best course of action would be to liquidate the troubled franchise. But Gerard is grateful that, in the midst of what everyone involved agreed was a devastating set of circumstances, he opted to stay the course. His take: "Get fit, be clever, and run the race." He's rejoicing today that the Nissan Ireland group of companies is up on market share, and that Chevrolet, a respected global brand, is doing very well on his turf.

PART 12

THE CHANGE AGILE LEADER
WHAT IT REALLY TAKES TO LEAD CHANGE

■ ■ ■

Change agile leadership may well be the single most important leadership competency in contemporary organizations. Today's change is radical, disruptive, and externally driven. It is totally unlike the incremental, nondisruptive, internally driven change that characterized Industrial Era organizations. Incremental change could be cascaded down the organization with a single memo from the top executive. People rarely resisted such change, because it didn't pose a threat to the status quo, much less to jobs or the way work got done. Today, all bets are off. Change impacts the work, the way it gets done, who does it, and where it gets done. Skill sets and job descriptions can become obsolete almost overnight, and leaders are expected to reinvent the workplace with lightning speed to stay ahead of the market.

There is a huge gap between what most managers were trained to do and what must be done today to effectively lead others through change. What are the attitudes and skills of the leaders who lead successful change efforts? How do they engage the commitment of reluctant employees who understand that as a result of their active engagement their jobs could be sent overseas? How does a leader create a vision of a credible future when everyone isn't in that picture of success? These are the really tough questions that leaders must address in their change initiatives today. And there is more. New and different skills are needed to communicate and execute change. They are the important and highly salable skills that leaders appearing on the following pages exemplify.

Leading change is not a job for those lacking courage and tenacity. Moreover, it requires tough-mindedness balanced with truthfulness and compassion for people. Indeed, no leader can effectively lead change in an emotional vacuum. To lead change is to immerse one's self fully in the work and in the heart of change. It's tough work leading radical change today. Some say it's the toughest work they've ever done. All seem to agree that the most successful change efforts are informed by a clear vision, highly effective communication, and thoughtfully executed strategy that is reinforced through robust metrics and rewards.

84. "ENVISION SUCCESS AND ENGENDER HOPE IN THE FUTURE"

■ ■ ■

Charles Barrentine always starts his transformation message with two questions: "Raise your hand if you've ever shot a roll of Kodak film." Typically, 100 percent of the hands shoot up. Then he follows with, "Keep your hand *up* if you shot a roll of Kodak film in the past few weeks." Usually, only one or two hands remain in the air. The answers to these two questions sum up his mission at Kodak: Help others recognize the need for change and lead the way. Known as CB to his associates and friends, he's Kodak's chief KOS officer. (KOS is short for Kodak Operating System, the company's program for institutionalizing lean methodologies and practices across Kodak.) CB is leading the charge, which began in manufacturing, by expanding and applying lean thinking to business processes. It's no job for the faint of heart. In fact, CB professes that no one can be successful as a lean change leader without a passion for the work and a fierce resolve to "do the right things the right way."

But what is lean anyway, and why is it so important to Kodak's future? CB defines lean as quite simply, the elimination of all non-value-added activity. In the lean world, this is often viewed as waste. "Kodak's commitment," CB says, "is that everything we do will be focused on creating value for our customer." For him and those he leads, lean is a way of thinking. It's a philosophy that guides everyday actions in serving the customer, eliminating waste, and creating a winning and inclusive workplace that fosters employee commitment. He explains that through a disciplined focus on lean, Kodak has taken hundreds of millions of dollars out of inventory and costs through improved productivity since the implementation of KOS in 1999. And while Kodak has had many lay-offs because of shifts in its traditional film business, he says the company, through KOS, has made work simpler and easier, while improving the quality of work life for employees.

CB has some very specific views on leading change in a fast-paced, highly competitive environment. For starters, *in order to lead change, a leader must move from what a vision* is *to what it* does. For him, it's about answering some fundamental questions: "What does it mean to be number one in the world? How is the vision actionable? What does it drive in the organization? How do I see myself in the vision?" As CB sees it, vision creates the reality of the results a company generates.

CB offers what he believes are the critical behaviors that are necessary for a leader who is driving transformative change in the organization:

Demonstrate effective strategic leadership. A leader must clearly and compellingly communicate the big picture about the aims and intentions of the change to keep the organization moving toward the desired state. CB says that at Kodak, leaders understand that KOS is the methodology that enables the corporate vision and applying lean is how the company is being transformed. Leaders use a strategic planning framework that incorporates lean as the road map to run the company and drive business results.

Make values-based decisions. Kodak's values as a company are respect for the dignity of the individual, integrity, trust, credibility, continuous improvement and personal renewal, recognition, and celebration. These values form the foundation or anchor points for all decisions. CB observes that while every company needs governance, it won't take you all the way. Values should be the strongest part of a company's operating philosophy.

Articulate what must change and communicate constantly—in person. It's important when driving transformative, disruptive change that a leader consistently, clearly, and honestly shares the scope of the transformation and breaks it down into key components so everyone can understand what is changing and what is expected through the transition. A leader must also be highly visible and able to correct any false assumptions that are created. False assumptions are counterproductive, often creating distrust because they often paint a picture that's worse than the reality. CB insists that a leader has to "reach out and grab folks." He explains that he and other Kodak leaders have been brutally honest with employees about what's happening with the traditional film business and where the company is heading. He insists that even though it's been very difficult for employees, they need to know what's happening and why.

Help people to learn, unlearn, and relearn. With radical change, mindsets and behavior have to change. Different skills and behavior are needed to meet the new requirements in the business. A leader must destroy old paradigms, articulate the skills required for the future, and invest in people by allowing them to relearn. CB explains that for decades Kodak was primarily a technology company in which *technical expertise* was a critical success factor in its traditional film manufacturing. "In the digital company, we still need technical experts, but we also want leaders who can innovate and who have experience in managing and leading the full extent of the supply chain. We want leaders who have a broad perspective on markets and who are able to build strong relationships with our customers. They need to understand what it takes to be a part of the future and be able to develop those skills and mind-sets."

Make change inclusive. This means that everyone who will be touched by change needs to understand their part in it. Values must be evident in everything leaders say and do. They must demonstrate integrity and honor their commitments. CB believes that making change inclusive also means ensuring fairness in your dealings with employees. "You must engender hope for the future of the company and hope for their individual futures, even if they are not in the picture of the company's future."

Be a change agile leader. Perhaps most important to effective change leadership is the leader's personal change agility. For CB, it comes down to having a passion for the future and the discipline to stay the course. He adds, "It's a bumpy ride. It's a transformation of enormous magnitude, and it's been the most difficult transformation I've ever undertaken but also a time of tremendous learning." He is quite clear about one thing though, and it is that leaders who allow themselves to be consumed with fear and dread and who carry that angst around with them simply cannot be effective in inspiring and engaging the hearts and minds of others. "You've got to believe it for yourself if you expect anyone else to believe you."

85. "YOU MUST MANAGE THREE CRITICAL FACTORS IN ANY RADICAL CHANGE PROCESS"

■ ■ ■

When **Nora Denzel** took over the reins as vice president of Hewlett-Packard's Software Global Business Unit in 2002, the company was in serious need of a turnaround. The business, which had not been profitable historically, was growing at –5 percent, well below the rate of the market overall, and it was not taken seriously in the software industry. The group's managers didn't see a need for change inasmuch as it had been largely viewed as a research and development group. Moreover, because of the way the business was structured, performance data was not reported to Wall Street, and the group's managers simply didn't understand their own metrics. Nora explains, "Software development is essentially a publishing business. There were these 'random acts of software' being developed, but we didn't have a number one or two hit." Not only that, but the company's customers were wary because HP had entered and exited the software market over the years. Fundamental questions about things such as responsive technical support and product upgrades nagged at customers. Nora says she understands that thinking quite well. "Customers don't buy what you have now; they buy based on where you're headed in the future." She explains that the lack of clarity extended to the top of the company. "Senior executives weren't clear about what kind of software they wanted to focus on."

Nora's charge was to convert the software group from a cost center to a profit center. It was full steam ahead for this intrepid change leader. Nora maintains that in any radical change initiative, three areas have to line up: strategy, structures and processes, and metrics and rewards.

On the first point of strategy, Nora explains that everyone must be clear on the need for change, the end state that is envisioned, and how change will impact people and the business. In the beginning, she spent enormous amounts of time discussing the desired end state with people at all levels of the organization. She says, "I went to every single board meeting since HP's merger with Compaq." She spent a lot of time in the software business unit itself discussing the business strategy and the end state. As she saw it, people were quite complacent. "Everyone thought they were doing well, and I had to penetrate that blind spot." She relates that she did a lot of handholding during this early period, adding, "This kind of change is not a spectator sport."

But what Nora did to rally her employees is in itself a feat. She deliberately fostered the creation of an enemy outside the company by showing people the performance data for best-in-breed competitors. She explains, "We showed them what other companies were doing and what we would be compared to. We impressed upon them that there were a lot of fast runners out there." Nora says she was clear that she didn't want people to be angry at HP, so she endeavored to make it possible for them to put those emotions outside the company.

Nora shares that it was very difficult in the beginning, but that she and her colleagues were able to unite around the end state and the company's increased competitiveness. The external competitive reference point made all the difference. It made both the end state and the strategy for getting there real and palpable. She adds that it's important that a change leader be clear about strategy with customers and stockholders as well as employees. She quips, "The difference between a hallucination and a vision is how many people can see it." In her view, the vision of the end state must be evident to everyone, even when the leader isn't present.

After a few months, Nora was able to turn her attention to other aspects of the change initiative, notably the structures and processes to support it. She is adamant that structures and processes follow strategy, and that you can't lead a radical change without them. Structures and processes create the accountabilities. They are the organizational design and work elements that make the change initiative real and actionable. She adds, "You have to ensure that structures and processes are not convoluted. People have to understand what their roles are, how budgets will be allocated, etc. It's very detailed work."

On her third point about metrics and rewards, Nora advises that metrics and rewards must be aligned with the core business strategy. This involves detailing the answers to such basic questions as, "Who's going to buy the product?" She explains that her group was developing a suite of software products, so the metrics had to be realigned to support an integrated strategy. Nora insists that it comes down to the simple fact that people will act in accordance with how they are being paid.

Nora maintains that a change leader's job is to keep the team energized despite the noise in the system. The leader has to address the ambiguity that surfaces, demonstrate unwavering optimism, and be personally well grounded emotionally. She remarks, "You have to have confidence in the outcomes and yet be able to tack to the right and to the left, because you're not just dealing with the unknowns, but the unknowable. With radical change, there's no way to control every variable, but you have to maintain momentum and manage through the cycle." In Nora's mind this is important because people can get excited about the change and then become paralyzed because there is so much to do. Being crystal clear about the priorities enables people to get focused on what's most important right now. On this last point, Nora advises that the leader must be constantly communicating about the work elements and the metrics. She also advises that the thresholds for metrics need to be monitored because metrics will shift over time because of a shifting of priorities.

So how did HP's Software Global Business Unit perform after the radical change Nora led? She rejoices that the business hit all its targets, going from –5 percent to +25 percent in an industry that's been growing at the rate of 10 percent. "We hit two and a half times the industry growth rate." While she's extremely proud of that accomplishment, she admits that it wasn't all pretty. She says, "We exited eight businesses and acquired eight companies. There was a lot of reshuffling, and there were job losses because some existing employees couldn't scale up to the new demands on the business. We had to hire to our skills gaps, but at the end of the day HP is a stronger, more profitable company."

86. "LEAD CHANGE, DON'T LET IT LEAD YOU"

■ ■ ■

Dan Middleton is senior vice president for Wells Fargo's Business Direct Division. Business Direct sells unsecured credit to small businesses, including loans, credit cards, and other credit instruments. It is one of the company's most profitable divisions, with double-digit growth in each of the past ten years.

A little less than two years ago, Dan, who's been with Business Direct for six of the ten years it's been in existence, had a sort of epiphany. He says he was grappling with a deep question, "Am I going to lead change, or am I going to let it lead me?" He realized that, given his division's explosive growth, conventional wisdom would suggest hiring more people to fulfill the increasing demands on the business. But Dan saw something different. "I could get a lot more people working for me, or I could find a way to help the people I had be more effective." Dan saw an opportunity to bring coaching into his organization to support leaders to enhance their contributions. He'd completed a professional training program in corporate coaching, so he envisioned that he'd play a different leadership role than he'd played previously. He observes, "I realized that my value to the company could be exponentially greater if I focused on supporting other leaders to be more effective in their roles rather than just managing more people myself."

Dan was keenly aware that his vision of creating a coaching culture represented a dramatic change at Wells Fargo. Sure, the company had contracted with external coaches for selected leaders from time to time, but coaching had not been deeply embedded in his company's culture. Moreover, Dan knew from personal experience that some managers don't naturally gravitate towards developing younger managers, or their strengths simply lie in other areas. He saw a way to make coaching available on an organization-wide basis while freeing managers to do what they do best: run the business. So how did Dan Middleton lead the change in Business Direct?

"The most important thing when championing any significant change," he says, "is to *go right to the top*. In my case this was the executive VP–level division head. When the top person buys into something, other people take notice. They take the change initiative more seriously." Dan approached his division head and executed what he says is the second most important strategy in leading change: *sell the benefits.* To Dan Middleton, the benefits to the business were clear and compelling, including retention of valued talent, increased productivity, enhanced customer relationships, and improved morale. Dan's division head was immediately receptive. Dan observes, "He realized that we were missing some important opportunities to develop our up-and-coming leaders, and he authorized me to move forward."

Many organizational change initiatives are doomed to fail at the outset because they are not executed well. There is inadequate planning, poor communication, and ineffective systems to support them. So Dan advises that when launching into new and uncharted territory, *"Do a pilot."* In his pilot, 14 individuals received coaching, and the results were carefully documented. The results were impressive: increased leader retention, increased stretch goals, and improved relationships with internal customers.

When asked what he believes made other organizational stakeholders willing to refer their people to him for participation in the coaching pilot, Dan quickly responds that it's credibility. *"Being credible,"* he says, "is another critical factor in leading a successful change initiative."

So what is the basis of Dan Middleton's credibility? He says, "I know the business, and I've been a highly successful manager. Moreover, I honestly believe I bring a servant leader orientation to what I do, and people seem to trust that." Dan is also convinced that self-confidence is an important dimension of credibility. True enough. No one can really get behind a change initiative that a leader doesn't have full confidence in. That confidence has to be demonstrated in every communication and in every action.

On a final note, Dan asserts that for any change initiative to be sustainable—i.e., become embedded in the organizational culture—the change leader must *sell a system-wide solution.* In his case this means garnering broad support of second-level stakeholders and aligning the coaching initiative with organizational strategy. One of Wells Fargo's ten company-wide strategies is PACA, which is shorthand for "People as a Competitive Advantage." Dan Middleton struck gold on this one.

What's next for Dan and coaching at Wells Fargo Business Direct? Dan's vision is a full-time coaching service organization that supports a number of strategic goals. His next steps will be to increase the number of internal coaching clients, hire an additional coach, and make the coaching service organization an official department.

87. "LEAD CHANGE WITH BOLDNESS"

■ ■ ■

When **Adam Drost** was director of national accounts with Norrell Corporation, now Spherion®, he led change initiatives that helped to take the then $0.5 billion regional company to a $1 billion global business in five years. Now president and founder of eCareerFit.com, Inc., he's presiding over another global organization that is changing at the speed of need.

On leading change, Adam says that it's important to *go in boldly, capture attention, and maintain a level of boldness in your actions and communications.* He adds that all too often, leaders enter the change game boldly but then get beaten down by organizational politics, losing steam in the process. It comes down to a simple truth of organizational life, and that is you are looking at other people's sandboxes, and nobody wants their sandbox interfered with. In Adam's estimation, there's nothing bold about maintaining and sustaining, even though the natural tilt of most organizations is to do just that. He says, "It's important, therefore, to *push continuous change.* It keeps people on their toes, and it prevents them from getting too comfortable."

According to Adam, "You must *understand the organizational structure and its top leaders' priorities.* The best change initiatives are tied to corporate objectives." So he advises that the place to start any major change initiative is at the top of the organization. *"Sell your ideas at the top,* and if you get agreement there, you can expect that there will be a trickle-down effect." He's quick to add that selling to the top is where you begin, but it's not where you end. *You've still got to sell down the organization, and the way to do that is to understand others' objectives and link your agenda to them.*

Now, here's where it can get a little tricky. Adam advises, *"Don't take 'Yes' for an answer.* You often get nods of agreement from people, but you can't assume that the appearance of agreement represents real buy-in." He's convinced that this is the case because people are motivated first and foremost to protect their self-interests. "If you aid and abet people's self-interests, they will love you; but if the change you're championing is perceived to be detrimental to them, their need to protect themselves will outweigh the desire to advocate in the organization's best interests." In Adam's view, true organizational change of the kind that is disruptive to people, systems, and structures is very difficult. So what advice does he offer for those who want to cut through this?

Adam maintains that it takes real guts to interrupt self-interested behavior, and if it is entrenched enough, it requires senior executive-level action, including at times a change in leadership. The consequences of not taking the necessary action can be the downfall of the entire enterprise. Naturally, the threat of loss of livelihood should be an action of last resort, and most change efforts don't require such drastic action. According to Adam, there is a kinder, gentler way that preserves morale and gets people energized and on board with a change initiative: *"Lead, serve, and facilitate"* are the behaviors of a leader that support the most successful change efforts. He says, "You can't manage people, and you can't motivate with fear." He offers the following tips for those who want to lead change using his theme:

- *Inspire with a bold direction*—create a powerful vision of the future and paint the picture with bold strokes.
- *Serve others' needs*—find a way to align your objectives with others' objectives in service to the organization.
- *Focus on others' strengths and understand their weaknesses*—playing to strengths is energizing, and people will more naturally and willingly shift behavior and grow skills in areas representing their strengths; trying to play to weaknesses is deenergizing and demoralizing, so don't put people in that position.

Adam believes that organizational leaders have to do more than pay lip service to the notion of supporting people to play to their personal strengths. "They must do a better job of assessing individual strengths, and then tailor jobs so that people can play to them." He advises that organizational leaders should give as much attention to their human talent inventory as they do to their parts inventory. After all, talent is the company's most important asset!

88. "MINE FOR THE GOLD"

■ ■ ■

As vice president for human resources for Canada's Miramar Mining Corporation and previously TELUS, a major Canadian telecommunications company, **Heather Duggan** has had plenty of experience leading change in difficult environments. Heather's story about leading change points to her time at TELUS. The company had undergone a painful downsizing of 3,000 employees, work-related accidents were at an all-time high, and there had been a fatality in the construction-heavy organization. The Canadian government had shut down part of the business pending a safety investigation, and several hundred employees were out on disability. As Heather puts it, "Everyone was nervous. We were losing a million dollars every day that that part of the business remained shut down. We had a mandate to do a complete change around."

Heather relates that the organizational mandate was to protect and preserve the safety of company employees. Her advice for selling the mandate is instructive. "You can't sell a change message about saving money or executives' and board members' backsides. *The change message needs to be compelling on an emotional level.* You have to craft messages that explicitly convey concern for employees." This means that a leader must create a personally-felt need for change by creating a personal business case for every employee to engage in the change process. She goes on to describe her approach for engaging others in a significant change initiative.

- *Use the top-level executive to communicate the mandate.* An organization-wide mandate must be communicated broadly by the person with the most organizational authority.
- *Enroll the organization's key stakeholders to embrace the change imperative.* In Heather's case this was the head of the union, organizational division/functional heads, and employees. The union head was a particularly important stakeholder because he had enormous influence over those whose job roles regularly place them at personal risk. Functional heads were important because they were the critical link for translating strategy, and employees were

important because they execute decisions on the front line every day.

- *Make others a part of the solution.* Heather asserts the importance of inviting broad participation in planning an effective strategy. She adds, "It's important that you resist the tendency to cherry-pick participants. Take a risk in allowing the group you're trying to influence select who will participate."
- *Empower stakeholders.* Grant them the authority they will need and help them develop the skills that will enable them to act with confidence back in their own work areas. Heather believes that folks like her help to put the change process in place and then stay in the background.
- *Make the change objectives real and present.* Ensure that change objectives are translated into individual performance objectives, and communicate progress widely and often through such vehicles as the company Web site, bulletin boards, and intranet discussion boards. "It's important to give people a way to discuss what's happening and communicate their progress."
- *Establish a recognition and rewards system.* Recognize and reward accomplishments tied to the objectives of the change initiative. Share the credit with everyone who makes a contribution in the desired direction.

Heather believes these strategies will support effective change, but she warns that leaders must avoid the pitfalls, including trying to over-manage people and processes, failing to share the stage, and not meeting people where they are with change. Heather suggests, "It's important that a leader know when to be patient and when to act with a sense of urgency."

Heather has some additional insights about what it takes for a woman leader to effectively enroll others in a highly technical, male-oriented organizational culture. "It was critical that I get the men to work with me," she says. "I didn't know what they knew, and I didn't initially have any credibility with them." She advises women leaders to consider the following when enrolling the men in a male-dominated organization:

- *Be willing to admit what you don't know and ask for help.* It can be quite humbling to do this, but it is critical in building bridges with others in the organization.

- *Be willing to go where they are to see what they see.* In Heather's case this meant literally climbing telephone poles and going down into manholes. "I established credibility by doing this."
- *Demonstrate your desire to learn from them.* "By treating the men as trusted advisors, I fostered a desire in them to be helpful."
- *Create a picture of success.* This is about more than describing a desired outcome. It's about placing people in the success scenario as members of a broader organizational team. She asserts, "Make them feel important."

Heather says the outcomes of the change initiative at TELUS were transformative. There were no more fatalities, accidents were decreased, disability-related absences were reduced, and, perhaps most important, morale was dramatically improved.

89. "EMBRACE COMPETITION AND USE IT TO IMPROVE YOUR ORGANIZATION"

■ ■ ■

As director of the Office of Information and Management for the Federal Highway Administration, a division of the granddaddy U.S. Department of Transportation, **Paula Ewen** is accustomed to the demands of managing a service organization serving 3,000 internal customers located in Washington as well as in offices in each of the states' Department of Transportation. Her staff of 66 full-time and 200 contracted employees provide information and management services, including marketing communications, regulatory policies, management studies, information technology, and facilities management.

Paula explains that as a result of the U.S. Government's emphasis on "pay for performance," jobs in every sector of the government are being reevaluated. As she describes it, it's fundamentally a competitive review process where jobs that were historically full-time government positions could go out to the private sector on contracts. When she learned that jobs in her government organization were slated for competitive review, she jumped at the chance to go first. She says, "I knew this could be a frightening experience for people who had grown accustomed to the safety and security of a government job with predictable pay increases, but I also knew that we were heading into a different world—a world where we would need to continually demonstrate our value in a highly competitive environment. I felt my people were up to the task."

Paula goes on to explain that ten individuals and their jobs were selected to be studied as part of the competitive review process. "I went to them and told them what was up, and I encouraged them to fully participate in the process. The message was that we must manage results as opposed to activities, and we need to have a competitive attitude." Paula also says she used her considerable enthusiasm and belief in her people to inspire their confidence and willingness to literally "put their jobs on the line." She says she made the business case for change with candor and optimism. She also supported individual choice by telling people that if they chose not to compete, she would help them figure out a different career direction. Most important, she says, she asked people to ruthlessly examine how their jobs could be done more efficiently. What most impressed Paula was how the real threat of job loss galvanized her employees. It caused them to be more alert to the opportunities to be resourceful.

The potential impact of the competitive job review in Paula's organization was much broader than the ten people whose jobs were selected to be reviewed. As she puts it, "The impact was in reality a substantial number of the 66 full-time employees in my organization. Because of seniority issues, people not directly involved in the competitive job review could have gotten bumped in the process. So I talked with every one of those 66 individuals."

Not only was there the very real threat that a number of full-time jobs could have gone out to the private sector on contract, there was also the potential for major disruptions to internal organizational systems that had been put in place to manage the work. Paula agrees that this level of change is quite distinct from the incremental change characteristic of more traditional organizations. "This kind of change is dramatic, disruptive, and it requires a different kind of leadership." The kind of leadership she felt was called for was up close and personal, with frequent communication.

Paula is proud to report that the outcome of the competitive job review was that all ten of her employees kept their jobs. She doesn't think this is any accident. She has created an expectation in her organization that people will maintain a high degree of performance stretch. She explains that her organization uses the Malcolm Baldridge award performance benchmarks to identify improvement opportunities each year in the key areas of leadership, strategic focus, customer focus, human resources, information and analysis, process management, and business results. "The employees select the projects; I don't control the process. By not attempting to control it, the employees create shared ownership for the improvement opportunities they select."

In addition to the stretch that is built into her organization through the annual benchmarking process, Paula says she endeavors to foster change agility in her organization by being a champion of change herself. She does this by being a model of optimism, creating a high level of expectation for stretch performance, and, of course, installing metrics that will keep everyone focused on the outcomes, not just the activities.

90. "DO A PILOT TO PUSH THE ENVELOPE EVER SO SLIGHTLY WHEN LEADING INCREMENTAL CHANGE"

■ ■ ■

Richard Brenner is a man with a mission. His mission is nothing less than innovating America's agriculture. As a senior executive with the U.S. Department of Agriculture and a doctoral-level scientist in his own right, Richard knows the landscape well. He is the director of the USDA's Office of Technology Transfer, a role he's held since 2004. He's responsible for managing intellectual property, facilitating the process of agricultural technology transfer to public- and private-sector partners, and overseeing marketing, licensing, and patents for agricultural technology development. He shares that his bosses evaluate him on how well he promotes economic development of U.S. agricultural industries. Richard's cadre of highly accomplished scientists must deliver on the mandate to create value for the country's taxpayers, right at the dinner table and in the garden. What it boils down to is finding the win-wins between the government and the private sector. Technology gets developed and patented by the government and is then licensed to private-sector firms, typically small businesses.

While Richard is clear that his organizational mandate requires out-of-the-box thinking every day, he's equally clear that out-of-the-box thinking must be coupled with the patience to execute incremental change. He says, "You don't turn a large ship on a dime." That's where things get tricky. Doing the hard science is one thing, and that's something the USDA's scientists and its university partners do very well. But it's quite another thing to get the science into the hands of those who can make the most economic gains from it. Moreover, deciding who gets license to control agricultural technology has enormous global competitive implications. Richard explains that the USDA used to make new plant releases broadly public. The trouble with that is you're making them available to everyone in the entire world, and that can hurt small businesses and taxpayers alike. Richard adds, "We don't want to create international trade barriers, but by being thoughtful about licensing agricultural technology to U.S. businesses, we're ensuring that those businesses can then sublicense but have the control they need to protect their business interests."

Which agricultural technology to bring public and whose hands to place it in represent big decisions, as do the government policy changes that might be necessary to support the transfer of technology. All this requires strong public- and private-sector partnerships, which Richard and his organization facilitate. As he puts it, "It's a multidimensional team of scientists, engineers, attorneys, business owners, and other external stakeholders. To be successful leading the kind of measured, incremental change we're about, we must get the broadest input from the most trusted people and have the patience to stay the course."

So what does Richard's experience suggest about strategies for leading incremental change? For starters, he points out that as a leader you have to recognize that you may have the questions, but you don't have the answers. It's important that you surround yourself with the best-qualified people. He adds, "It's your role to provide the vision and then solicit the expertise, ideas, and judgments of others." He advises that incremental change can often be effectively spearheaded by doing a pilot.

A pilot doesn't require a change in policy or even the buy-in of all the stakeholders you might eventually need to fully implement the change. A pilot allows you to push the envelope ever so slightly to test the veracity of a new idea. The success of the pilot will enable you to build broad consensus on full implementation more easily.

Richard advises that it's important to not get discouraged by the naysayers in your midst. Instead of seeing them as people who need to be convinced of the merits of your great ideas, see them as a source of new ideas that can be blended with others to build broad-based consensus. The trick, Richard believes, is to get enough diversity of thought on the team that people see themselves as part of a whole, but not *the* whole. They have to be willing to let go of the need for individual control and work with others. "Collaborative skills don't just happen," Richard observes. So, as a leader you have to see it as a part of your role to expand people's horizons and develop them to be more effective resources and change agents within a multidimensional team. Then you must make sure that everyone understands that you value their backgrounds and experience. Richard asserts, "Valuing people promotes self-empowerment. You have to value the richness of others' perspectives, and that means you nurture, guide, and appreciate."

On a final note, he advises the leader who is leading incremental change to maintain perspective in the midst of setbacks. In his view, setbacks represent an opportunity to tweak a process—to learn something that can positively impact the final outcome. He says, "Okay, so others may not always share your passion, and you may need to rethink the project. The chances are it will be better as a result."

91. "DEMONSTRATE PRIDE, PASSION, AND PERSONAL COMMITMENT"

■ ■ ■

Clayton Tychkowsky is vice president and general manager for the European operations of Eaton Electrical. The Canadian native is on an expatriate assignment in the United Kingdom, where he spoke with me about leading change in a global manufacturing environment. He offers three fundamental things that every change leader needs to fully understand and embrace to lead change successfully:

- *Create the business case and focus the organization on the need for change.* Clayton relates that he has seen leaders derail early on by forging ahead with execution in the absence of presenting a rational business case for change. He maintains that at the most basic level people need to know why and how the change will impact them—they need to know how processes, responsibilities, and organizational reporting will change.

- *Create employee engagement and commitment.* In Clayton's view, how communication of a change process occurs is critical. Very early on, it's important to get stakeholders at all levels involved in crafting the communication and implementation plans and actions. "Show the plan to those who will be directly impacted by change and get their ideas on how to implement it and communicate it."

- *Execute with a clear plan.* Clayton advises that, early on, a leader needs to identify and communicate when a change initiative is expected to begin *and* end. "People need to know how much time it will take—in effect, how long it will be before we're over the pain." It's also important that the right people are on the team to lead the execution and that change leaders are visibly involved and leading by example. Finally, it's important to conduct a continuous review of the plan, communicate how targets are being met, and celebrate successes. Clayton says that you could liken a change initiative to the sport of mountain climbing. It's not just about reaching the summit, but about all the little steps it takes to get there.

According to Clayton, there are special considerations for the leader who is leading change in a multicultural environment, as he is. "I'm a North American leader working in the United Kingdom, and I've learned that I can't underestimate the importance of cultural differences. I must understand the issues, but at the same time not allow them to be a barrier. It's important to understand people's work ethic and the incentives that matter to them." In Europe, for example, people are motivated more by the rewards that derive from the work itself, while in North America, monetary rewards can play a bigger role. Clayton offers a case in point:

"We had a plan to shift from a salary-based compensation model to an incentive-based pay system. In some regions, however, our employees couldn't understand why they needed an 'incentive' to do their jobs. As a result, we slowed the change process down. They are still on a traditional salary structure, but we put a small bonus system in place to reward those who exceed their targets. Earning additional personal incentives can be a source of discomfort for people, as they view the team reward to be far more important than the individual reward. Their satisfaction comes from achievement on the job and collaboration with their peers. They like to be acknowledged in front of peers and also privately by their manager. We use the process to reinforce positive behavior change in ways people most want to be acknowledged."

On the subject of what it takes for a leader to be personally change agile, Clayton offers several strategies that have served him well:

- *Be open to input from all stakeholders.* Don't assume you have all the answers, because you don't. Reach out to the management team, employees, customers, and suppliers and question and probe. You have to be willing to not only question but also to ensure that you understand what you're hearing. You can't simply give lip service to communication. It's about having an attitude of inclusiveness and leading by example.
- *Demonstrate pride, passion, and personal commitment.* Clayton believes that these attributes underscore the personal effectiveness of any change leader. A leader needs to show pride in the organization, in people, and in their accomplishments. Then, a leader must be visibly passionate about the vision of the end state and what they are doing. Finally, it's not enough to simply issue directives from the corner office. A change leader must get directly involved in the work and be visibly present at all levels of the organization. For Clayton, this means taking time to talk with employees and getting involved with employee teams.
- *Invest in preparing both your mind and your body for change.* Clayton relates, "As a mountain climber, I may spend up to a full

year preparing myself mentally and physically for a major climb." In his mind, a change leader should take personal preparation in anticipation of a major change initiative just as seriously. This involves getting as much input as possible through reading and talking with colleagues. It also involves taking care of one's self physically by being mindful of diet, exercise, and rest. In Clayton's experience, employees can be inspired by a leader who actively pursues work/life balance, but who also consistently moves outside of one's comfort zone.

- *Find ways that help you and others stay the course.* In Clayton's view, a good change leader finds ways to encourage people to keep going despite discomfort and also ways to take their minds off the discomfort they might be feeling. And that starts with a leader being able to do that for himself or herself first. It can involve celebrating small steps and early successes, or reinforcing the end goal by repainting the picture of success. It almost certainly means having the capacity to anticipate and recognize trouble and adjust the route as necessary.

Finally, Clayton offers that leading change, like climbing mountains, doesn't happen in a giant rush. It's a measured course with a lot of little steps and obstacles that must be overcome—step-by-step.

92. "RESPECT THOSE WHO'VE HELPED YOU GROW YOUR BUSINESS WHEN GOING AGAINST THE GRAIN"

■ ■ ■

The Insurance Corporation of British Columbia insures 3 million drivers in Vancouver and the rest of the province through its 52 branch offices. In the mid-1990s, **Doug Downing,** who is now vice president of customer service for ICBC, was asked to oversee a radical change in the claims-processing side of the business through the creation of a centralized customer call center. The driver for this change was a mandate to increase business volume and decrease the costs associated with brick-and-mortar facilities. Each branch office cost at least a million dollars to put up, and the number of drivers and driving accidents was increasing steadily. What made the initiative unconventional is that, in implementing it, the traditional way customers were served in the business would be entirely uprooted.

Usually, customer calls were taken in each of the branch offices by a clerk who set up a face-to-face appointment for an insured driver to initiate a claims-adjustment process. Doug points out that while centralized call centers are commonplace today, they were a novel concept in his province in the mid-1990s. Most call centers at the time handled outbound sales-driven calls rather than inbound customer-driven calls. ICBP branch managers were not initially very receptive to the idea of a centralized call center. Doug explains that the branch office managers felt threatened by the possibility that they would lose control over their customer bases. Moreover, there was a pervasive belief that size, as measured by the number of employees, mattered more than output.

The concept of a centralized call center represented not only a change in where calls would be taken, but also who would take them. In the old model, a clerk functioned more or less as an "order taker," funneling calls and setting walk-in appointments for insurance-claims adjusters. In the new model, calls would be taken by highly trained adjusters who would provide a comprehensive level of customer service. Services would be expanded, and they would be available province-wide via the telephone. Doug points out that 75 percent of all vehicular accidents are relatively straightforward, and they can be managed in an expedient manner.

Doug says the first thing he did was to pull a planning team together to fully develop the new model. The team was comprised of the senior operations person, two field managers, and Doug. He also secured the services of "technical visionaries" to create user-friendly database tools for claims processing. The second thing he and his team did was to craft a communications strategy for selling the change up, down, and across the organization. Selling up was by far the easiest part. Senior management was already supportive of the concept, but Doug needed to win their support for the investment required to build a centralized call center and fund the claims-processing database development.

Doug and his team sold the change initiative to the branch managers by first addressing their concerns about internal competition. Doug says, "The biggest struggle was people learning to share the customer. It's the company's customer after all. That said, we were invested in creating win-wins. We wanted the branch managers and their teams to feel valued for their experience and expertise. By freeing them up from handling the high percentage of relatively straightforward claims, they could apply their considerable talents to the more highly complex cases involving serious injury and requiring extensive investigation."

Selling the change down the organization was a slower process, Doug says. It involved people having to physically move their location of work. "We took advantage of natural attrition and then used technology to hook up people in more remote locations to the central call center. They functioned as part of the central call center, but they worked in branch offices." Doug is quite proud of the fact that he and his team carried out the entire change initiative without forcing anyone to forfeit his or her job. Today, the centralized call center uses the Internet and telephone to process claims involving more than 4 million calls per year.

In Doug's view, respect for individuals is a critical success factor in a change process. "Your employees have helped to make your company successful thus far, and you owe it to them to support them in the process of adapting and learning to contribute differently." Doug believes that it's critical to reject what he calls the "replacement mentality." He maintains that if you want loyalty from your employees, you've got to demonstrate your loyalty to them.

93. "TAKE A CREATIVE CUSTOMER STANCE WHEN IMPLEMENTING A STEP CHANGE IN A COMMODITIZED BUSINESS"

■ ■ ■

Bob Hedley, now the corporate vice president of leadership at Toronto-based Maple Leaf Foods, has a clear perspective on what it takes to lead change in highly commoditized businesses. He asserts that leaders who understand the value of growth make change happen. They get smarter, wiser and faster than their competitors. His story of a successful change initiative takes him back to the mid-1990s when he was senior director of leadership at Canadian Tire Corporation, a large hard-goods retailer selling automotive components, sporting goods, and home and gardening products.

In 1993, Canadian Tire had 300 retail dealers, only 80 of which were in large retail markets such as Toronto. When Wal-Mart and Home Depot entered the market, Canadian Tire was suddenly and dramatically experiencing a sea change in the retail hard-goods business. Bob says, "We needed Canadian Tire dealers to commit to investing tens of millions of dollars to create a successful retail model to deal with intense competition by the big discounters. We clearly needed a performance-based model to replace the handshake agreements that had characterized many of the dealer relationships made with the company's original owners. Moreover, we wanted dealers to double and triple the size of their stores, and we wanted to put more stores in place. We were convinced that same store sales would increase with the changes we proposed, even with the addition of new stores." If only it were that simple. Bob describes the dealer stance as distrustful and disinterested. After all, most of the 300 stores at the time were not in the markets threatened by the onslaught of Wal-Mart and Home Depot. He admits that dealers just simply didn't see the need to make a quantum leap. They were, in fact, content to stay the course and accept single-digit, incremental growth. This was something that wasn't acceptable to stakeholders, but Canadian Tire executive leaders couldn't use the force of will to make change happen. Bob quips, "We wouldn't have scored any points by running dealers out of business."

Bob shares that the leadership stance in this circumstance was to embrace the dealers' resistance to change without becoming mired in the details. "It was not a war strategy, but a strategy of taking the dealer relationships to a different level—a level that would promote a profound culture-driven change. We had to shift the conversations from debate and negotiation to reflection and dialogue to build shared ownership of a fundamental shift in the way we would do business in the future." Initially, it was necessary to bring in a third-party facilitator to establish a dialogue with dealers aimed at identifying common issues and concerns.

Canadian Tire's CEO then worked one-to-one with key dealers and the dealers association to build trust with those who were key influencers and to establish leverage with dealers who had multiple dealerships. But there was more.

It was necessary to examine the competencies required to be a dealer in an entrepreneurial environment versus simply being a store manager. Bob says, "What we recognized was that entrepreneurship, especially in smaller communities, is a barrier to entry for large commodities-based retailers such as Wal-Mart. It's about legacy leadership in an environment where there are strong community and family ties. Careful selection of new dealers could enhance our competitiveness in these communities. But we also recognized that, going forward, our dealers needed to be able to deal with rapid change."

Taking a creative stance, forging relationships, and leveraging influence with key dealers resulted in small, initial wins that Canadian Tire executives were able to build on. What they did next was to come up with a compelling and highly attractive investment for dealers to create momentum for growth. Bob says, "We eventually got to a place where dealers were willing to reinvent their businesses using a new performance-based model that provided the right incentives and protected their interests."

What was the company-wide impact of the change initiated in 1993? Bob shares that Canadian Tire grew from 300 to 550 stores in less than 5 years, and by 10 years out in 2003, sales had grown from less than $4 billion to more than $9 billion.

PART 13

LEADING HIGH-PERFORMANCE TEAMS
SECRETS FOR OPTIMIZING GROUP INTELLIGENCE

■ ■ ■

Teamwork is perhaps one of the most misunderstood and mismanaged aspects of organizational leadership. Teamwork is routinely invoked in the absence of a clear mandate for teamwork, and groups of people who work in close proximity to each other are often incorrectly labeled as teams. And that's not all. Teams can fail to deliver for a host of reasons, including the absence of a charter, poor team leadership, undeveloped teaming skills, unclear working agreements, mismanaged conflict, lack of sponsorship, lack of resources, and failure to integrate the work of the team into the organization. What's clear is that successful organizations today must be able to harness the intelligence of teams, and it's in everyone's interest to learn the skills and apply the discipline of teamwork. It all starts with understanding what a team is and what it isn't and when teamwork is most effectively employed.

Each of the leaders on the following pages has had extensive experience leading teams, some in extremely high-stakes circumstances where there is little margin for error. What's compelling is how crystal clear they are about what works and what doesn't work when the goal is to optimize team intelligence. They offer secrets on everything from getting the right people on the team to managing conflict to developing team skills. They debunk the myths of teamwork and provide practical strategies for creating shared ownership and accountability and bringing the work of the team to the organization. Ironically, they also point to the importance of developing individuals' skills and confidence as a prerequisite for their being effective team players.

The development of team leadership skills deserves as much attention as the development of teamwork skills because when teams fail, the culprit is often ineffective team leadership. The leaders on the following pages offer insight into this all-important area and how to avoid the pitfalls of ineffective team leadership.

94. "ESTABLISH THE DISCIPLINE AND THE FOCUS"

■ ■ ■

Rick White has had plenty of experience working with teams in high-stakes circumstances. He spent a total of 24 years on active and reserve duty in the Air National Guard as a jet fighter pilot and flight commander. Today, he is first officer for the Airbus A320 for United Airlines and CEO for Afterburner UK, a training company that specializes in supporting high-impact team performance in hospital emergency departments and operating rooms.

Whether it's in the high-stakes world of aviation or the hospital surgical suite, Rick maintains the same principles apply. He observes, "Mistakes or errors in judgment can endanger lives and damage property. But whenever these things happen, the source is almost always a poorly defined process for effective teamwork and a lack of proper communication among team members."

Rick suggests that we first should determine what a team is and how it is distinguished from what he calls *a high-performance team.* In his view, a *common goal* defines the *need* for teamwork, but it's the attitudes and behavior of team members that create the performance. In a high-performance team, the stakes are high, and there is little margin for error. Things are happening very quickly, but they are formalized enough that the level of output is predictable, achievable, and replicable. Moreover, team members are fully engaged, they can think creatively, and they can operate independently from direct guidance. Think *Top Gun,* and then think again about your team.

Rick worries that his take on high-stakes teamwork will be perceived as cold and impersonal. "But," he says, "when lives and property are at stake, it's no time for a tea party." He believes that high-performance teamwork of the type he mastered in piloting and commanding jet fighter planes demands a discipline and an intensity of focus that renders emotions superfluous and counterproductive. If you start to fret when you're in a dogfight (militaryspeak for being engaged in air combat), you're going to lose the battle and probably your life as well.

That said, Rick relates that the principles of a high-performance team that have influenced his work in the aviation world and in his training company can be generalized to any setting where the proper conditions for teamwork have been established:

First and foremost, it's about the talent. The right people with the right talent have to be at the table. Subject matter expertise and work experience are factors to be considered, as are communication and work style. While it's tempting to put people on a team who know and like each other, diversity of thought and experience will take the team a lot further.

Align the talent with the team's mission. The team must create a mission statement that defines the purpose of its work. It answers the question, "Why are we here?" When teamwork breaks down, one of the first things a leader should examine with the team members is if the purpose of their work is clear, because if it isn't, confusion, strained relationships, inefficient meetings, and poor results are sure to follow.

Analyze the talent. While this may seem redundant with the first principle, Rick suggests that this is really the process of evolving the team by determining how it needs to be developed to generate the next level of performance, or how the team's composition might need to be modified in response to changing demands. A team can become insular and stagnant when there is an overreliance on existing team members and resistance to recruiting new blood. Reviewing the team's talent needs in light of the performance objectives and accomplishment of major milestones represents a way to systematize this process.

Develop the objectives. The team creates formal plans and actions, assigns responsibility, and establishes accountabilities and timelines. Everyone knows their role and how their talent contributes to successful results. Rick suggests that the best objectives are *SMART*—specific, measurable, achievable, resourced, and time-bound.

Establish norms. Norms reduce confusion and create efficiency in such areas as how the team will conduct its work, how decisions will be made, how team members will be held accountable, how briefings and debriefings will occur, and how the work of the team will be communicated and implemented. Establishing norms requires a certain discipline on the part of team members and a willingness to invest the time up front creating a shared understanding of how they want to work together.

Authorize and empower. Team members must be authorized and empowered to act in direct proportion to the responsibility that has been placed on the team. An authorized and empowered team is self-directed, has the resources to do its work, and has had major organizational obstacles removed. The removal of obstacles is critical to a team's successful implementation of its work in the organization. A team that is focused on the technical aspects of its work can find itself derailed when it's time to integrate its work across the organization. Authorizing and empowering a team also means that the team has a road map for implementing its work.

Manage morale. Rick maintains that morale isn't a driver of team performance; it's an indicator. When morale plummets, this indicates a deficiency in one of the other areas previously mentioned. Rick says, "Morale will self-generate when the other areas are managed well." He adds that it's possible to boost team morale on a short-term basis with a celebratory event, but it's not sustainable unless it is self-generated. So while it's not possible for a leader to literally manage morale any more than he or she can manage organizational culture, a team leader can influence the conditions that, when optimized, will result in positive morale.

95. "BUILD A STRONG TEAM FOUNDATION BY BUILDING INDIVIDUALS"

■ ■ ■

Brian Foster, who spoke with me from his office in Calgary, Alberta, is general manager for Maxwell Drummond's Canada operations. The United Kingdom–owned firm specializes in executive recruitment for the oil and gas industries worldwide. He wears the hats of both team leader and team sponsor of a high-performance team whose mission is "delivery, capacity, tenacity, passion, and solutions."

Brian fervently believes that the foundation of any team is the capability of its individual members. So he places a lot of his attention on recruiting the best talent he can find and developing that talent so that members are able to step into powerful team roles. He feels that the most important thing a team leader can do is *invest in sustainable relationships*— provide training and development and create incentives for top-line performance. Brian also believes that it's important for a team leader to *stretch individuals through challenging assignments* that require active collaboration and that provide a safe landing when mistakes are made.

He suggests that supporting an individual to build a strong foundation that can contribute to high-performance teamwork includes developing product and process knowledge, creating a strong professional role identity, and building confidence through increased responsibility. In Brian's experience, when people are confident, they bring passion and pride to their work on a team.

Brian advises that it's also important to *match the talent to the performance demands of the team and the organization's cultural context.* An individual can possess the right skills, but if his or her experience in other firms has created expectations about the workplace and patterns of behavior that are out of sync with your organization's cultural context, tensions will mount, and teamwork will be diminished. Brian admits that he's made two big mistakes as a team sponsor and leader: failing to properly match the talent to the cultural context of his firm and tolerating a marginal performer on a team. He says he understands all too well now that a marginal performer becomes a disabler to everyone, and that a leader must summon the courage to change the constitution of the team. "Performance goes down and morale deteriorates to the level of the weak link." Brian feels there's no way for a team leader to deflect the responsibility for this. In his view, very few teams are mature enough to be entirely self-auditing and self-regulating. He says, "The buck stops with the team leader and sponsor to ensure that the team has the right talent and that the talent is able to perform."

Once the talent is in place and the team has established norms for conducting its work, the team must *establish measures of success and a plan for generating outcomes.* In Brian's estimation, this is where building shared ownership is critical. People cannot perform on a team where everyone is working at cross-purposes or with different metrics. More-over, the team needs to *establish a process for reviewing its work and making course corrections at regular intervals.* Brian also advises that the rewards for outstanding team performance be communicated early on. "Knowing up front what the rewards will be creates an incentive and also encourages fairness and respect among team members."

In Brian's world, teams work hard and play hard. They *celebrate their successes* and they know how to have fun. His advice: "Don't forget to laugh. A great sense of humor elevates people and increases connection. Humor also allows people to be vulnerable within a safe space. It's a great balancer for any team."

96. "DEFINE THE NEED FOR TEAMWORK BEFORE CHARGING A TEAM"

■ ■ ■

As assistant vice president of communication and change management for AIM Trimark, **Libby McCready** works with teams to put the structures and processes in place that will support high-impact team performance. She notes that teamwork does not occur simply because people come to-gether in a group. People can get together on a regular basis to share in-formation or coordinate their activities, but these activities in and of themselves don't constitute high-performance teamwork. Groups that can sometimes be mistaken for teams include natural work groups where people pursue individual goals but cooperate with each other from time to time, or single leader–led groups where multiple individuals reporting to a single leader come together as needed to share information, coordi-nate activities, or receive direction to accomplish individual objectives.

Libby defines high-performance teamwork as a group that has a clearly defined charter that includes a shared purpose—a common goal. To be even more specific, a high-performance team has three important elements:

■ *A project mandate from the sponsor.* A sponsor is anyone with the authority to allocate people and resources to work on a project.

- *A clearly articulated purpose and measurable outcomes.* The purpose is broader than can be accomplished with individual effort.
- *Ground rules that support the group's work and that can be used to hold team members accountable.* Ground rules articulate the way a team will work together, including how the team will make decisions and solve problems, how technical skills will be employed, what interpersonal skills will best support the team's efforts, how conflicts will be managed, and how change will be implemented.

Libby points out that *it's the work itself that drives the need for teamwork.* She believes that many of the problems groups have can be traced to *incorrectly labeling a group as a team or not defining the need for teamwork.* It's little wonder, then, when individual morale deteriorates in the absence of a clearly defined team charter or when there is a low level of cooperation among individuals.

Other difficulties can arise when there is an *absence of mutual accountability.* This can be seen when individual agendas, driven by a need for personal control, usurp a team's process. Behavior such as overinfluencing and coercing may be common. When this happens, it indicates that the group has not established clear ground rules for getting its work done or that individual team members have not developed important interactional skills for engaging in teamwork.

Libby suggests that several things can prevent team derailments or can be used to make course corrections:

- *Take the pulse of the team.* This is a process check by the team leader to determine how the team is working. Team members may resist engaging in this important activity because they are concerned that taking time out will prevent them from getting their work done. But the process check can often be the very thing that uncovers tension in the group or a lack of clarity around roles and responsibilities and in so doing enhances the team's performance.
- *Provide training and coaching in team process.* High-performance teamwork doesn't come naturally to many people. Skills such as making group decisions, managing mutual accountabilities, communicating with sponsors, negotiating organizational politics, and implementing team outcomes must be learned.

- *Provide tools and templates.* Tools and templates can provide a basis for easy-to-implement, highly repeatable processes. They also accelerate the work of a team by simplifying an action or process. Tools and templates that can be useful to a team include those that support fact-based decision making and problem solving, mind mapping, communication style, conflict management, and project management.
- *Provide individual development of team members.* Some skills necessary for high-performance teamwork, such as the skill of building shared understanding, can be hard to learn within a team environment because of the "rush of ideas" as well as the tendency to build on or negate ideas offered up within the team. In either case, ideas do not get fully heard. When individuals learn these skills outside of a team environment, they are better equipped to resist their natural tendencies to talk more than they listen when working with the team.
- *Develop the team leader who is new to a team-leader role.* A new team leader may need the support of a mentor or coach to be able to effectively anticipate and identify team challenges, build robust but achievable agendas, and manage himself or herself in a manner consistent with good team leadership. Without such support, the new team leader may default to other interactional patterns that don't serve the needs of the team.

97. "GET THE TEAM TALENT AND STRUCTURES RIGHT"

■ ■ ■

When you are a vice president with one of the Big Three consulting firms, leading high-performance teams *is* your job. **Herb Schul** is an expert in global automotive consulting and in the management of multilevel teams delivering complex solutions to Fortune 100 client companies. The projects Herb's teams have worked on include process and technology transfers across multiple business units with employees numbering in the thousands. Examples of projects include redesigning processes that are enabled by a new technology, creating shared service centers, or designing the interface when an organizational process or function is outsourced. The work involves design through system-wide integration. It's about large-scale organizational change.

Herb's experience in working with multilevel teams delivering complex system-wide solutions can be instructive to any leader whose charge is to deliver broad-based solutions requiring the active participation of stakeholders at multiple levels of an organization. He says there are four important considerations for leading a high-performance team working with complex solutions:

Talent and structures. The team leader needs to consider both the capabilities of team members as well as the technical components needed on the team. From a capabilities standpoint, effective team members are those with strong subject matter expertise who also know the business. They know what the process steps are, how to employ technology, and how to orchestrate a plan for change management. Moreover, effective team members bring expertise in one of four primary team components:

- *Functional*—concerned with process or system design
- *Technical*—focuses on the technology transfer in a complex solution
- *Change management*—responsible for creating work plans, coordinating meetings with change sponsors, designing and delivering formal training for stakeholder groups affected by change, and creating important communications pieces to support the change initiative
- *Infrastructure*—works with all the other components on logistics related to those areas as well as supporting system design

Herb suggests that when these components are covered with the right talent mix, the work of organizing the team to support a complex change initiative is still not done. Identification of a team internal to the organization with team members representing each of the affected business units is critical to the eventual implementation of the solution. These "extended team members" function as more than points of contact—their support is critical to the successful implementation of a complex solution.

Building in stretch. The second important factor for consideration by a team leader is building in stretch for team members. Why is this so important? In Herb's view, it is critical to keeping team members motivated, learning, and growing even as they are performing. He explains that everyone on the team brings specific subject matter or technical expertise. They work on processes within their defined area of expertise. To do that continuously, however, does not grow their breadth of knowledge and experience. Moreover, it does not keep people energized, particularly in the middle and later phases of a project. So to grow talented, promotable team members, individuals are assigned to certain "work streams" that cut across all team components. A work stream is a major project phase that requires the input of all team components and multilevel team members for the phase to be completed. Team members garner an understanding of a broader slice of functional areas, and they become conversant in disciplines other than their own. More important, they can make mistakes without failing.

Harness the group's intelligence. This is much more than a matter of assigning the right talent to the team and aligning the right components (functional areas). Herb maintains that what's important here is that a group's process be iterated or facilitated to concentrate the best methods and approaches. He explains, "You'll never get the right answer the first time you go at a problem, and you'll never get it right if only one person produces it." So what exactly is involved in iterating a team's process? A variety of tools, including formal group facilitation, surveys, testing, simulation, and model creation, represents the ways a group's process can be iterated and the collective intelligence harnessed.

Manage the team through its phases on a complex project. In Herb's experience, individuals in a high-performance team environment bring strong personalities with equally strong experience and expertise. As he puts it, "They think they know, and if all this ego and energy are not properly channeled, you can end up with a powder keg instead of a high-performance team." Definitely preferring the latter outcome, Herb says it's important to put processes in place to manage the group dynamics—like social events, celebrations, and additional activities or learning events that directly address people's career aspirations.

98. "FIGURE OUT HOW TO BE A SERVANT TO INSPIRE HIGH-PERFORMANCE TEAMWORK"

■ ■ ■

Bill Jamieson should understand how to communicate and apply the principles of servant leadership better than almost anyone. As president of the Institute for Servant Leadership in Asheville, North Carolina, for ten years, he spearheaded the development of programs to teach these principles to leaders from a broad range of public- and private-sector organizations. But Bill maintains that he received his inspiration for servant leadership during the years he spent working in government. He served as the assistant commissioner of health and social services for the state of Georgia during Jimmy Carter's term as governor. He then served in Carter's presidential administration as head of the Department of Health, Education, and Welfare's social services regional offices. In 1978 he went west, where he served in the state government of Arizona as director of that state's Department of Economic Security. He spent a total of six years working in the Arizona state government, and he says that during this time, he saw firsthand the results of enacting the principles of servant leadership as a leader of high-impact teams.

Bill says that the first thing a leader must do is *build the right team for the job*. "Even though easing people out of their roles is a difficult task, it's imperative that the team be fitted with the right talent for the job at hand," Bill says. He's also quite clear that a leader must communicate and honor a set of core values that guide the work of the team. Ordained as a deacon in the Episcopal Church, Bill shares that he felt a call to the ministry, but not a traditional pulpit-based ministry. He saw his *job* as a ministry in which his spiritual values could be incorporated into his work. Those values are respect for the dignity of every human being and his or her inherent worth. Bill believes that government can give voice to these values through just laws and compassionate programs.

In Bill's view, it takes a strong, confident leader to hire people who are smarter than he or she is and who could succeed the leader. But Bill believes that the success of a team depends on the leader's being willing to balance his or her weaknesses by hiring people who bring those smarts to the table. Someone who is worried about the security of being in control might feel threatened about having really smart people around, but Bill thinks the benefits are compelling. Not only is the leader freed from dwelling in the house of details and looking over people's shoulders, but the team's talent is fully leveraged for the benefit of stakeholders. Bill is proud of the fact that one of the talented individuals he recruited succeeded him in his job, and others went on to serve as state-level department heads.

Beyond hiring the right talent that balances a leader's strengths and weaknesses, Bill asserts that a leader's role is to be the keeper of the team's vision and to continually uphold the mission of servant leadership for the team. In his experience, it's easy for people to get seduced by the power of their office and to misuse that power for personal aims. But he says he made sure that people knew that wasn't the path to success on his watch.

Bill believes that a team's full contribution can be unleashed only when the leader is *hands-on with people but not hands-on with their work*. For him, this means that a leader shows up, gets involved, but lets others do the work they were hired to do. It also means being willing to serve as a buffer and "take the heat" from above for the team. "Once people know that their backsides are covered, they will step up to take the risks that are necessary to advance important initiatives." For Bill, this included understanding the politics of the organization and being able to demonstrate that he had strength behind him. "The governor would show up whenever I needed him to," he says.

Being hands-on with people without being hands-on with their work also means creating stretch assignments that showcase team members' accomplishments and give them visibility. Bill says that he regularly put people in roles that they were not quite ready for. He says he could do this because when people have ambition and drive, and when they care passionately about their work, they rise to the occasion when the bar is raised for them.

99. "MAKE CORPORATE SOCIAL RESPONSIBILITY YOUR LICENSE TO OPERATE"

■ ■ ■

Corporate social responsibility has taken on a higher profile in **Bonnie DuPont's** organization. Bonnie is the group vice president of corporate resources for Enbridge, Inc., the Canadian-based energy processing and distribution company. Not only is corporate social responsibility in her job description, it's the basis of high-performance teamwork at Enbridge. Bonnie explains that while her organization's leaders have always strived to have Enbridge be a good corporate citizen, there wasn't a really good definition of what corporate citizenship meant. That is, until it became clear that the company's future growth depended on getting both form and momentum with it. The company's CEO issued a mandate that corporate social responsibility would be defined, resourced, and measured, and that it would be the company's license to operate. Concerns of *all* stakeholders would be addressed. Bonnie explains that this mandate has enormous implications. "We have a number of projects on the docket involving billions of dollars, including the 1,500-mile Gateway pipeline that will go through aboriginal land and environmentally sensitive land."

Bonnie explains that within the past two years, Enbridge leaders have made the commitment that the organization will be transparent in its dealings with all its stakeholders. Moreover, a board committee was created to provide oversight and governance, and a corporate social responsibility steering team of dedicated Enbridge employees representing all geographical slices of the organization was chartered. A team leader was hired and subsequently promoted to vice president. Bonnie says that senior leadership wanted to signal the importance of the initiative by placing the team's leader at a high level as well as creating a board committee with broad oversight and governance power. Bonnie notes that making the team inclusive of the broad geographical dispersion of the organization across four American states and six Canadian provinces was important to the success of the initiative. "A centralized approach would not have been practical or well received. We needed the people who had rightful ownership involved right from the start."

Bonnie goes on to relate that corporate social responsibility teamwork at Enbridge emphasizes three central organizing principles: a company-wide approach, adherence to the highest standards of practice in each geographical area, and an auditable reporting process. Moreover, there is strong commitment by managers of Enbridge business units and senior-level executives, and resources have been allocated to cover community investment and publishing of the team's annual reports. Something else that has been critical to the success of the team is team members' ability to be self-managing. Bonnie shares that the team creates a set of common objectives, and plans are executed at the business unit level and then reported up. So business unit managers have the autonomy they need to execute within their geographical areas.

Has corporate social responsibility at Enbridge paid off? You bet it has. Bonnie exclaims that it has given her organization a distinct competitive advantage. Not only that, but the organization has been selected by the World Economic Forum in Switzerland as one of the world's most sustainable companies for the past two years. Bonnie delights in saying, "We want our name in lights, and we want our stakeholders to see us as socially responsible neighbors." She concludes by saying that she and her colleagues don't just feel good about what they're doing, they know they're doing the right thing. "Social responsibility is one of our defining characteristics. It's teamwork plus."

100. "SURVIVAL IN A GLOBAL ENVIRONMENT REQUIRES A SHIFT FROM A CULTURE OF SELF TO A CULTURE OF SERVICE"

■ ■ ■

Martin Darby is managing director of the Coates Division of Sun Chemical Corporation, a manufacturer of printing inks for flexible packaging. He fervently believes that high-performance teamwork is the product of leaders who "empower, enable, and entrust" and embrace the principles of servant leadership. Martin's story is one of personal redemption and renewal in the wake of a failed traditional management approach.

He shares, "I used to report into London in the early 1990s. One of my employees, a young woman in a technical role, resigned. I tried to persuade her to stay, but her mind was made up. I subsequently made a trip to London to see my boss. When I arrived at his office, he asked me to go to his house where he said his wife was waiting to pour me a drink. He put a letter in my hand and said he'd be along in a little while. On the way over to his house, I read the letter. It was from the young woman, and it was nothing short of a scathing attack on my management approach. My boss came in a little while, and he asked me how I was doing. I told him that I needed another bloody drink! He said only that he wanted me to think about the letter, learn from it, and then decide what I wanted to do about it. I realized in that moment that my boss was being a servant to me. I thought hard about that letter and how my boss had handled it with me, and I determined that I wanted to be a different kind of leader. That wake-up call began my journey into being a servant leader." Martin acknowledges that it wasn't easy ridding himself of the persona he'd come to believe was required of a leader. He says he had to be willing to ask people to help him and grant them permission to stop him if he shifted back into old behaviors. So how has Martin shifted his organizational culture from a culture of self to a culture of service?

Martin explains that his modeling of servant leadership begins with new-employee orientation. "I meet with every new employee, regardless of job role. We always meet in the break room or the cafeteria, and we sit at a round table. I serve them coffee or tea. I tell them how glad I am to have them and how their gifts and talents are valued. I tell them that my job is to provide the vision, but they will tell us how to get there, and they will take us there."

Martin believes that compassion for individual circumstances is a critical factor in an environment that empowers, enables, and entrusts. He shares the story of a female employee who was repeatedly late to work because she was having trouble getting a reliable sitter for her child. "Her boss came to see me to report the problem and ask what he should do about it. I asked if her peers were having a problem with her lateness, and his answer was that they were covering for her until she could get to work. I told him that it seemed that he was the only one having a problem with it. My recommendation was that we give the young mother the time she needed to straighten out her sitter problem. What good would it have done to add another burden on her by threatening her with disciplinary action?" Martin admits that this approach is far different from what most managers would do in similar circumstances, but he is convinced that expressing caring for employees through words and gestures accrues extraordinary benefits in any business.

He shares that a regional manager called him to report a quality issue with a high-profile customer. "I went in to see the customer service team and asked them to dig in and examine how we'd previously handled similar issues. We met an hour later, and they gave me the history and a path forward that they had all agreed on. They immediately set to work to correct the problem. The next day, the regional manager called to say that the customer, who had been historically quite difficult to deal with, was delighted with what our team had done on a short turnaround. I went in to see the team, and I told them that what they had done by serving each other had served the customer so well that the customer had been moved to respond. I reminded them that this was a customer who had never before complimented us as a supplier in the history of our relationship." Martin believes that outcomes like these are the result of engendering employee trust through respectful behavior. In his mind, it's the opposite of coercive management built on silos and hierarchy. He adds, "Empowerment isn't enough. You have to enable people to do their best work by removing obstacles that get in their way."

So what benefits of modeling servant leadership have accrued to Martin's business? He exclaims with pride that high performance teamwork in his division has led the way in creating the customer value proposition, with performance exceeding six other divisions last year.

101. "STAY CLOSE TO THE TEAM AND POINT TO THE FUTURE DURING DISRUPTIVE TRANSITION"

■ ■ ■

As the corporate controller of Volkswagen of America and Canada, **Lori-Ann Roxburgh** leads a high-performance team of accounting professionals that has had to reinvent itself. Lori describes what happened to her team when a decision was made in the mid-1990s to integrate and centralize the company's accounting functions into one location in Canada. "We had to downsize the accounting function by 45 percent, even as it was decided that we would implement SAP enterprise software across the company's operations in Canada, the United States, and Mexico." Lori says that anyone who's ever implemented an enterprise software system understands the complexity of what she and her downsized team confronted. Not only that, but the U.S. team had to train their Canadian counterparts on the business processes, and they knew going into it that they were going to lose their jobs. She reflects, "It was a very challenging time for all of us, but I knew that it was critical that I be able to get the team excited about where we were heading. I knew that my role was to communicate a clear vision and set a tone that would energize and inspire people to be able to move past the tough setback they had experienced."

By holding frequent meetings with her team, including a team-building event, Lori was able to reinforce the message of success and keep the team motivated. Given that the team was being asked to implement a major computing upgrade with diminished staffing resources, she explains that it was important for her to set clear expectations with time frames that aligned with the overall strategy. She adds, "Under the circumstances, it was vital for people to understand that they only needed to bite off one piece of the elephant at a time. I coached the team through the big milestones and entrusted them with the goal of working out the details. Because there was less of us to go around, everyone had to learn to depend on each other." Lori explains that she worked with the team to establish clearly articulated deliverables that everyone had ownership of. She adds, "Everyone understood what their impact was and what the dependencies were. My role was coaching and encouraging— supporting dialogue around process and necessary course corrections." Lori also invested time with those who were slated to lose their jobs. She shares that she dialogued with them about their personal futures and encouraged them to choose paths that would enable them to play to their strengths. By investing in these individuals, she believes that she not only helped them to move on gracefully, but she also created ambassadors for Volkswagen.

Lori believes that a critically important factor in her team's success was her involvement as a leader. "People bought in because they saw me doing what was right for the company, I talked straight with them, and

I helped them create a personal picture of success. They felt good about helping and about being part of something big." Lori maintains that politics and game playing have no place in building a high-performance team. She believes that people respond to clean, clear communication, even when it hurts. Beyond that, she advises that team members need specifics, and they need to feel trusted and empowered to act. In her mind, especially when the going is tough, a team leader needs to be able to let go and let people execute. Empowering them in this way is what gets them mobilized and focused on the future instead of what's happened in the past.

Lori's team successfully implemented SAP, and the following year, the company received a clean audit letter. She exclaims, "It's a well-run, efficient team we have in Canada."

INDEX

A

Abbott Laboratories, 11, 136
Accessibility, 5
Accountability, 24, 88, 226
Adversity, 40–44
    communication and, 43
    management of, 48–50
    not taking personally, 43–44
    overcoming fear of, 46–48
    positive attitude during, 41
    preserving dignity, 42
    transforming, and paying forward,
        50–52
Affiliated Computer Services, 68
Afterburner UK, 221
Agriculture, U.S. Department of, 209
AIM Trimark, 225
Almatis, Inc., 115
American Red Cross, 25
AmerUs Capital Management, 57
Anger management, 123
Anticipatory skills, 81
Anxiety, 82
Army Medical Service Corps, U.S., 58
Assessments, 25–26, 39
Attitude
    of employee *vs.* leader, 19, 21
    of levelness, 45
    positive, 7, 152, 168
    of team members, 221
Authoritative power, 31, 38–40
Authority to act, 75

B

Balance, work/life, 83
Bandwidth. *See* Leadership bandwidth

Bannwolf, Chris, 100–101
Barbie Collectibles, 62–64
Barrentine, Charles, 195–97
Bauccio, Fedele, 156–57
Bauer, André, 171–72
Behavior
    adversity and, 40–42
    from aggressive to persuasive, 128–30
    from delivering to facilitating results,
        134–36
    from local to global plans/actions,
        136–38
    of new management/leader, 21
    overplaying or overusing success
        formulas, 125
    from personal to organizational, 127–28
    from personal to shared ownership,
        132–34
    psychological shifts, 21–23
    reinforcing positive change in, 213
    from self-interests to shared interests,
        139–40
    from tactical to strategic, 130–31
Bellamy, Terry, 139–40
Benes, Russ, 11–13
Benson, Gary, 128–30
Bertoch, Vicki, 68–69
Biltmore Company, 151
Blockbuster Inc., 3
Blonsky, Doug, 117–19
Boal, Greg, 57–58
Boeing Telephone Company, 167
Boldness, 203–4
Bon Appetit Management Company, 156
Bornhorst, Don, 48–50
Brand image, 157

239

Brand management/reinvention, 62–66
Brenner, Bill, 25–26
Brenner, Richard, 209–11
Broadening your perspective, 84
Broadway National Bank (San Antonio), 100
Buckanin, Dorothy, 95–96
Business acumen, 131
Business model changes, 178
Business publications, 61

C

Canadian Heritage Arts and Culture
    Programming, 87
"Can do" attitude, 7, 152, 168
Career path, 7–8
Cassano, Sherry, 13–15
Central Park Conservancy, 117
Chandler, Larry, 173–74
Change
    business case for, 212
    communicating process of, 212, 215
    inclusive nature of, 197
    shift from reacting to leading, 23
    team leadership and, 25
Change agile leadership, 193
    boldness in, 203–4
    commoditized businesses and, 216–18
    competition and, 207–9
    corporate objectives and, 203
    courage and, 193
    creativity and, 216–18
    credibility and, 202, 207
    critical factors in, 198–200
    emotionally compelling messages, 205
    envisioning success/engendering
        hope, 195–97
    measured, incremental change, 209–11
    pilots, 202, 210–11
    pride/passion/commitment and, 211–14
    priorities and, 200
    recognition and rewards system, 206
    respect and, 214–16
    structures/processes and, 199
    top leadership support for, 201
Charisma, 56, 58–60
Chase Home Finance, 29
Chevrolet, 191
Christopoulos, Kostas, 111–13

Citigroup Smith Barney, 64
Clarica Financial Services, 163
ClientSkills®, 21
CoachInc., 177
Coaching, 162, 187, 201, 226
Colgate-Palmolive Company, 23
Collaboration, 44–45, 159
    as choice, 163–65
    creating opportunities for, 168
    derailing, 170–71
    humility and, 171–72
    as organizational imperative, 173–74
    resources and, 169–71
    support for partners, 164
Comair, 48
Comfort zone, stretching beyond, 55, 57
Commercial Communication Services, 149
Commitment, 5, 212, 213
Commoditized businesses, and change,
    216–18
Communication
    broad-based, 57, 137–38
    change agile leaders and, 196, 205, 215
    clear thinking and, 75
    credibility and, 37–38
    downtime conversations, 166
    effective collaboration and, 165–66
    engaging the conversation, 37–38
    finding common ground, 139
    jargon and, 95
    leadership bandwidth and, 56
    lower vs. higher levels of leadership, 145
    managing complexity and, 71–72
    managing up, 95–96
    mastering the subject matter, 38
    new leaders and, 28
    open, 163
    presentation skills, 62
    process of change, 212
    professionalism in, 123
    sensitivity to personalities and, 100
    shift from possessive to open, 22
    situational awareness, 82
    strategy, for complex situations, 78–80
    of success, 30
    timely, 95
    in time of crisis, 49–50
    trust and, 24

validating understanding, 170
when challenging the status quo, 149
Community involvement, 8, 11
Community of practice, 149
Company culture, 224
Competitiveness, 165
Competitive review process, 207–9
Complacency, 78
Complexity, management of, 71–72
    annotating the process, 80
    broadening your perspective, 81
    communications strategy, 78–80
    critical information and, 76–78
    disaster scenarios, 79
    environmental management, 81–83
    exiting the leadership role, 84
    gradations of action, 75
    manufactured complexity, 87–89
    outsourcing, threat of, 90
    planning for, 74–76
    priorities, 88
    response plan simulation, 79
    review and debriefing, 75–76
    shared ownership and, 73–74
    vision and, 90
Compromise, 139–40
Concessions, 101
Confidants, 80
Conflict resolution, 170–71
Connective leadership, 121–22
Consistency, 143–44
Cook, Julie, 163–64
Coordinated Care Services, Inc., 31
Cormier, Mike, 27–28
Corporate social responsibility, 232–33
Corporate values, 3
Costco, 46
Cotton, Eldon, 74–76
Courageous conversations, 165–66
Cox, Steve, 134–36
Cracker Barrel, 44
Creativity, 124
Credibility, 56
    change agile leadership and, 202, 207
    collaborative behavior and, 44–45
    communication and, 37–38
    feedback implementation and, 112
    knowledge of business and, 102–4

managing up with, 93
shifting mind-sets and, 150
Credit
    giving unearned, 98
    sharing, 96, 114
Crisis. *See* Complexity, management of
Critical path, 91
Critical thinking skills, 61, 62–63
Cross Bros. Company, 55
Cross-functional
    experiences, 60, 66–67
    orientation, 33–34
    relationships, 138
Cultural differences, 212

D

Daewoo, 190
Dale Carnegie public-speaking course, 46
Darby, Martin, 233–35
Decision making, values-based, 196
Decision rights, 32–33
Decisiveness, 29
Delegation, 28, 32, 62, 86, 138
Delta Air Lines, 48–49, 76–78
Demoralizing behavior, 119
Denzel, Nora, 198–200
Developmental experiences, 35
Difficult coworkers, 11
Dignity, 42
DiMarzo, Richard, 64–66
Disaster scenarios, 79. *See also*
    Complexity, management of
Discipline, 31, 221–23
Divergent opinions, 163–64
Donaldson, Carolyn, 15–17
Downing, Doug, 214–16
Downtime conversations, 166
Drake Beam Morin, 4
Drost, Adam, 203–4
Duggan, Heather, 205–7
DuPont, Bonnie, 232–33
Duvall, Joe, 73–74

E

Eagle Ideas, 123
Eaton, Janet, 130–31
Eaton Electrical, 211
eCareerFit.com, Inc., 203

Edwards, Bill, 33–34
Ego conflicts, 82
Ejection envelope, 76–77
Emergency Preparedness and Continuity of
    Operations Plan (COOP), 179
Emergency situations, 75. *See also*
    Complexity, management of
Empathy, 185
Employees, needless demands on, 88
Empowerment, 37, 124
Enbridge, Inc., 232
Enerflex Systems, 40
Energizing, 37
Energy, 164
Enthusiasm, 164
Entrepreneurship, 83
Enviromedia, Inc., 50
Erwin, Maureen, 29
Ethics, 3
Ethox Corporation, 128
Ewen, Paula, 207–9
Executive coach, 65
Executive presence, 56
Expectations, 24, 28, 34, 144
Experience, 35
Experts, 80
Exposure. *See* Visibility
Extracurricular interests, 86
Exxon Mobil, 187

F

Fairness, 33
Faith, 43
Family-owned businesses, 153
Fast learners, 7
Fear
    of failure, 55
    overcoming, 46–48
Federal Aviation Administration, 38, 95
Federal Highway Administration, 81
Feedback, 24, 32, 86, 187
    failure to implement, 111–12
    private, 116
Figueroa, Jaime, 38–40
Flexibility, 9, 49
Flora, Kathy, 177–79
Focus
    strategic, 68–69
    team leadership and, 221–23

Forest Service, U.S. Department of
    Agriculture, 78
Foster, Brian, 223–25

G

Garcia, Pedro, 4–6
General Motors, 191
Generosity, 9
Gilliland, Liz, 119–20
Global perspective, 61, 233–35
Goals
    collaboration and, 161–62
    from delivering to facilitating results,
        134–36
    joint personal/organizational, 127
    linking to boss's, 96
    planning and staying the course, 124
    professional, 5, 9, 14
    teamwork and, 221
Gregory, Janey, 46–48

H

Hallahan, Jim, 187–88
Hanna, Ana, 3–4
Hard work, 5
Health, 178
Healy, Barbara, 21–23
Healy, Jack, 104–6
Hedley, Bob, 216–18
Heitzman, Karen, 6–8
Helping others, 9
Hewlett-Packard's Software Global
    Business, 198
Hicks, Marlow, 115–16
Hines, Pamela, 113–14
Holtz, Shel, 98–100
Hospira, Inc., 134
Humility, 5, 171–72
Humor, 101
Hutensky Group, 97

I

Ideas
    challenging assumptions with, 145
    recasting your message, 101
    submitting, 16
Identifying, with role, 86
Incentives, 213

Inclusion, 185–86
Inclusiveness, 28
Independent thinking, 103
Individual development, 166, 227
Individuality, 157
Industry trade groups, 6
Influence management skills, 135
Initiative, 97
Innovation, 122
INROADS, 13–14
Institute for Servant Leadership, 230
Insurance Corporation of British
   Columbia, 214
Integrity, 27–28, 65, 107
Interacting upward, 127
Interdependence, 130
International University of Professional
   Studies, 147
Interpersonal skills, 65
Intuition, 190–91
Investing in future, 11–13
ITT Industries' Space System Division, 113
Ives, Steve, 132

J

Jamieson, Bill, 230–31
Jargon, 95–96
Johnson, Marci, 66–67
Joy, Bob, 23–25
Judgment, rushing to, 28
Jumping to conclusions, 113–14

K

Katz, Irv, 147–49
Kellogg Canada, 121
Kern, Tony, 78–80
Kitchell Contractors, 73, 181
Knowledge
   admitting what you don't know, 44–45
   adult learning styles, 10–11
   broadening, 61
   of broader business world, 56
   of company, 3–4, 12
   following a personal strategy, 84
   of function and business, 102–4
   importance of, 5–6, 7
   of limitations, 168
   mastering the subject matter, 38

   relearning skills, 197
   of self, 10–11
   shift from personal to networked, 22
   of strengths/weaknesses, 118, 164, 204
Knowlton, Tom, 121–22
Kodak, 195
Kreutzfeldt, Shirley, 136–38

L

Leadership
   see also Leadership bandwidth
   bad/dysfunctional, 88, 109
   behavior. *See* Behavior
   broadening your impact, 27–28
   collaborative, 159
   connective, 121–22
   dealing with issues while manageable,
     28
   decision rights, 33–34
   derailing behavior, 28
   developing young leaders, 155
   exiting role of, 84, 184
   family-owned businesses, 153
   from heart, 150–51
   legislative, 99
   lessons learned from bad leadership, 109
   making transition from peer to leader,
     29
   making your boss look good, 96
   self-confidence, optimism, and focus,
     29–31
   shared model of leadership, 163
   situational leadership, 79
   strategic planning and, 185–86
   understanding your boss, 96–98
Leadership bandwidth
   brand management, 62–64
   communication and, 56
   credibility and, 56
   critical thinking and, 61, 62–63
   cross-functional experience and, 61
   defined, 53
   education and, 61
   interpersonal skills and, 65
   networking and, 59–60
   personality and, 58–60
   presentation skills, 62
   reinventing brand to gain, 64–66

sensitivity to opportunities, 63
strategic focus, 68–69
strategic thinking capacity, 56
stretch assignments and, 55, 60–62, 66–67
success in, 55
Learning
mastering skills, 14
styles, 10–11
Lee, John, 31–33
Legacy, 41
Legislative leadership, 99
Levelness, 45
Listening skills, 102–3, 161
LoJack, 37, 185
Loyalty, 216

M

McCready, Libby, 225–27
McDonald's, 10
Malcolm Baldridge Award, 209
Managing up
advisory role, 98–100
communication and, 95–96
defined, 93
guidance, 100–101
identifying the synergies, 104–6
integrity, 107
knowledge of function and business, 102–4
playing to boss's ego, 99
showcasing your boss, 105–6
stakeholder analysis, 106–7
understanding your boss, 96–98
Manufactured complexity, 87–89. *See also* Complexity, management of
Maple Leaf Foods, 216
Maple Leaf Sports and Entertainment, Ltd., 154
Maritz, Inc., 161
Marriott Corporation, 127
Marsh@WorkSolutions, 143
Martin, Kimberly, 169–71
Mattel, 62–64
Mauro, Joe, 60–62
Maven, 80
Maxwell, Terry, 44–45
Maxwell Drummond, 223

Meetings, 88
Mentors/mentoring, 10, 13, 27, 30, 178, 188
Merit raises/promotions, 154
Methodical approach, 149–51
MetLife Inc., 106
Micromanagement, 133
Middleton, Dan, 200–202
Miller, Steve, 151–53
Minority programs, 13–14
Miramar Mining Corporation, 205
Mission, 148, 153, 222
Missteps, 175
Mistakes, owning, 168
Montague, Sarah, 37–38
Moore, Rachel, 40–42
Morale, 223, 224
Muhleman, Fred, 55–56
MulvannyG2 Architecture, 46

N

Nationwide Lending, 42–43
Networking, 6–7, 12, 17, 30, 168
diversifying, 8
leadership bandwidth and, 59–60
risks and, 180
shift from personal to networked knowledge, 22
Nissan Ireland, 190
Norms, 222–23
Norrell Corporation, 203
Northern California Power Agency, 74
Noven Pharmaceuticals, Inc., 15

O

Obstacles, removing, 234–35
Olejar, Becky, 161–62
Opportunity
in enjoyable work, 81–82
sensitivity to, 63
Optimism, 32
Organization, knowledge of, 3–4, 5, 12
Organizational identity, 58, 224
Organizational politics, 177–79, 188, 203
focusing on, to exclusion of work, 114
O'Toole, Gerard, 190–91
Outsourcing, 90
Overanalyzing, 153

P

Parker, Neil, 76–78
Parker Pen Company, 188–90
Partnering, 3, 5
Passion, 5, 118–19, 213
Patience, 26
Paul, Ross, 83–84
Pay It Forward project, 51
Pearl Meyer & Partners, 6
Peddie, Richard, 154–56
Peer relationships, 27, 68, 103–4, 159–74
    aligning goals, 161–62
    collaboration, 163–64, 173–74
    creating win-wins, 167–68
    environment of support, 165–66
    humility and, 171–72
    resources and, 169–71
Peil, John, 123–24
People's Bank, 13–14, 21
Performance, creating all-star, 23–25
Persistence, 9
Personal attributes, 5
Personal boundaries, 89
Personal brand, reinventing, 64–66
Personal development, 9
Personal incentives, 213
Personal interests, 86
Personality, 58–60, 100
Pfeiffer, Irene, 183–84
Pfizer Global Research and Development, 15
Pilots, 202, 210–11
Pisarcik, Steve, 181–83
Planning, 9, 16
Point of view, 38, 145
Political astuteness, management of
    complexity and, 71
Political undercurrents, 29–30, 39
Politics, new initiatives and, 177–79
Portsmouth Abbey, 85
Positive attitude, 7, 41, 168
Potential, 179–81
Power
    overuse of, 28, 53, 118
    reverence vs. authoritative, 31
    seductive nature of, 117–19
Presentation skills, 62
PricewaterhouseCoopers, 169
Pride, 213

Proactive approach
    to career, 4, 5
    to leadership, 81
Professional association memberships, 6, 7
Professionalism, 123
Professionals, leading, 83–84
Profit and loss considerations, 30, 69
Public speaking
    leadership success and, 62
    overcoming fear of, 46–48

R

Radical change initiative, 198–200
Railton, Drew, 8–9
Reeson, Dale, 102–4
Relationship building, 3–4, 11–12
    see also Peer relationships
    with all constituent groups, 118
    conversations and, 187
    cross-functional, 138
    vision and, 122
Renken, Anne, 127–28
Replacement mentality, 216
Resourcefulness, 17
Resources, 38–40, 169–71
Respect, 5, 9, 60, 93, 101, 144, 163, 170,
    174, 191, 214–16
Response plan, 79
Reverence power, 31
Reynolds, Cindy, 149–51
Riley, Rich, 185–86
Risk, 4, 7, 45, 55
    courage and, 107
    management of, 143–45
    organizational growth and, 124
Roxburgh, Lori-Ann, 235–37
Rule breaking, 147–49
Ryder System, Inc., 102

S

Safety, 166
Schul, Herb, 227–29
Self-assessment, 87
Self-confidence, 32, 103, 169–70, 202
Self-defeating thinking/behavior, 7
Self-development, 22, 31
Self-discipline, in personal reactions, 89
Self-esteem, 124

Self-interest, 114, 174, 204
September 11 terrorist attacks, 51
Serna, Mark, 85–87
Servant leadership, 50–52, 230–31, 233–35
Setbacks, 175–91
    lack of work/life balance, 188–90
    overmanagement, 181–83
    realizing potential, 179–81
Shared leadership model, 163
Shared ownership, 73–74, 118, 132–34,
    144, 162
Shell Canada, 183
Sherwood, Brian, 167–68
Siciliano, Mario, 10–11
Situational awareness, 82
Situational leadership, 79
Skills
    anticipatory, 81
    collaborative, 159
    influence management, 135
    mastering, 14, 78
    mix of, 164
    relearning, 197
    soft skills, and leadership, 131
    team balance and, 24
SMART objectives, 222
Smith, Manville, 188–90
Smith, Willie, 81–83
Sobrino, Pablo, 87–89
Social responsibility, 232–33
Soft skills, 131
Speaking, overcoming fear of, 46–48
SPIRIT AeroSystems, 66, 89, 130
Spirituality, 86
Stakeholder analysis, 106–7
Stakeholders, 34
    empowering, 206
    forging relationships with, 178
    input from, on change, 213
    needs/concerns of, 174
Standing up for beliefs, 4
Stasior, Matt, 42–44
Status quo, challenging, 141
    and appeal to target audience, 148
    breaking rules, 147–49
    clarity and, 154–56
    community of practice, maintaining, 149
    environment for, 151

fresh perspectives/talent, 151–53
learning on the go, 145–47
managing risk, 143–45
methodical approach, 149–51
opposition and, 148
organizational culture and, 156–57
teamwork and, 151
Stewardship, 81
Strategic behavior, 21–22
Strategic focus, 68–69
Strategic planning, 196
Stress management, 71–72
Stretching/stretch assignments, 9, 12, 35,
    66–67
    as developmental experience, 45
    leadership bandwidth and, 55, 60–62
    organizational politics and, 39
    for team members, 229, 231
    understanding complexity of, 38–40
Strimling, Ethan, 145–47
Success
    overcommitment and, 87
    paradox of, 125
    personal interpretation of, 6, 7–8
Sun Chemical Corporation, 233
Sutton Place Hotels, 111
Synergies, creating, 104–6
Synthesis, 53, 63
Systems thinking, 119
System-wide solutions, 178, 202

T
Tactical behavior, 21–22
Talent, 222, 224
Team leadership, 22–26, 219
    discipline and focus, 221–23
    method of getting results, 115–16
    preparing team for change, 25
    sharing credit, 114
    status quo challenges and, 151
    team building and, 59
    team rather than leader support, 57–58
Teams/teamwork
    authorization and empowerment, 223
    balanced skills and, 24
    channeling individuality, 157
    conflict resolution, 170–71
    decision rights, 32–33

defining need for, 225–27
ground rules, 226
high performance teams, 221–31
maintaining diverse skills/experience, 84
morale and, 223, 224
overmanagement of, 181–83
primary team components, 228
review and corrections, 225, 226
shared ownership, 73–74
team talent, 222, 224, 227–29
TELUS, 8
Templates, 227
Temporal distortion, 76
Time management, 172
Tools, 227
Toombs KWA, 8
Toronto Maple Leafs, 154
Toronto Raptors, 154
Toys "R" Us Canada, 165–66
Trade publications, 61
Transportation, U.S. Department of, 207
Trust, 24, 86, 163
  abuse of, 103
  effective collaborators and, 166
  leveraged for shared success, 93
  shift from self-trust to trust in others, 57–58
Truth, 27, 86
Tuerff, Kevin, 50–52
Tychkowsky, Clayton, 211–14

U

United Airlines, 221
United Way, 104
University of Windsor, 83
U.S. Army Medical Service Corps, 58
U.S. Department of Agriculture, 209
U.S. Department of Agriculture Forest Service, 78
U.S. Department of Transportation, 207
U.S. Federal Highway Administration, 81

V

Value, for customer, 195

Values, 3, 65, 74
  -based decisions, 196
  employee *vs.* leader, 21
  illuminating core values, 146
Vanderbilt, George, 152
Via, Tom, 165–66
Visibility, 5, 12, 14, 231
  in time of crisis, 49–50
Vision
  action and, 195–96
  creating a shared, 24, 130
  focused, 84
  innovation and, 122
  managing complexity and, 90
  passion and, 85–87
Volkswagen of America and Canada, 235
Volunteer Calgary, 10
Volunteering
  community involvement, 8, 10–11
  within company, 68

W

Walk the talk, 3
Wayne Water Systems, 60
Weatherington, Lisa, 58–60
Weatherington, Walt, 179–81
Wells Fargo, 200
Weyers, Bill, 143–45
White, Ellston, 89–91
White, Rick, 221–23
Wiltshire, John, 106–7
Win-win relationships, 167–68, 178
Women, career acceleration of, 15–17
Women in Leadership, 47
Woolley, Cathy, 96–98
Workaholics, 88
Work/life balance, 83, 188–90
Work stream, 229

X–Z

Xerox, 33
YMCA, 132
Zwiers, Nancy, 62

Share the message!

Bulk discounts
Discounts start at only 10 copies and range from 30% to 55% off retail price based on quantity.

Custom publishing
Private label a cover with your organization's name and logo. Or, tailor information to your needs with a custom pamphlet that highlights specific chapters.

Ancillaries
Workshop outlines, videos, and other products are available on select titles.

Dynamic speakers
Engaging authors are available to share their expertise and insight at your event.

Call Kaplan Publishing Corporate Sales at 1-800-621-9621, ext. 4444, or e-mail kaplanpubsales@kaplan.com

PUBLISHING